Keith Martin on
COLLECTING ALFA ROMEO

Bob Dunsmore, Colorado Grand

Keith Martin on

Modena Cento Ore Classic

COLLECTING ALFA ROMEO

FOREWORD BY MARTIN SWIG

Featuring **Pat Braden, Donald Osborne, Craig Morningstar, Raymond Milo** and the editors of

Sports Car Market

MOTORBOOKS

This edition published in 2006 by Motorbooks, an imprint of MBI Publishing Company, Galtier Plaza, Suite 200, 380 Jackson Street, St. Paul, MN 55101-3885 USA

Motorbooks titles are also available at discounts in bulk quantity for industrial or sales-promotional use. For details write to Special Sales Manager at MBI Publishing Company, Galtier Plaza, Suite 200, 380 Jackson Street, St. Paul, MN 55101-3885 USA.

ISBN-13: 978-0-7603-2383-0
ISBN-10: 0-7603-2383-6

Front cover: 1994 Alfa Romeo Spider by Ron Kimball Stock

Designed by Kirsten Onoday

Printed in China

If You're Lucky, an Alfa Will Choose You

Alfa Romeo cars have figured in my life more than I could have imagined in February 1958, my first day as a salesman at the Alfa Romeo dealership in San Francisco.

That was a time when the VW Beetle dominated the less-than-10%-market-share imported car business, with the Renault Dauphine a red-hot second best seller. I recall we used to implore Fiat, which we also sold, to make their cars more like Renaults. And we always hoped next years Alfas would be as sturdy as TR3s.

A Giulietta spider was about $3,500 and Veloce spiders a hard upsell at round $4,000, in a market where MGAs and TR3s sold in the mid-two thousands.

The Giuliettas were so much more sophisticated—DOHC, five-bearing crank, all-synchro transmission, and those unbelievable finned drum brakes. This was a time when the cheapest Plymouth still used a flat-head six introduced in 1933. Studebaker-Packard, Nash and Hudson were disappearing, and the hot new brand for 1958 was called Edsel.

Swig and his 1928 6C 1500

I had been in Italy in 1955—my first exposure to that country, and to Fiats, Alfas and Lancias, all of which I love to this day. What a country—perfect cars, lovely roads and competent drivers who were always up for a little go.

So I was really ready for the Alfa in 1958, although I could only afford a Fiat 600 as an everyday driver. But selling the Alfas gave me the chance to learn about all their endearing qualities, and to demonstrate them vigorously to prospective customers. Giuliettas morphed into Giulias, then into GTVs and Duettos. It's hard to believe that a company that was so good then is an also-ran today.

Think of all the talk today of differentiating same-platform cars. Then imagine the Giulietta Berlina, Spider and Sprint Coupe of the 1950s. Three totally different cars using the same brilliant mechanicals. Alfa had earlier experimented with their first volume product, the 1900, introduced in 1950. The "family car that wins races" was actually the world's first sports sedan, a category that BMW "discovered" more than ten years later and exploited so effectively. The 1900 platform was supplied to every coach builder you ever heard of, and many of those cars are all time greats.

In 1975 I bought a 1900 Zagato for $3,500. Twenty thousand dollars later I was on the starting grid at the 1978 Monterey Historic Auto Races. I remember people saying something to the effect of "why did you waste all that money on a car that will never win a race?" I loved that car so much that I didn't even bother to answer. And although I never won, it was a rare 300SL or XK 120 (unless it was a lightweight) that could get by.

In 1982, my 1900 Zagato got me into the first retrospective Mille Miglia. John Lamm (long-time contributor to *Road & Track*) and I had the time of our lives. It changed my life; I've since participated in the Mille Miglia 18 times, along with multiple visits to the Melbourne Mille in Australia, the Festa Fille Miglia in Japan, and the Mil Millas Sport de la Republica Argentina, usually in an Alfa. And now, our own California Mille has completed 15 years, providing this Alfa enthusiast still more magic in life.

Given all the richness that Alfa has brought to my life, the $20,000 I "blew" on the 1900 Zagato now seems like a pretty good investment, even if only in terms of life experiences. But it didn't stop with the 1900. During the '78 Monterey Historics, a 1928 6C 1500 Alfa Romeo Zagato spider caught my eye. Today, I'm lucky enough to own that 6C, and it is teaching me all about what Alfa was and meant as an enthusiast-driven car company in that era. And you can see where Ferrari got their shift gate.

Commercially, by 1969, I had started my own dealership and in '71 I got the Alfa franchise, which I kept until Alfa withdrew from the U.S. in 1995. It was never much financially. But I had "good" franchises like Toyota, Nissan, Mazda and others, which fed my wallet while Alfa took care of my heart, along with providing the chance to have one of every new Alfa as a daily driver.

After the emission-control strangling of the 2000-cc models, we got the GTV6 in '81, the Milano in '87, and the 164 in '91—great and memorable cars all. And at this writing, any of those are available at four-digit prices. One of the great mysteries—why are they so cheap? Recall that Giuliettas used to be cheap, too. Now they're scarce and good ones have crept up significantly in price—into the low five-figure range. Many Alfa 1900 coupes are now six-figure cars. I'm not saying that a GTV-6 will be $100,000 in twenty years, but they certainly have a better chance to appreciate than cars with boring mechanicals, tepid styling and a total lack of excitement when you are behind the wheel—things the GTV-6 will never be accused of.

Finally, the best part of Alfa ownership is the friends you'll make. One especially good result has been my crossing paths with Keith Martin. I first met him when he slapped a muffler and windshield onto his 1958 Giulietta Spider Veloce and drove it in one of the California Milles. Just like me, he's got Alfa in his blood, and I've been pleased to watch his career develop over the years.

In the end, I believe that the cars choose the people. Some makes choose gold-chainers, others like the Peter-perfect types. But if you're an all-round great motorhead, and want a car that provides some of the best-balanced driving experiences in the world, sooner or later an Alfa will choose you as an owner. Then, drive your Alfa to any gathering of Alfa fanatics, and be prepared for a whole new dimension in your life.—*Martin Swig, San Francisco, California*

Table of Contents

Section III: The Modern Era

Section IV: Resource Directory

My Snake and Cross Compatriots

W ho would have thought that my journey with Alfa Romeos, which began as a young man enjoying a red sports car, would have ended up including so many fellow travelers? This is the fourth book in the *Keith Martin on Collecting* series, the first three focusing on Porsche, Ferrari and Jaguar.

As with the previous books, *Keith Martin on Collecting Alfa Romeo* pulls the very best from the pages of *Sports Car Market* magazine, and adds some contemporary observations. (If you're not currently a subscriber to *SCM*, you'll find a special offer to become a member of our gang of irreverent enthusiasts in the back of this book.)

Sports Car Market magazine was born in 1989 as *The Alfa Romeo Market Letter*, printed in black on blue paper. In 1993, *ARML* morphed into *SCM*, which allowed our peripatetic contributors to make observations on the entire car market, instead of just those built in Arese.

One of the key supporters of *SCM* in its various incarnations has been Martin Swig, iconoclastic lover of all things automotive. Although best known in collector circles as the founder of the California Mille, Swig is also a tireless enthusiast, for whom a stint behind the wheel of a 1950s Fiat or '30s Chrysler is the best time of all. I thank him for kindly contributing the foreword to this book.

The profiles in *On Collecting Alfa Romeo* offer an educated and incisive look at a variety of Alfa models, built from the 1920s to the 1990s. The authors include Carl Bomstead, Pat Braden, Dave Brownell, Miles Collier, Michael Duffey, Keith Duly, O. Delmas Greene, Raymond Milo, Craig Morningstar, Donald Osborne, Giuseppe Tomasetti and Doug Zaitz.

As with *SCM*, a critical and unique component of this book are the market reports, which consist of first-hand visual inspections of cars being offered for sale at auction, the sale or no-sale result of each transaction, and the auction reporter's analysis of the result.

Each of this group has spent many weekends in blazing sun and freezing rain looking at cars, jotting down notes in the field, taking photos and later transcribing it all for your benefit. They include Scott Abts, Dennis Adler, Steve Ahlgrim, John Apen, Chip Baldoni, Carl Bomstead, Pat Braden, Dave Brownell, B. Mitchell Carlson, Trevor Clinard, John Clucas, Scott Featherman, Dan Grunwald, Haig Haleblian, Richard Hudson-Evans, Dave Kinney, Bob LeFlufy, Cecile Nierodzinski, Marit Peterson, Steve Serio, Phil Skinner and David Slama.

Of course, without auction houses there would be no auctions, so we thank the following for graciously allowing our analysts free rein to examine their offerings: Artcurial, Barrett-Jackson, Blackhawk, Bonhams (in all its various incarnations), Cheffins, Christie's, Coys, eBay/Kruse, Gooding & Co., H&H Classic Auctions, Kruse International, Mecum, New York Auto Salon, McCormicks Palm Springs Exotic Car Auctions, Poulain Le Fur, RM Auctions, Russo and Steele, Shannons, Silver Auctions and The Auction.

The material in this book was assembled by the indefatigable David Slama, director of special projects at *SCM* and recently appointed as its first General Manager. Bill Neil, Kathy Karapondo and Jeff Sabatini performed the magic of copy editing which brought nearly two decades of prose into a consistent style.

The cover photograph was taken by Ron Kimball, *SCM* legal analyst John Draneas snapped the photo of me standing next to his handsome red Giulietta.

As with the previous books, the impetus for this one came from our good friends Tim Parker and Zack Miller at Motorbooks

Ken Shaff (1929 - 2005), a friend to all of us

Company (MBI Publishing), whose constant phone calls and e-mails have acted as a catalyst for this entire process.

If this book is helpful to you in your collecting, the credit goes to all of the enthusiasts above who have worked so diligently to create the material presented. If there are any errors or omissions, they are mine alone.

I would like to dedicate this book to two people. The first is my 13-year-old daughter Alexandra, who continues to be a source of sunlight and freshness in my life, and whom I hope has the chance to have her own Giulietta some day.

The second is to Ken Shaff, who recently passed away. He has been a mentor to me in so many ways over the past 20 years. A highly successful publisher, he founded *Competition Press,* which later evolved into *AutoWeek.* Ken was always been there for me when I was dogged by questions about how to grow first *ARML*, and then *SCM*, from a little newsletter into the magazine it is today. At the same time, Ken was a true enthusiast, and he and delightful wife Jeri always brought a spark of excitement and good cheer to every event they were a part of. *SCM* wouldn't be what it is today if it hadn't been for his caring and thoughtful advice.—*Keith Martin*◆

"Why Don't You Get a Real Sports Car?"

Like a trusty golden retriever, my Alfas have been by my side through times both good and bad. At the age of 19, I recall a non-stop, 12-hour drive from San Francisco to Mercer Island, WA, in my red 1962 Giulietta Spider Veloce to pick up my then-girlfriend for a trip across Canada. When I got to her house, she told me she had fallen for someone else. The drive back home was a long and lonely one, with only the smooth sounds of the chain-driven camshafts to comfort my broken heart.

On the happier side of the equation, a few years later my best buddy Larry Gilbert and I took my white 1967 Duetto on a memorable spin through Yosemite National Park, continuing on to Reno, where we discovered that motels which rented rooms by the hour weren't necessarily doing that as an economy measure. We cruised across the desert at a steady 100 mph for hours, enjoying being two young men in a hot-looking Italian sports car, drinking in adventures as fast as we could.

Martin and a 1957 Giulietta in Central Oregon

My career as an automotive writer began through an Alfa connection. During a stint as president of the Alfa Romeo Owners of Oregon. I wrote for the club newsletter, Overhead Cams. My first editors, Bob and Margaret McGill, offered continual encouragement.

But my affair with these lithe sports cars really started in 1968 when good friend Bjarne Holm looked at my Bug Eye Sprite and said, "Why don't you get a real sports car?"

I loved my little Sprite, although at a purchase price of $30, its body looked like it had come out on the losing side of a demolition derby. But I had just turned 16, the Sprite was a sports car, and best of all, it was mine.

But Bjarne, far older and wiser at 19, dismissed it with hardly a glance. "Look under the hood of my Alfa and you'll see what kind of engine a true sports car should have." And as he lifted the hood, I had my first look at the world of Webers,

Extracting a GTV engine, circa 1970

alloy heads, twin camshafts and headers. I was hooked.

A year later, I acquired my first Alfa, a red 1963 Giulia Spider Normale, and I have never been without an Alfa for more than a few days since.

What sets serial production Alfas apart from all other cars is their combination of entry-level values with first-rate exotic car engineering. Post-1950s Alfas can rightfully claim to be the initial rung on a ladder that leads to Lancia, Maserati and finally Ferrari. Every Alfa is imbued with the right kind of DNA that results in precise steering feel, state-of-the-art braking, excellent handling, more than adequate acceleration, and a mouthwatering visual package both in styling and under the hood.

It's no secret that for Alfa the years after 1967 saw nothing but a gradual slide into overpriced, outdated mediocrity as the once-proud carmaker cobbled together the cheapest, crudest methods of meeting U.S. safety and smog regulations. And while there's always talk of Alfa someday coming back to the States, I simply don't foresee it. The issues of re-establishing a dealer body, providing warranty service, and offering the kind of quality expected in this increasingly competitive market are, in my opinion, simply insurmountable for this Italian company.

But Alfa lovers can continue to gather around fireplaces late into the night, to glory in a marque whose history extends back to the dawn of motoring. A marque that has produced Mille Miglia winners and World Champions. A marque where even the lowliest $2,500 Berlina has the same disc brakes, dual camshafts and alloy block as the thundering, all-conquering GTA.

This book is my way of saying thank you to Alfa Romeo for being a good friend to me all these years, and for offering a taste of the exotic at an affordable price to hundreds of thousands of enthusiasts all over the world.—*Keith Martin*◆

Section I
The Grand Classics

For those who came of age during the era of Alfettas, Milanos, Spider Quadrifoglios and 164s, it's hard to imagine that at one time Alfa was the Ferrari, Bentley and Bugatti of the automotive world—all rolled into one.

Starting with the supercharged six-cylinder 1750s and continuing through the magnificent 8C 2300 and 2900s, prior to World War II Alfas were simply the best cars in the world. They had unmatched style and performance, and a full trophy rack to prove it.

Today, outstanding examples of any of the above cars sell for values far above a million dollars. My sources tell me that most recently the 8C 2900 once driven by Phil Hill changed hands for more than $12,000,000—the same amount it will take to buy a first-rate Ferrari 250 GTO.

Yet today these cars are seen mostly in museums or on vintage race tracks. No one uses their 8C Monza as a daily driver, although it sometimes seems like marque expert Paul Grist tries to.

For the serious student of automotive history, these early Alfas bear some study. More than six decades ago, Alfas were being built with superchargers, overhead cams and transaxles, and the factory made liberal use of alloys in their construction. They had haute couture styling by the leading coachbuilders of the time, including Touring and Zagato. If you were truly wealthy and wanted a car that embodied high-time style and performance, an Alfa was your only choice.

The cars in this section all have something to teach us about the history of high performance cars, and the history of Alfa Romeo. And for those of us who own Alfas from the post-war years, we can learn just where the DNA of all the performance kist in our later cars came from.—*Keith Martin*◆

1928 6C 1500 Sport Zagato

Hired to develop a sports car based on a winning Grand Prix Alfa Romeo, Jano delivered—beyond Nicola Romeo's wildest dreams

by Pat Braden

Chassis number: 0231191
Engine number: 0211462

After joining Alfa Romeo in 1923, Vittorio Jano created the all-conquering P2, an expedient design based largely on Jano's experience with Fiat's 1923 Tipo 805 GP car. Jano refined the best elements of the Tipo 805 and designed around some of its weaknesses. But this was not the creative Jano, it was the practical engineer going only as far as necessary to achieve the objective in the time available.

The P2's 1925 championship initiated a long series of victories. Jano next turned to passenger cars to succeed the Merosi-designed RL and RM series. Merosi's L-head six- and four-cylinder cars were now dated and Alfa needed something better. For 1927, Jano created a legendary six-cylinder that was to set new standards for lightweight, high-performance motorcars: the 6C 1500.

The 6C 1500's engine was a masterpiece of design and construction. The iron cylinder block and head were each single-piece castings. The block mated to a light-alloy crankcase and sump. Initially a single-camshaft design, a twin-camshaft supercharged powerplant, designated "Super Sport," quickly became the standard for performance. Unlike the P2 and later 8C designs that used a geartrain to drive the camshafts, Jano utilized shaft and bevel gears for the 6C.

The chassis was low and lightweight, featuring semi-elliptic springs front and rear. While Alfa Romeo could, and in many cases did, clothe these artistic machines with its own bodies, most were supplied in chassis form. They were the basis on which the best coachbuilders of the era expressed their ideas for both open and closed automobiles. Touring, Castagna, James Young and Brianza produced coachwork for this chassis, but most of all it was Zagato whose Spiders have come to epitomize the sporting 6C series. These cars were a triumph of balance, quickness and controlled responsiveness over ponderous leviathans, and were potential winners in any event.

This Alfa is one of only a few, perhaps as few as four, known to survive. According to Angela Cherrett, Registrar of the VSCC Alfa Section, this 6C is the oldest of them. Fortunately, its inherent quality and presence has kept it in the hands of Alfa enthusiasts who have preserved it. The panels still carry their original Zagato job numbers.

Sympathetically restored by Hill and Vaughn more than a quarter century ago, this car has been shown, raced and toured in historic events, and driven by such luminaries as World Champion Phil Hill. It has garnered many Best of Show trophies and a first in class at Pebble Beach.

The SCM Analysis: This car sold for $112,200, including buyer's premium, at the RM Monterey sale on August 18, 2001.

Merosi was a master of designing passenger cars but his Grand Prix cars were disasters, and Nicola Romeo wanted a change. Jano was hired with the understanding that he was to develop a sports car based on a winning Grand Prix Alfa Romeo. He delivered beyond Romeo's wildest dreams, for his 6C 1500 and 6C 1750 Zagato-bodied Spiders became the standard against which all pre-war lightweight sports cars were measured. Because they reflected many features of the P2, contemporaries regarded the 6Cs as road-going versions of the Grand Prix car.

On the other hand, this car is proof that performance really matters. While the "standard for performance" 6C 1500 SS claimed a top speed of 87 mph, the 100-hp 6C 1750GS, first introduced in 1929, could almost reach 100 mph. The unsupercharged Sport model, pictured here, with twin cams but only 60 hp, offers no more than 78 mph.

Few people want to spend more than $100,000 for a sports car that can barely outrun an early VW Beetle, but this car also proves that intelligent marketing is an essential element of a successful sale. This is the oldest Jano-designed car in private hands, a Hill and Vaughn restoration that has been maintained with few expenses spared. However, it has also been seeking a buyer for years, finally selling in Monterey for $112,200. The sale price can be compared to a supercharged 6C 1500SS Zagato that sold for $230,683, including buyer's premium, at the Brooks Goodwood Festival of Speed auction on December 18, 1999.

The owner responsible for restoring this car, Jack Becronis, was a great Alfista. At the time of his death, his wife knew little about his cars, and listened to some very bad advice. The initial asking price was more appropriate for a supercharged car, yet the widow, probably fearful of being taken advantage of, refused to consider lower offers. A stalemate between seller and buyers continued for years before reality dawned. By that time, every reasonable offer had already been refused and the car's market was threadbare.

Whether or not $112,200 is an appropriate value depends entirely on how you regard the car. As the oldest example of a fabulous series, designed by one of the automotive greats and restored to perfection, it's an absolute bargain. As a practical piece of sporting entertainment, that kind of money will buy you more testosterone. The new owner will probably want to keep the car for a while, until marketplace memories have faded.

(Editor's note: We are advised by the auction company that the high bidder in Monterey failed to perform, and that this car was subsequently sold to the underbidder, an SCM subscriber who is known for creating California-based vintage road rallies.)

(Historical and descriptive information courtesy of the auction company.)

From the January 2002 issue of SCM. ◆

1929 6C 1500 SS

Bless the Brits for their meticulous attention to the details of history. In this case, they have conserved one of the rarest of Jano's delectable confections

by Pat Braden

Chassis number: 0312873
Engine number: 0312872

Unequalled in their class in the 1927-1930 era were the superbly engineered, extremely light and very quick Tipo 6C twin-camshaft, supercharged Alfa Romeos from the design board of the brilliant Vittorio Jano.

Alfa Romeo's concessionaire in England, Fred Stiles, imported four "works" cars with Zagato racing coachwork, chassis numbers 0312871 to 0312874. The cars were picked up in Milan, photographed outside the factory with Mrs. Stiles at the wheel of this car and Johnny Lurani and Giulio Ramponi in two others. The cars were driven back to England, where 0312873 was sold to Edgar Fronteras and registered GU9699.

Fronteras was invited to participate as a "works" driver in the Junior Car Club's Double Twelve Hour race at Brooklands in May, 1929. He placed 12th, while Ramponi won outright. Ramponi later took a 6th on the Tourist Trophy Ards circuit. The car appeared at Shelsley Walsh in the same year and at Brooklands in 1930 before being retired. At some time during its racing career, the original engine was replaced with the powerplant from 0312872. In 1933, the car was rebodied as a two-seater by Freestone & Webb, then sold to Mrs. Beryl Leitch, who kept the car until 1937. After the war, Mic Comber rebodied it to its original Zagato configuration. After being campaigned throughout England and Europe, the car was sold to a Japanese collector in 1989. Remaining with the car are its V5 registration document, old log books, FIA and FIVA identity documents. While presently equipped with an SU carburetor, the original-type Memini is included.

The SCM *Analysis: This Alfa sold for $230,683, including buyer's commission, at the Brooks auction held on June 18, 1999 as part of the Goodwood Festival of Speed in Chichester, Sussex, England.*

When Jano joined Alfa Romeo, his assignment was to create a Grand Prix car that could beat Fiat, then develop a passenger car along the same lines, as racing success generates sales. Jano's P2 earned Alfa its Championship wreath in 1925 and sired the 6C 1500 and 6C 1750 cars which first appeared two years later. Among the 6C 1500 model's first wins, Enzo Ferrari led the field at Modena in 1927, with Marioni just behind in another unsupercharged 6C 1500. Campari and Ramponi took a first overall with a supercharged model in the 1928 Mille Miglia. Other 1928 6C 1500 wins included the Essex Six Hours at Brooklands and the Belgian GP at Spa. By 1929, the 1750s were dominant, but Ramponi still managed the win at the JCC Double Twelve with his 6C 1500 Super Sport.

I have always felt that the soul of the Alfa Romeo mystique has been Jano's 6Cs, which dominated the racecourses in their era, and set a reputation for lightness and performance that has carried Alfa through some very lean years indeed. The 6Cs were available as sedans, convertibles and roadsters, with single- or twin-cam engines, the latter with a supercharger option. The larger-displacement 1752-cc cars have always been more popular, but the 1487-cc version differs only in its slightly smaller bore and stroke.

The original engine configuration of the supercharged cars (3rd series) included a Memini carburetor on the driver's (right-hand) side and a deeply-finned inlet pipe which did a U-turn over the top of the supercharger and then made a right-angle turn back along the head. A more direct path was adopted beginning with the 51st car of the third series 6C 1750, when the ports of the supercharger were swapped, echoing the layout of the P2.

After so many years, we're pretty sophisticated about the differences between the P2s and the passenger 6Cs. This, I think, was not at all true of the motoring public in the early 1930s, most of whom would never have seen the P2's straight-8 powerplant. One of the secrets of Jano's early success may have been the widespread belief that the 6C cars were really road-going versions of the P2. Certainly, Varzi's use of 1750 Gran Sport parts on his 1930 Targa Florio-winning P2 only confirmed this popular belief.

Although 0312873 now carries replica Zagato bodywork, English bodies on the 6C Alfas are not unknown. James Young bodied several phaetons and drophead coupes. It's a shame that so many of these less sporting cars have been rebodied as Zagatos, primarily to increase their value. With its Freestone & Webb bodywork, this car would be even more rare, though certainly not more valuable.

The third series configuration is rare, and a third series 1500 SS is one of the rarest of Jano's delectable confections. A large part of the value of this car is its well-documented provenance. Bless the Brits for their meticulous attention to the details of history. In this case, they have conserved an important Alfa icon. The price paid, while on the high side for a 1500-cc SS, was fair given the outstanding history, beginning with the day it was delivered, of this particular car.

(Photo, historical and descriptive information courtesy of the auction company.)

From the March 2000 issue of SCM. ◆

1930 6C 1750 Convertible Coupe

The most common fate of Castagna and James Young convertibles was to be parted out for spares by owners of supercharged, Zagato-bodied 1750s; it's a wonder any of them survive at all

by Pat Braden

Chassis number: 6C861336

The Castagna-bodied 6C 1750 Alfa shown here is a triple masterpiece: its magnificent Vittorio Jano-designed engine, Alfa Romeo's superb chassis, and the beautifully constructed and subtly detailed Castagna body. In addition, it has been fastidiously restored in Australia by marque specialists Double J.

Vittorio Jano put the P2 GP project behind him and turned his talent and creativity to Alfa Romeo's commercial products, still derived from Giuseppe Merosi's designs of the teens. Jano took advantage of the carte blanche assignment given him by Alfa Romeo and, for 1927, created a new engine from scratch, an engine of great potential and adaptability. Conceived and developed to accept both single and dual overhead-camshaft cylinder heads, Jano's original 1.5-liter six-cylinder expanded slightly to 1.752 liters in 1929 and was designated 6C 1750. It would take three forms, from supercharged twin-cam racing versions that demonstrated their prowess in race after race to reliable, naturally aspirated twin- or single-cam sporting models, touring cars and sedans. During a period of rapid evolution in performance automobiles at Alfa Romeo and others, the eight-year production life of Jano's six-cylinder cars is remarkable and offers ample evidence of the design's quality, a pedigree that attached to all of Jano's 6C series engines.

The chassis into which Jano's little masterpiece was placed was itself a model of Alfa's mastery of contemporary technique. Renowned to this day for their delicate handling, responsiveness to driver input and roadholding, the Alfa 6C 1750 chassis was at once refined and exuberant. The competence of the chassis in diverse and demanding conditions is illustrated by its four victories in the Mille Miglia, a race that demanded much of its drivers and rewarded automobiles with stability and predictability.

While Zagato and Touring turned out lightweight competition and sports models on Alfa's six-cylinder chassis, it was Castagna that delivered the elegant yet sporting coachwork favored by many Alfa buyers of the time. Castagna had been in existence for nearly a century in 1930, and was noted for the exceptional quality of its coachwork and its meticulous attention to detail in design and execution. Elegant, comfortable and practical, without being stodgy, Castagna's coachwork was the mark of a discerning owner who appreciated both style and function.

The 1930 Alfa Romeo 6C 1750 Castagna convertible coupe shown here was imported into Australia in the late 1980s in unrestored condition, where it was restored for a noted European collector, then living in Australia. It gained many awards in Australian concours before coming to the U.S., where it was proudly displayed at the 1997 Concorso Italiano in Carmel Valley, CA. Carefully maintained since, it is still in show-quality condition and is ready to use and enjoy whether in shows and concours, or in the many vintage tours for which it is eligible.

The SCM *Analysis: This car sold for $82,500 including buyer's premium at RM Auctions held on January 18, 2002 in Phoenix, AZ.*

It's a pleasure to see restored 6C 1750 Alfas that do not carry Zagato bodies, or recent facsimiles thereof. A Castagna-bodied Alfa in its original configuration is now very rare. There's a reason for this: heavy Castagna 1750 convertibles were considered worthless by enthusiasts in the '50s and '60s, especially if not supercharged. These cars were completely vulnerable to the dismantler in an era when you could buy supercharged Alfas for less than $3,000. Over the years, the most common fate of Castagna (and James Young) convertibles was to be parted out as a source of spares by owners of supercharged, Zagato-bodied 1750s, and it's really a wonder that any of them survived that era. I once owned the front half of just such a sacrificial convertible, and finally sold the front frame section to designer Dick Teague for his own 1750 Zagato.

In point of fact, the huge gap in value between sporty and staid still applies. This car sold for $82,500, including buyer's premium, at the RM Phoenix sale on January 18, 2002. At the same auction, a 1750 supercharged Zagato, also restored to a high level, was bid up to $319,000 and went unsold. Even today, the less sporting cars may be in danger of being sacrificed into oblivion by well-heeled owners of old Alfas in need of parts.

This particular car has recently had two very different valuations by the market. It was declared sold for $162,000, including premium, at the 2000 Brooks Amelia Island auction, a price that we considered quite high, given the double curse of great weight and little power. Then, at the RM Biltmore sale, the car sold for just half that amount, at $82,500.

The second sale was somewhat of a bargain, but probably more in line with current values than the first sale. In any event, for those Alfisti who will never be able to afford a supercharged Jano Alfa, an unsupercharged one with non-sporting bodywork may be a happy compromise. The buyer got a sterling piece of late 1920s engineering, and a slow-speed tourer of satisfying reliability and charm.

(Photo, historical and descriptive information courtesy of the auction company.)

From the June 2002 issue of SCM. ◆

1930 6C 1750 DHC

Profoundly shadowed by their superstar siblings, and ignored by collectors, these are rare indeed, and can draw larger crowds than supercharged Zagatos

by Pat Braden

Chassis number: 0412061
Engine number: 0412294

Tempted to join Alfa Romeo from Fiat in 1923 by the opportunity to head his own department and a three-times salary increase, the brilliant Vittorio Jano became part of the racing department in Milan in the autumn of that year. His first major project was the six-cylinder P2 racing car, winner of the 1924 European Grand Prix at Lyon and AIACR championship Grand Prix car of 1925. Jano had been brought on by Nicola Romeo with the understanding that he would develop a passenger car based on his race car. By the time of the Milan Salon in 1925, the new NR, or 6C 1500, was displayed in chassis form.

Deliveries commenced in early 1927 and the car was enthusiastically received. In the following year, the original single-cam engine was joined by a twin-cam version which could be had normally aspirated or supercharged. In 1929, a 1752-cc version of the engine appeared in single-cam, twin-cam and twin-cam supercharged stages of tune. This model, the 6C 1750, was a truly great car that was to dominate its class in competition from 1929 to 1931, and yet was also a most desirable road car. For 1929, the 6C 1750 was offered in various forms, including the long-wheelbase (10 ft. 2 in.) SOHC Turismo, a short-chassis (9 ft.) DOHC Sport and the short-chassis DOHC supercharged Super Sport.

The chassis number of this car makes it a 1929 Turismo, of which 327 were produced. However, its engine comes from a 1930 Turismo. Finally, a DOHC head has been fitted: not a casual conversion, since the Turismo cast-in cam-drive tower has a different spacing from the DOHC unit's alloy tower.

This car is well known in British Alfa circles, having been in the David Black family since 1972. It carries drophead coupe coachwork by James Young of Bromley, Kent and offers 2+2 seating, wind-up windows, external pram hood irons and rear-mounted spare wheel. The car retains a delightful patina to the interior with original leather upholstery that reflects careful ownership, and wooden dash and door cappings representing the skills of the finest British craftsmen.

Presented in silver-gray livery with black hood, this snug vintage Alfa is described as being in good order throughout.

The SCM analysis: This car sold for $106,650, including buyer's premium, at the Brooks auction in England, on April 27, 2000.

The pedigree of this car, as outlined in the auctioneer's description, is one of the finest possible. However, the road-going versions of Jano's championship P2 had little more than overall specification in common with the P2. The 1750 series included single-cam engines powering sedans and even limousines.

This car is a collection of the less-sporting components in the line. Initially a long-wheelbase, single-cam model developing 46 hp, it is burdened with a heavy drophead body. At some point in its life,

it has gained a twin-cam head that raised its output by about 4 hp. The top speed of this car in its original configuration was barely 65 mph, and the twin-cam head probably allows it to attain 70 on a good day.

These pedestrian 1750s are profoundly shadowed by their superstar siblings, and have been largely ignored by collectors. In the 1960s, Castagna and James Young dropheads were regarded as cheap sources of spares for the supercharged Super Sport or Gran Sport models. The fact that any of these donor cars has survived intact is truly remarkable. Now, because they were never highly valued, these models are very rare indeed, and they can draw larger crowds than the supercharged Zagatos when they appear at shows.

This car's worth—its survival, actually— is due entirely to its ownership by David Black, who appreciated and conserved it for decades. If the auctioneer's description of original leather interior is correct, then this car is a veritable time capsule. That alone qualifies it as a collectible.

What did Black see in this car, to have cherished it so? Jano's hand. A finely crafted design that was decades ahead of its time. The 6C 1750 set standards for comfort, performance and handling that were not bettered until well after the War. The trade-off for the Zagato's wind-in-the-hair sportiness was roll-up windows and a degree of elegance shared with the likes of Hispano Suiza, some Isotta Fraschinis and a few Bugattis.

This car embodies both the best and the worst of its breed. Its pedestrian performance is counterbalanced by pedigree. The price paid, well above SCM's guide, indicates that pedigree and provenance prevailed.

(Photo, historical and descriptive information courtesy of the auction company.)

From the August 2000 issue of SCM.◆

1933 Tipo 6C 1750 Supercharged Gran Sport Spider

The steering is precise, the brakes are excellent for the era, and the handling as good as it gets for an early '30s car

by Keith Duly

Chassis number: 121215048
Engine number: 121215048

The 1750 Gran Sport is regarded as one of the finest sports racing cars of its time. Its race record is nothing short of legendary, with numerous wins in the Mille Miglia, Tourist Trophy and other races coming at the hands of such famed drivers as Nuvolari, Campari and Varzi.

This sixth series supercharged model of 1933 was the most powerful 1750 of the series with some 85 hp at 4,400 rpm. It was capable of reaching 145 kph. Modifications common to all sixth-series cars were boxed chassis frames of all-welded construction, synchromesh gearbox with freewheel device, telecontrol shock absorbers and three-spoke steering wheels.

Based upon the chassis sequence, this is the 18th of 44 built. Early history for this car is currently not confirmed, although it is believed that Major Ayers of England purchased the car new. The next known owner was Henry Harrison, brother of renowned car collector Bob Harrison, who kept the car for some twenty years. On his passing in 1987, the Alfa was acquired from his estate by Mr. Charles Mallory, himself a well-respected collector from Connecticut. The car was then sold to a collector by the name of David Van Schaick, of Pennsylvania, from whom the current owner purchased it about six or seven years ago.

The car was subject to a superbly detailed restoration to the very highest concours standard. The Alfa Romeo is said to run and drive extremely well, as it was mechanically rebuilt with the goal of participating in long distance events such as the Mille Miglia. The engine was rebuilt with new Carillo rods, as original ones are known to be weak in design. The crankshaft and camshafts were reground, new-old-stock tappets were sourced, and new pistons were fitted. The supercharger was rebuilt with new bearings. The original Memini carburetor was overhauled, and an electric fan was fitted as a consent to modern driving conditions. The original coachwork has been fully restored, but retains the "Monza cowl" which is thought to have been fitted in the 1950s. The coachwork also has a fin over the twin spare wheels to give the car an 8C look.

The Alfa has been driven only 50 miles since the rebuild and has been shown just three times: at Pebble Beach in 1999, where it took a third in its class; at the Greenwich Concours, where it won Best In Class and was voted most exotic Italian car; and at a recent Hershey event where it won a Junior First Place award from the Antique Automobile Club of America.

With matching numbers, uncomplicated history, much sought-after Touring coachwork, sixth series refinements, and the aforementioned restoration, this example has all of the best ingredients. These supercharged Alfa Romeos are highly eligible for vintage events around the world and justifiably rank very high among pre-war sports cars.

The SCM analysis: This car sold for $436,500, including buyer's commission, at the Christie's New York sale on June 5, 2003. Though this car found a new home for less than the auction company's opti-

mistic estimate of $450,000-$550,000, the price was consistent with current market values.

The sixth-series Gran Sport cars could really be considered the "last gasp" of the small capacity supercharged sports cars from Alfa Romeo. As the Depression started to bite hard in Europe, the firm was trying to move toward more economic production methods. This resulted in changes like the chassis being fully welded, rather than the traditional and more expensive flanged and bolted construction of the preceding series. The front and rear track were both widened a bit—again, probably to save money by making components more common to other production models. Even so, these cars were expensive to build and fewer than 50 were constructed.

By this time, Alfa had embraced Touring as the body manufacturer of choice—only some four chassis in this sixth series carried the more traditional Zagato configuration. Another new departure was the use of a synchromesh gearbox and the introduction of a freewheel on the output shaft, a system soon to be found on more mundane Alfas. The engine, however, was essentially the same as for the fourth and fifth series 6Cs, a direct descendant of the 1500-cc engine that powered the first 6Cs in 1927.

To drive one of these cars is a pleasurable surprise. The steering is precise, the brakes are excellent for the era, and the handling as good as it gets for an early '30s car. Alfa has always had a reputation for making cars that are fun to drive, and we can see from this car just how ingrained that is in their manufacturing culture.

The early history of this car is uncertain, which is unfortunate. What we're looking for here is the answer to a simple question: Did it race? This has become crucial to the value of such cars, because so many Alfas did well in the Mille Miglia, Targa Florio, and other races of the era. With a documented racing provenance, this Alfa might be worth $100,000 more.

However, the car is a fine numbers-matching example of its type, even if the "Alfa Red" chosen in the restoration was a bit on the bright side for my taste. Though 1750 prices have been a little soft recently, I'd call this one well bought and well sold.

(Photo, historical and descriptive information courtesy of the auction company.)

From the December 2003 issue of SCM.◆

1938 6C 2300B

Any time a dolled-up 6C 2300 with a short chassis sells for less then 200 grand, something stinks—and it's usually the car

by Raymond Milo and Keith Martin

Chassis number: 815022
Engine number: 823251

Carrozzeria Touring of Milan developed and patented Superleggera body construction, working with light alloys and sparingly dimensioned components to lay up aluminum panels over a cage-like steel frame. The earliest of these bodies ever made included those for Alfa Romeo's 6C 2300B chassis in 1937.

The 6C 2500 was introduced as a follow up in 1939, with this beautiful Torpedino Brescia-style bodywork appearing in summer of that year. Touring originally gave this name to the identical type of bodywork found on an Auto-Avio-Construzioni type 815 chassis. Indeed, two cars of this type took part in the Targa Abruzzo race of that year, with one example winning the competition.

Using the 1938 6C 2300B Mille Miglia second series in shorter form, the car on offer here has recently had its engine completely rebuilt by Chris Leydon of Lahaska, PA, at a cost of $36,803. With full photo and written documentation, it was completed with three-port 6C 2500 cylinder head with correct triple-Weber 36 DCO 2 carburetors and air cleaners, together with a new set of Carillo rods. Engine output is understood to be 110 hp from a second series 1935 6C 2300B short-chassis example.

FIA papers have now been applied for, anticipating enjoyment of this car to the fullest in continental events. It is described as good in all respects and ready to use.

The SCM analysis: This car sold for $179,904 at Bonhams' London sale, held Dec. 6, 2004.

Let us get right to the point. Just as a Pontiac Tempest rebadged as a GTO is a fake, and a 383-ci 'Cuda with a Hemi stuffed in it is a clone, this car is a complete fakey-doo.

We've watched it cross the block at three auctions now, and each auction company has danced neatly around the central issue. The basic engine from this car originated in a sedan, the chassis probably the same, subsequently shortened by someone who is never named, and the coachwork is a fairly recent creation by someone who spent too much time staring at real cars in the Alfa Romeo Museum.

Result? At best, a recently-built speciale. *At worst, a fraud.*

As collectors become more sophisticated, if auction companies wish to retain their trust, it is recumbent upon them to simply tell it like it is when it comes to the merchandise they are offering. Oddly enough, American auction companies are taking the lead here, with clear statements of "non-numbers matching," "re-creation" and "clone" becoming ever more prevalent in the lead line of auction company descriptions.

As a demonstration of the pitfalls of non-disclosure, our Editor Martin recalls his experiences with S/N 815022: "Back in my buying and selling days, I got offered this car when it had just been finished and was part of a Swedish collection. What stuck in my mind was the Model T taillight treatment, jarring compared to the voluptuousness of the rest of its lines.

"At that time, it was described to me as a total fabrication using a modified Alfa sedan chassis and engine, and clothed in freshly-made coachwork. I don't recall what the asking price was.

"Another replica from the same batch later appeared at a World Classic Auction at Blackhawk, sitting in their Expo tent, Model T taillights glaring balefully at potential buyers.

"A couple of years later, I was at a private reception in Florida, and lo and behold, there was 815022. The proud owner asked me what

I thought of the car, and I told him it was very shiny. The next day, he asked for more information, and I used the data in the back of the Fusi book to show him the pedestrian origins of the chassis and engine. He was not happy to know that instead of a fabled 6C 2300MM, he had a fakey-doo, and immediately consigned it to the 2002 RM Biltmore sale.

"To RM's credit, its catalog clearly stated that 815022 is 'bodied in the Torpedino Brescia style,' and that the engine is fitted with a three-port cylinder head from a 6C 2500. The car sold for $151,800.

"Later, it was offered at the February 2004 Christie's Retromobile sale, where it was carefully described as 'a stylish and evocative restoration,' but remained unsold at $165,474.

"Then we come to the December 2004 Bonhams London sale. Nowhere in the catalog description is there any reference to the coachwork being non-authentic. I only hope that the new owner knew exactly what he was bidding on, and doesn't discover it by reading this."

What should make any astute buyer most suspicious of this car is its body. It is likely that in the period any short chassis would have had a beautiful, aquiline body built by one of dozens of coachbuilders. If this car started its life as a short chassis, it must have had a unique and sporting body. Yet it is clear that the metal it wears now is a rebody.

Though the work is very good, the form misses by a country mile. Imagine the cheerleader whose looks drove you wild in high school. Now you see her 20 years later—with an extra 20 pounds in the wrong places.

It is also strange that there is nothing mentioned in the catalog description of past history, no name of the first owner, absolutely nothing but the name of the recent engine builder—who may or may not have done an excellent job. Add to this the fact that the car has a 6C 2500 head, a much easier item to find then a real one from a 2300, and the case is as good as closed; this car is not red.

If we are wrong, may the Lord and the new owner forgive us. But our accusations aside, the market has spoken, loud and clear. Any time a dolled-up 6C 2300 with a short chassis sells for less then 200 grand, something stinks—and it's usually the car.

But let us take a look at the car itself, not as an example in authenticity but as its sits, a nice and shiny speciale *with 110-plus ponies under the hood. Could this buyer be a smart guy who knows that for a relatively modest amount of money, he bought a nice Franken-Alfa that he can enjoy in many events? If that's the case, I wish him happy motoring.*

(Historical and descriptive information courtesy of the auction company.)

From the April 2005 issue of SCM.◆

1939 6C 2500 Cabriolet

This pre-war Tücher-bodied Alfa is a link between the angular styles of the 1930s and the aerodynamic bodies after the war

by Pat Braden

Chassis number: 913014

Vittorio Jano's 1927 6C 1500 provided the foundation for a series of engines that form the basis of Alfa Romeo's great prewar reputation. Expanded to 1752 cc, it became the 6C 1750. With two added cylinders, the 6C 1750 design became the 8C 2300. The Tipo B 2.9-liter Grand Prix expanded upon these principles and was ultimately adapted to the famed 8C 2900 sports cars.

However noble, the performance attributes of the 6C 1500 and its derivatives became dated. In 1934, Jano created a new generation of Alfa Romeo powerplants: the dual overhead camshaft 6C 2300. With a 70-mm bore and 100-mm stroke, the 6C 2300 continued the long stroke that gave Alfa's engines high-end torque for drivability while adopting an improved light alloy cylinder head with chain-driven camshafts. Reliability was a priority in its design, and Jano gave it hollow camshafts for superior lubrication, seven main bearings for rigidity, a single-piece block and head castings, and an innovative dual-level sump that acted as an efficient oil cooler. In 1939, the bore was increased to 72 mm, creating the 6C 2500 with 2443-cc displacement.

The new 6C series engine was complemented by a brilliant chassis reflecting all that Alfa had learned from its dominant GP and sports cars: four-wheel independent suspension; parallel trailing arms at the front and swing axles at the rear. Springing was achieved by torsion bars at the rear and coil springs in hydraulic cylinders at the front.

Most 6Cs were provided on special order to favored clients for custom coachwork, among them the 1939 6C 2500 offered here. Chassis number 913014 was discovered by the current owner in Nova Scotia in 1976. Years of research traced the car back through its prior owners in England to a Heathrow Airport parking facility where it had been abandoned with a broken axle. The Alfa's attractive cabriolet coachwork was an even greater mystery. Again, painstaking and lengthy research by the owner finally traced the body to Gebruder Tücher in Zurich, Switzerland. The company, still in existence building bus bodies, provided copies of the original records showing delivery by November 1, 1939, to Herr Direktor Weber in two-tone gray, the same colors it displays today.

With the combination of Vittorio Jano's powerful yet reliable engine and race-bred, fully independent suspension, prewar 6C 2300 and 6C 2500 models are superb road machines. The Tücher-bodied example shown here is not only rare, it is unique. It is faithfully presented, appearing much as it did when it was delivered to Herr Direktor Weber 61 years ago. Angelo Tito Anselmi's authoritative book, *Alfa Romeo 6C 2500,* indicates that this is the earliest surviving 6C 2500.

The SCM analysis: This car sold for $121,000 at RM's Arizona Biltmore sale, January 19, 2001, including buyer's premium. There should be a law that prohibits invoking the ghost of Vittorio Jano every time an Alfa crosses the block. While Jano is credited with the 6C 2300, *he was fired from Alfa two years before the 6C 2500 appeared. Certainly the 6C 2500 engine is a minor elaboration of Jano's earlier powerplant, but the honor of its development goes to Bruno Trevisan, who also created the more sporting Corto and Super Sport versions. Furthermore, the 6C 2500 was not a very distinguished race car, nor was it the obsolescence of the great Jano cars that prompted the 6C 2300 and 6C 2500, the Depression instead being the cause. Alfa needed cheaper cars for the economy, and that is exactly what the 6C 2300 and 6C 2500 were.*

It would be fascinating to know exactly what Herr Weber "directed" (S/N 915521 went to Albert Speer; two earlier 6C 2500s anonymously to the Deutsche Wehrmacht). Hopefully, the new owner will continue the dedicated research undertaken by the individual who restored this car. Without the supplied provenance, including the identified body builder and, indeed, the original owner's name, this car would have brought much less.

This provenance is probably more valuable than the claim that this is the oldest 6C 2500 known. A quick read of Anselmi's book fails to reveal a reference to this car, but Anselmi does state that the official factory register, covering the years 1939-42, was destroyed during the war. This leaves Luigi Fusi's personal records as the most authoritative resource. Fusi lists the first 1939 6C 2500 Turismo five-seater chassis as S/N 913001, which means there are potentially 13 other chassis waiting to dethrone this car as the oldest of the litter.

This pre-war Tücher-bodied Alfa deserves better than a fawning, Jano-laden description that misleads more than it informs. The car is a handsome and distinctive link between the angular body styles of the 1930s and the seminal, aerodynamic bodies that clothed the same chassis after the war. Given the decent condition of the car (SCM's Dave Brownell described it as being an "older restoration still quite presentable" in the April 2001 issue) and its rarity, it should be considered very well bought in today's market.

(Photo, historical and descriptive information courtesy of the auction company.)

From the September 2001 issue of SCM.◆

1947 6C 2500 Berlinetta Touring Sport

At a hefty 3,000 pounds and with only 95 horsepower, the 6C 2500 Sport was far from an AA Fuel dragster

by Ramond Milo

Chassis number: 916015

By the later 1930s and during the early 1940s, thanks to the high-profile successes won in motor racing by its sports and Grand Prix cars, Alfa Romeo had earned a well-deserved reputation for producing outstanding road cars. The groundbreaking and innovative engineering of Vittorio Jano was responsible for one of the most outstanding designs of all time, the 6C 2500.

This 6C 2500 with Berlinetta Touring Sport coachwork by Milanese coachbuilder Touring was made by Alfa Romeo in 1947, supplied new to Luigi Ledosti and Company, also of Milan, and first registered in the U.K. in September 1951.

The coupe is claimed to be an original and unrestored example, hence its appearance, which was described by a previous owner as "used." Incredibly, the 13,889 kilometers displayed when consigned for this sale are believed to be the genuine total for this car from new. The current condition of the chassis, coupe bodywork, and red paintwork is reportedly very good. The interior is original and the 2,443-cc, six-cylinder engine and four-speed manual gearbox are in very good order.

The SCM *analysis: This car sold for $69,865 at the H&H Buxton auction held on April 7, 2004.*

Early in the '20s, automotive engineers became aware that the four-cylinder engine could never be fully dynamically balanced. (The same was true of eight-cylinder engines, which were really just two joined fours.) However, the inline six (and its derivative V12) were naturally balanced. The slightly higher cost of a six, as opposed to the four, was more than offset by its quicker revving and higher output. Thus many sports car manufacturers, including Alfa Romeo, favored sixes.

Beginning in 1920, Alfa produced six-cylinder cars continuously through the end of 1953. The 6C 2300 engine was developed under the auspices of one of the great automotive engineers, Vittorio Jano, and powered Alfa to a string of international victories. In 1937, after Jano's departure, Bruno Trevisan took charge of the design and development of Alfa's six-cylinder cars and the 6C 2500 was the next logical step. By 1939, production was humming along.

In typical Alfa fashion, the 6C was offered in a variety of body styles, ranging from four-door sedans called "ministeriale" (these tend to be donor cars today), to the honest-to-goodness factory race cars. With some exceptions, all 6C 2500s shared the same chassis with various wheelbases ranging from 325 cm (about 128 inches) to the 270-cm (about 106 inches) Super Sport. Power ranged from a low of 90 hp at 4,200 rpm in the "coloniale" (to be used primarily in African colonies) to 110 hp at 4,800 rpm in the Super Sport. The difference between the engines was due to the usual factors, like camshafts, compression ratios and the number of carburetors.

Standard Alfa construction practices continued: a four-speed gearbox (the top three gears were synchronized after World War II), large hydraulic brake drums, independent front and rear suspension, 18-inch wheels, and right-hand drive. (Myth has it that this was done in imitation of the great touring and sports cars from Britain, including Jaguar and Bentley, but we would be interested in hearing other theories on this subject.)

The sportier, two-door versions of the 6Cs rode on wire wheels, which for some strange reason always had hubcaps hiding them. The bread and butter of the 6C production range was the Sport model, with a 95-hp motor and a 300-cm (118-inch) wheelbase. It came with many different body styles, but the most frequent were factory built (as in the Freccia d'Oro two-door coupe) and Berlinetta by Touring. Because of the rather generous wheelbase, the rear seats were even comfortable.

Depending on the number of grappas consumed, a claimed top speed of 155 km/h (96 mph) was obtainable. However, at a hefty 1,350 kg or thereabouts (roughly 3,000 pounds), the 6C 2500 Sport was far from a AA Fuel dragster. I don't have any contemporary acceleration tests, but would guess that 0-60 mph was pushing 20 seconds. The late Pat Braden called the car a "sheep in wolf's clothing."

According to various records, a total of 1,256 cars were produced. (This is a guesstimate—never take production figures from this era as absolute.) Excluding the pure race cars, the most interesting and valuable examples came from the last three years of production. These 109 examples built from 1951 to 1953 were fitted at the factory with the SS engine (triple carbs, 110 hp), and predominantly had interesting bodies by the finest coachbuilders. Some Alfisti consider these SS-engined cars a separate sub-series, with an appropriately much higher market price than plain vanilla examples. The most valuable of these are the Touring-bodied cabriolets, which, when in perfect condition, can command upwards of $200,000.

Which brings us to chassis #916015. According to my records, this example was built as a 1948 model (finished in November 1947) and "officially" sold in the beginning of 1949. One should not take the time gap between completion and sale date seriously. More than likely the enterprising first owner drove the car with a junkyard title to avoid the dreaded value tax.

At almost 70 grand, I would say this car sold for fair money. It's a large, comfortable car that needs to be capital-D driven to achieve maximum performance—just sitting behind the steering wheel and adjusting the radio won't do it. If, for less than $50,000, the new owner can make the car presentable and reliable, he has a car that will be accepted into nearly any vintage event in the world. The late Tom Congleton had a magnificent 6C 2500 SS Berlinetta that he drove in the Copperstate 1000 and the California Mille numerous times, and it always attracted a great deal of attention.

So for the right buyer, who isn't looking for a big Alfa that handles like a Giulietta, this sounds like a nice, low-mileage, well-patinated driver. Regardless of value, one rarely sees them offered for sale. As the market is beginning to value unrestored cars, the new owner should be okay here provided the surprises he is sure to find are small and inexpensive ones, and that he doesn't decide that a full nut-and-bolt restoration is needed. I wish him the best, and I hope to see this unusual car, from a relatively unknown period of Alfa's history, back on the road.

(Historical and descriptive information courtesy of the auction company.)

From the September 2004 issue of SCM. ◆

1947 6C 2500 SS

This last of the hand-built Alfas was a favorite of Middle Eastern royalty and Hollywood movie stars

by Pat Braden

Chassis number: 915417

One of the most beautiful cars of the late 1940s, the Alfa Romeo 6C 2500 was among the first Italian sports cars to go into production after World War II. The superbly styled coachwork by Pinin Farina earned the 6C 2500 dual honors: it was one of the last cars to be recognized by the CCCA (Classic Car Club of America) and one of the first to be honored by the Milestone Car Society as a post-war collectible.

Subtle in its design, most Alfa Romeo 6C 2500s, such as this award-winning example from the Jerry McAlevy Collection, had only minor exterior embellishments. Even the bumpers, as on this 1947 auto, were little more than metal strips. Equipped with a four-wheel fully independent suspension and four-wheel hydraulic brakes, the 6C 2500 Sport and Super Sport models were powered by a race-proven, 2443-cc, six-cylinder dual overhead-camshaft engine with hemispheric combustion chambers. Sport models had a single two-barrel carburetor and 7:1 compression ratio, and developed 90 hp.

The car's striking shape was actually narrower at the rear than the front, which led to the unusual three-passenger front bench seat. Alfa owners had to be well coordinated since the cars were right-hand drive with a four-speed shifter mounted on the left side of the steering column. The interiors were superbly appointed with jewel-like instruments, faux yellow-ivory control knobs and luxurious upholstery of glove-soft leather. Such fine detail was a hallmark of these last hand-built Alfa Romeo tourers.

The SCM Analysis: This car sold for $108,000, including buyer's premium, on January 20, 2001, at the Barrett-Jackson auction held in Scottsdale, Arizona.

Jano's fabulous 6C 1750, 8C 2300 and 2900 were world-class performance cars, but they were also prohibitively expensive for the depressed 1930s economy. To broaden its market, Alfa needed a cheaper car. The 6C 2300, introduced in 1934, offered the same displacement as Jano's 8-cylinder supercharged passenger cars, but with natural aspiration, two fewer cylinders, about half the horsepower and none of the sophistication (or fabulous castings) of those benchmark cars.

The 6C 2300 was still not a cheap car by any standard, though. Chassis were individually assembled by hand, and often shipped off to the body builder of the owner's choice, even though "factory" bodies were available. Initially introduced in 1934 with independent front suspension but a solid rear axle, the car received fully independent suspension as the 6C 2300 B in 1935. After Jano was fired, Bruno Trevisan enlarged its engine to 2.5 liters in 1939.

Even though this is the Super Sport version of a 2.5-liter engine, it only develops 110 hp and is capable of only 100 mph. By carefully picking its venues, Alfa was able to record some victories for the 6C 2500, but the description of the engine as being "race-derived" is more hyperbole than fact. In spite of its twin-cam configuration and triple carburetors, the 6C 2500 SS was mildly tuned. Brake mean

effective pressure for the Super Sport engine was only 7.26 kg/cm^2, compared to 8.55 kg/cm^2 in Colombo's development for the notorious 6C 3000 C50 coupe, and 10.62 kg/cm^2 for the more modern Giulia Super.

In 1946, Alfa's Portello factory, especially its foundry, was nothing more than rubble. Alfa had moved its huge inventory of cars and parts out of the factory before it was bombed, and cached them away in a number of caves north of Milan. As soon as the Germans were driven out of Italy, the horde of parts was rescued and assembly of cars recommenced. Three single-carburetor Sport models were assembled in 1945 and the number of cars for 1946 soared to 162. In the following year 281 6Cs were built, 71 of which were Super Sports. Thus, a majority of the parts in this 1947 car are actually pre-war and ex-cave.

The 6C 2500 is probably the most comfortable long-distance tourer Alfa ever built. A fully independent suspension combines rear torsion bars, front coil springs and a long wheelbase to give a luxurious ride. The bodywork by Pinin Farina, Touring and others on this chassis unquestionably set the direction of post-war automotive design. This model was also a favorite of Middle Eastern royalty and Hollywood movie stars. Furthering its desirability, this was the last of the hand-built Alfas, as the succeeding 1900 series was assembled on a production line. Notwithstanding, this model Alfa is the least appreciated of all the coachbuilt series, and the sportier models have always attracted more interest.

Beautifully restored some years ago, this particular car is starting to age once again. Paint bubbles are beginning to appear in vulnerable areas and a fabricated rear bumper detracts from its back view. The dash is superbly detailed with correct instruments, knobs and steering wheel, and it's hard to fault the leather interior. The fact that this presentable Alfa sold for less than SCM's Price Guide range of $125,000-$175,000 tells us that either the market for these large, comfortable cars is as soft as their ride, or else the muscle car fanatics in the Barrett-Jackson audience just didn't know what to make of this right-drive, left-shift car. Personally, I suspect a little of both.

(Historical and descriptive information courtesy of the auction company.)

From the May 2001 issue of SCM.◆

1950 6C 2500 Competizione

The buyer who anticipates a 'wolf in sheep's clothing' may be in for a shock. A 'sheep in wolf's clothing' might be a more appropriate description

by Pat Braden

Chassis number: 64251
Engine number: 924866

Alfa's 1934 6C model was conceived as a natural development of the successful 6C 1500 and 6C 1750 series, and set the pattern for post-war Alfas. With dual overhead camshafts and a 70 x 100-mm bore and stroke, Jano's final design of a production Alfa Romeo was robust: an engine with seven main bearings and a stiff, boxed-chassis frame. Though designed and built with costs in mind, it carried on the sporting traditions of the Milanese marque.

The success of the 6C 2300 models was demonstrated in 1938 when Pintacuda and Giuseppe Farina finished first and second in the Mille Miglia, just one leading example of many highly successful competition outings in the season. In 1939 the factory increased the cylinder bore to 72 mm, creating the 2443-cc 6C 2500. With an improved cylinder head for better breathing and compression ratio increased from 6.75:1 to 7:1, output rose from 87 bhp to 95 bhp in the Sport version, with a single-throat Weber carburetor, and up to 105 bhp in the Super Sport version, which sported three Weber carburetors.

In 1948 Alfa developed the 6C 2500 Competizione, of which only three were built. One of these cars had a more advanced chassis, developed and manufactured by Gilco Milano. Behind the company name of Gilco was the full name of Gilberto Colombo, who designed and manufactured racing Ferrari and Maserati chassis in the 1950s. In 1950 Alfetta gave the order for chassis 64251 to Gilco to build a special frame to accommodate the 6C running gear.

Meanwhile, on the motor racing competition front, 1950 was an unforgettable season for the Alfa Romeo team, which entered the newly designed type 158 in eleven Grand Prix and won them all, Fangio winning six and Farina five. In 1951 Fangio went on to win the first of his five world championship titles. As a result of this achievement, at the end of the season Alfa Romeo had the Gilco Tubolare chassis rebodied by Ghia and, after displaying it at a concours in Milano, gifted it to Juan Manuel Fangio as a present in recognition of winning the world championship.

At some later stage Fangio decided to sell the car, which was then exported to England. Years afterward it was discovered in an unrestored condition in a collection of Ferraris. Between 1995 and 1997 the car underwent a very thorough restoration, taking some 5,800 hours, which was fully documented and photographed.

It has since won many concours prizes, most recently winning its class at the famous Villa d'Este Concours this year against stiff competition, and taking second prize overall. This is an opportunity to acquire a magnificent and elegant sports car with a thoroughbred race car chassis, eligible for many of the international concours d'elegance and long-distance touring events around the world. A true wolf in sheep's clothing, both beauty and beast.

The SCM Analysis: The auction copy rings all the bells crafted to open the most truculent wallet: Jano-derived, racing heritage, one-of-a-kind competition version, special tubular chassis, custom body, ex-Fangio and—here's the clincher—a real barn find. Worth $220,000 to $260,000, asserts the auction company (in spite of the fact that SCM's own Price Guide tops out around $175,000).

Bidding stopped at $160,000 at Christie's Pebble Beach sale, August 19, 2001, and the car drove off a no-sale. Of all coach-built Alfa Romeos, the 6C 2500 is the least sporting Alfa, even when dubbed "Competizione." The buyer who anticipates a "wolf in sheep's clothing" may be in for a shock the first time he floors this car in fourth. A "sheep in wolf's clothing" might be a more appropriate description.

This car was built at a time when Alfa was not keeping precise production records, even by Italian standards, so I will not claim that this car's heritage is suspect. But I have looked in vain in Fusi, Tabucchi and Anselmi for a reference to a 6C 2500 engine number beginning with 924. The same goes for this car's chassis number. The "gift from Alfa" account is well known, but it was a 1900 coupe from the early 1950s that was Alfa's gift to Fangio, who has placed his signature on that car's firewall.

Finally, the mention of Colombo in relation to an Alfa suggests Gioacchino Colombo, who went on to do great things for Ferrari. The Colombo in this instance, however, is Gilberto, no relation to Gioacchino, and references to Gilberto's further successes with Ferrari and Maserati are, to say the least, sparse. Further, Gilco seems to have built frames only for the Ferrari 125, according to the official Ferrari 50th Anniversary book. Hopefully, the claims of ex-Fangio and ex-Gilco for this 6C are fully documented in the papers that accompany the car.

Suspicions aside, this is still an attractive 6C 2500. Its body is a refreshing departure from the frequently seen Pininfarina style, and hints at the tighter lines of the 1900 series that followed. That it was a no-sale only underscores the fact that the 6C 2500 is a slow mover in more ways than one.

(Photo, historical and descriptive information courtesy of the auction company.)

From the December 2001 issue of SCM.◆

1951 Villa d'Este Cabriolet

If there had been no war, Alfa would have soon replaced the 6C 2500; but Italian fortunes began to unravel, and bombs began to fall

by Pat Braden

Chassis number: 918089
Engine number: 928305

Destined to be the last of the separate-chassis Alfas, the 2500 debuted in 1939 as a development of the preceding 6C 2300B. The engine was, of course, the latest version of Alfa's race-developed twin-cam six, its 2443-cc displacement having been enlarged by boring out the 2300 cylinders by 2 mm for a bore and stroke of 72 x 100 mm. Maximum power ranged from 90 bhp for the single-carburetor Sport model to 105 bhp for the triple-carb Super Sport. Production of the model spanned the war, finally ending in 1953, with a total run of 2,594.

This handsome 6C 2500 carries Superleggera four-seater cabriolet coachwork by Touring of Milan, and retains its original 105-bhp Super Sport engine, as indicated on the chassis plate. Most Villa d'Este models were fixed-head coupes built on the short-wheelbase three-meter chassis, and a cabriolet such as this on the standard 3.25-meter chassis is rare. Distinctive styling touches include disappearing exterior door handles, door pulls and amber window winders and switchgear.

Chassis number 918089 was delivered new in October 1951 to Garage Conva, in Vaduz, Lichtenstein, subsequently spending much of its life in Chile. The current owner acquired the car in Santiago in 1983. The bodywork was restored six years ago by Los Hermanos Torres, of Santiago, and the mechanical refurbishment was undertaken by the owner himself. Only a handful of miles has been covered since completion. The car is in running condition, though would probably benefit from a service, and, apart from a few easily rectifiable cosmetic blemishes, the body, paint and brightwork are all in very good condition. The brown soft top is easily erected. This coachbuilt Italian Gran Turismo comes with Registro Internazionale Touring Superleggera letter of acceptance and Alfa Romeo factory production certificate.

The SCM *analysis: This car sold for $93,620 at the Brooks Goodwood Festival of Speed weekend on June 23, 2000. The sale price was twice the auction house's estimate, but below the SCM Price Guide of $100,000 to $150,000 for this model. The low initial estimate was due to the car's condition. SCM's Richard Hudson-Evans reports that the car showed only 5 km (8 miles) on the odometer, but was "incomplete and needed finishing. [It was] over-thickly painted and missing wiper arms and blades."*

An auction description containing phrases such as "running condition...benefit from a service...easily rectifiable cosmetic blemishes," signals that the new owner will have much to do before the car is truly reliable and presentable. Interestingly, the ex-Eric Clapton 6C 2500 SS PF-bodied cabriolet sold for $126,000 at the same show, perhaps raising the interest in the Villa d'Este.

There is probably not a single auction description of an Alfa Romeo that does not make reference to one of Alfa's "race-developed" features. In point of fact, the 6C 2500 model, like its predecessor, the 6C 2300, was conceived as a passenger car. Most of the models produced were somewhat slow and heavy for their heritage, in spite of model designations like "Pescara," "Mille Miglia" and "Super Sport." Even sporting 6C 2500s do well to approach 100 mph, and it was not until 1948 that the 6C 2500 Competizione appeared with an engine developing 145 bhp for a top speed of 125 mph. An experimental car, the 6C 3000 C50, was developed by Colombo from the 6C 2500 Competizione and ran in the 1950 Mille Miglia. By all accounts it was an evil-handling beast.

However, the significance of the 6C 2500 cars cannot be underestimated. The svelte, sparely decorated bodies from Touring and Pinin Farina on this chassis helped set the direction of the post-war automobile. The 6C 2500s offered fully independent suspension with rear torsion bars and a handsome twin-cam engine. Models included single-, dual- and triple-carburetor engines and short- and long-wheelbase designations. Styles ranged from two-place cabriolets to limousines.

The fact that 956 6C 2500s were produced in 1947 says something about Alfa's ability to protect its pre-war stock of parts, and a lot about the resilience of the Italian spirit.

If there had been no war, it is likely that Alfa would have moved quickly to replace the 6C 2500. The S11 model of 1938, designed to succeed the 6C 2500, featured a 90-degree V8 engine of 2260 cc that developed 94 bhp and could power the 2,300-lb, four-door sedan to 100 mph. The S10 sedan of the same year offered a 60-degree V12 engine of 3.5 liters and produced 140 hp for a top speed of just over 100 mph. As the Italian fortunes began to unravel, and bombs began to fall, Alfa moved its design department north to Lake Orta, where Wilfredo Ricart designed the more-modest 6C 2000 Gazelle, a six-passenger sedan powered by a 1954-cc engine in a fully independent chassis. Only one of these cars was ever fully assembled and it remains the last undiscovered grail of post-war Alfadom today.

This Villa D'Este, in its tired condition, brought all the money and more. The new owner has a rare piece, but paid a hefty price for that privilege.

(Photo, historical and descriptive information courtesy of the auction company.)

From the October 2000 issue of SCM. ◆

1932 8C 2300 Corto

In a world of instant 8Cs, where handsome saloon-bodied cars have new replica bodies slathered with instant patina, the fact that this is a real car is refreshing

by Pat Braden

Chassis number: 2111027
Engine number: 2111027

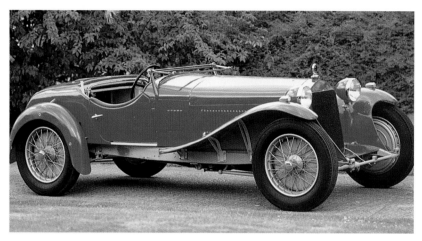

This is not just another mouth-watering classic Alfa. Offered here, absolutely fresh from 42 years in the ownership of one British enthusiast, chassis 2111027 is one of three Scuderia Ferrari short-chassis team cars prepared for the 1932 Mille Miglia. While this car did not enter that race, it was one of two cars to first carry the *Cavallino Rampante* in international competition, at the 1932 Spa 24-hour Endurance Classic. Works driver Piero Taruffi recalls: "For the last two hours, we drove with a broken piston; the mechanics had taken the sparking plug out of the offending cylinder and we finished on seven, coming in second behind the other Scuderia Ferrari Alfa driven by Brivio and Siena." The "seven-cylinder" car covered 1,675 miles at an average speed of 69.84 mph.

Though it ran at Spa as a Zagato Spider, the car was quickly rebodied with closed coupe bodywork for Luigi Scarfiotti, the father of Ferrari team driver Ludovico Scarfiotti. In 1936, someone, probably Africo Serra, again rebodied the car as a roadster with more modern, enveloping lines. The car traded hands several times again before making its way to England in 1938. The car's history during the war years is unknown, and its next registration appears in 1946, to a Grace Gertrude Danels.

In 1959, this Alfa was sold to Jack Hayward, who owned it for 42 years and began its full restoration. In the file accompanying the car, there is a letter dated March 9, 1959, from Frank Clissold Ltd. of Birmingham, detailing work done on the car: "...engine completely stripped, crank ground, new bearings fitted throughout, block bored, new pistons, rings, pins fitted, head stripped, valves ground in, supercharger stripped, new bearings and oil seals fitted and end float adjusted..." In the early '60s Hayward reported the renewed engine ran "sweetly," but it has not run since. With the chassis restored, Hayward decided to fit a replica Zagato body, but never completed it.

This is one of the most important and clearest-provenanced Scuderia Ferrari Alfa Romeos to have come onto the market in recent years. When completely restored to original form, 2111027 will once again be a truly lovely, significant, historic high-performance car of the utmost quality and value.

The SCM analysis: This car sold at the Bonhams & Brooks Silverstone auction, held August 25, 2001, for a price of $1,530,720, including buyer's premium.

To use the terms in Luigi Fusi's book, Alfa Romeo, All The Cars From 1910, *this is a Spider Corsa modification to the 8C 2300 Corto. The difference is in state of tune and final drive ratio: The standard* 8C 2300 Corto and Lungo cars developed 142 hp at 5,000 rpm with a 4.25 final drive. Spider Corsas were built to customer specification (presumably, Enzo Ferrari) and developed 165 hp at 5,400 rpm for the 1932 model cars, and the owner could select a 4.08:1 or 3.76:1 final drive. Additionally, this car is one of the first of three 8C 2300 series, indicated by the second digit of the serial number. Differences between the three series include the location of the oil tank and the radiator shape.

Though some body parts are included with the car, in practical terms, this is a chassis waiting for a body. Moreover, the fact that the car has not moved under its own power for more than 40 years means that, at a minimum, the chassis and drivetrain should be torn down and thoroughly inspected. The cost of this, as well as the cost of new bodywork and trim, represents a small percentage of the car's worth. This car's sale price of $1,530,720 suggests that the restored car could easily top $2,000,000 under spirited bidding. That would allow the new owner to spend about $500,000 before exceeding the car's probable market value. Clearly, this is a well-bought project and a solid investment.

Further, in a world of "instant 8Cs," where handsome saloon-bodied cars have their coachwork tossed off, their chassis shortened and their new replica bodies slathered with instant patina, the fact that this is a "real" car, with "real" provenance, is refreshing. It was born a race car, and no matter what body is ultimately fitted, the new owner will have a car with a provenance far superior to the chop-job 8C race cars built by enthusiasts who couldn't quite afford the real thing.

(Photo, historical and descriptive information courtesy of the auction company.)

From the February 2002 issue of SCM. ◆

1932 8C 2300 Corto Corsa

Such is the demand for 8Cs today that even highly compromised examples like this one command whacking great money

by Dave Brownell

Chassis Number: 2211080
Engine Number: 2211087

For many enthusiasts, no supercharged straight-eight Alfa Romeo has more visual appeal and flair than the short-wheelbase *Carozzeria Touring Spider Corsa* style, as offered here in chassis 2211080. For many experienced drivers of such cars, this specific sub-group comprises the best handling, most responsive, most nimble and best-braked of all the 8C series cars.

As researched by vintage Alfa authority Simon Moore, it seems likely that this car's first recorded appearance was as an un-numbered frame, listed within the Figoni coachbuilding files as having been delivered in the late spring/early summer of 1933.

Some features of this car's chassis suggest significant competition use before the car's first known road registration in Paris in 1933, including the lightweight chassis frame that still retains period competition stiffening about the front-end dumb-irons.

After being hidden from the Nazis during World War II, this 8C was imported into the U.S. around 1961 wearing Figoni four-seat cabriolet coachwork. The American owner removed the body from the car and traded the chassis and drivetrain for a Volkswagen.

In the late 1960s, the frame was modified to its current short-chassis configuration by British expert David Black, and a new engine was built up using the crankcase from 8C S/N 2211087. By 1971, our subject Alfa had been resurrected as a complete car, with its current replica Touring-style bodywork.

In the late 1980s it was disassembled again, and specialist Paul Grist was entrusted with the car's reassembly and complete restoration, which included the addition of the signature Touring fin ahead of the spare tires. It competed in the 1997 Mille Miglia, and is absolutely road-ready for any event.

The SCM *Analysis: This car sold for $894,375, including buyer's premium, at Bonhams' Goodwood auction on September 5, 2003.*

As SCM *senior auction reporter Richard Hudson-Evans remarked in his market comments concerning this car, it has a "complicated history." That's British understatement at its best. After reading and re-reading the catalog description for this car several times (a condensed version appears above), I was reaching for some aspirin to relieve the ache between my eyes.*

According to the catalog, this car may or may not have had a racing history prior to receiving the elegant and swoopy open four-seater Figoni coachwork mounted upon it in 1933. Furthermore, it may have raced in long-wheelbase form without a chassis number (!?) before being delivered to its alleged second owner, Count Januszkowski, who purchased it with the Figoni body in place. One thing is certain: The chassis and running gear are part of the 1932 production numbers.

The American who brought the car to the States actually got it as part of a package deal with two Type 57 Bugattis. (Those were the days.) As it was just a used-up used car, no one stepped up to buy

the Alfa, so after it was traded for a VW Beetle, it was broken up for parts. Then, as the values of 8Cs rose, all of the pieces necessary to make it a car again magically came together, drawn by the magnet of money.

So what do we have here? A well-documented pile of important bits that have somehow amalgamated themselves into a replica of an important car. Franken-Alfa doesn't seem an inappropriate term. Of course, the fact that the car exists at all is somewhat of a minor miracle in view of its checkered history.

Two things rankle about this restoration/conversion. First, the reverse-rim wheels and oversize tires give the car a somewhat heavy look instead of the litheness of line for which these cars are so admired. It's rather like wearing combat boots with a tuxedo. They cover your feet but a pair of patent leather shoes would be much more appropriate. Second, the new "Touring" body's doors don't have the right sweep and look a bit awkward to the experienced Alfisti's eye.

Such, though, is the demand for these cars today that even highly compromised examples like this one command whacking great money, as the winning bid demonstrates. Rumor has it that this car was bought by a U.S.-based SCMer who has already been offered a profit on his deal.

How much more would it be worth if it were a real car? Consider the famous Rimoldi Alfa 8C 2300 that was sold at a Christie's Pebble Beach auction a few years back. That car was so sublimely original and correct that merely contemplating subjecting it to a restoration, repaint or rebuild would rank as a mortal sin. At the time the successful bidder paid $1.75 million for this gem. Today it could be worth close to twice that.

(Photo, historical and descriptive information courtesy of the auction company.)

From the February 2004 issue of SCM.◆

1934 8C 2300

This 8C Alfa Romeo has matching serial numbers, but it isn't at all the car I owned 40 years ago

by Pat Braden

Chassis number: 2211133
Engine number: 2211133

Chassis number 2211133 was delivered on April 19, 1934 to Angelo Listori, with two-seat coupe bodywork that was shortly replaced by a drophead coupe body. In post-war Austria, the body was refurbished and the car eventually came to the U.S., where it was owned by Ed Bond, Pat Braden, Henry Petronis and Herb Wetson, who installed a Zagato body and sold the car to Canadian Mike Craven. After several other owners, Englishman Hugh Taylor commissioned Paul Grist to fit a Monza body.

Some purists may view this Monza as not entirely authentic. However, it should be noted that this is a correct, numbers-matching 8C 2300 chassis and engine, and 8C 2300 Monzas were being built as early as 1933 by none other than Scuderia Ferrari.

Inherently lightweight, powerful, responsive and quick, this 8C 2300 Monza is a beautifully presented memorial to the golden age of Italian automobiles. It is as competent today as it was 65 years ago, with lithe handling and gobs of power from its long-stroke supercharged straight-eight engine. Instantly recognizable by both cognoscenti and the uninformed as a Great Car, it is a ticket to the greatest historic racing and touring events, where its style, grace and performance will inspire onlookers, but most of all, thrill its driver. The new owner of this 8C 2300 Monza enjoys a direct connection with personalities like Nuvolari, Campari, Caracciola, Jano and even Enzo Ferrari—who drove his last race in an 8C 2300.

The SCM analysis: This car earned a high bid of $850,000 at the RM Amelia Island auction on March 10, 2001, but didn't sell. Buyers were not seduced by the boy-racer fantasy the auction catalog's copy tried to inspire.

Matching serial numbers have become a standard for evaluating the originality of a car. Matching numbers signify a virginal car, a mechanically noble savage. This 8C Alfa Romeo has matching serial numbers, but it isn't at all the car I owned 40 years ago. When I owned 2211133, it was a long-chassis car with a non-original heavy drophead body created somewhere in the bowels of Eastern Europe. It had burst out of iron-curtain Hungary full-chat, carrying its occupants and a few possessions to freedom in the West. It was a comfortable 100-mph tourer that I drove from Connecticut to Michigan over an unforgettable, snowy weekend. Its engine sounds, even when enveloped in a stodgy body, were music. I often lifted the hood and revved the engine just to hear all the gears work their magic. Its skinny tires gave it great traction in the snow, and I occasionally drove it to work to keep the battery charged and the mechanicals lubricated.

When I owned this car (from 1962-65, as I recall), it was still regarded as an interesting method of transportation, so practical

issues such as reliability and maintenance figured in the decision to buy. It never let me down. Gradually, however, the thought of the engine ingesting some incompressible object through the supercharger began to wear on me, and I finally traded it back to Ed Bond for an unsupercharged 6C James Young Phaeton, plus two other cars. At the time I let it go, my total investment in the 8C was about $2,500.

The estimated price range on this car before it crossed the block at Amelia Island was $1 to $1.3 million. That's long-chassis 8C money, not the $2.5 to $3.3 million a real Monza commands. In this case, the attraction of matching numbers seems to have had no influence on the value of the car, and the expensive Zagato and Monza modifications have produced absolutely no return on investment. If I had done nothing more than keep the car and then let it go for the $850,000 high bid, the car would have paid me just over $21,000 for each year I owned it. That's a great ROI by any standard. I would have saved a genuine slice of automotive history and the considerable expense of giving the world another imitation Monza. Moreover, I'd still be able to recognize the Alfa I once owned.

This 8C started life as a long-chassis (3100 mm) coupe. Keith Hellon shortened the chassis to 2750 mm to fit a replica Zagato body, and then Rodney Felton shortened it further to the 2650 mm Monza specification. So, the Monza body is really the fourth this car has worn, and the chassis has had three lengths.

Why in the world would anyone spend so much unrecoverable money to create a replica? Side-by-side with a real Monza, in the pits or on the track, this is an absolutely equivalent car in all respects (except for the magneto drive and, possibly, a 2.6-liter displacement). That makes this car a one-third-priced bargain that looks like a Monza, drives like a Monza and goes like a Monza. And it's got matching serial numbers, which is more than most Monzas (there were a debatable ten originals, six of which were converted to 2.6 liters) can now claim.

However, a more original car has been lost. Does the creation of another ersatz Monza justify the sacrifice of a long-chassis 8C? In this instance, the market's clear answer is no.

(Photo, historical and descriptive information courtesy of the auction company.)

From the June 2001 issue of SCM.◆

1934 Tipo B (P3)

Two million dollars is a lot to pay for anything, even one of the most desirable vintage race cars in the world

by Pat Braden

Chassis number: 50006

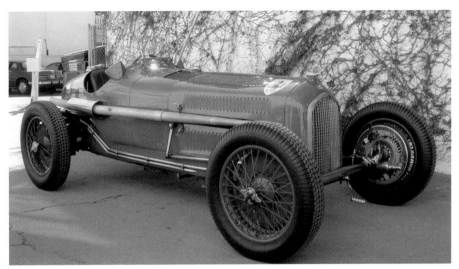

A design from the pen of the great Vittorio Jano, the Alfa Romeo Tipo B was a masterpiece on the drawing board and on the race track. It was not, incidentally, the first *monoposto* Alfa Romeo. That distinction belongs to the 1931 Tipo A, of which four were built, and none survive. There is a replica in the Alfa Museum.

The Tipo B first appeared at the Monza Grand Prix on June 5, 1932. Its engine was loosely derived from Jano's double overhead camshaft, straight-eight design for the road-going 8C 2300 and Monza Grand Prix cars. Unlike the 8C 2300s, however, the engine's intake was on the driver's left side, with dual superchargers serving the front and rear *testa fissa* alloy blocks. The stroke was increased from 88 to 100 mm to give a capacity of 2654 cc (65 x 100 mm).

Also, unlike the 8C 2300's conventional driveline, the Tipo B carried a single differential immediately behind a three-speed gearbox. Twin torque tubes splayed outward, enclosing separate driveshafts to a pair of bevel gears located near the ends of the solid rear axle. The Tipo B won Monza outright and continued to dominate the remainder of the season, including wins at the French and German Grand Prix.

The cars sat idle from the end of the successful 1932 season until the following August. At that time, Alfa Romeo transferred its racing activities to Scuderia Ferrari. Alfa built seven new cars for the Scuderia in 1934, the first year of the 750-kg formula. The engines for the 1934 cars were bored to 2905 cc, the displacement for which the Tipo B is best known, and horsepower rose from the original 215 at 5600 rpm to 255 at 5400 rpm. These cars were successfully campaigned by the Scuderia, with wins including Monaco, Tripoli, the Targa Florio, Avus and the French Grand Prix.

For the 1935 season, in response to the Mercedes and Auto Union efforts, Jano asked Ferrari to make additional modifications to the Tipo B. For the Pau Grand Prix in February, Nuvolari's car got a 3165-cc engine (71 x 100 mm and 265 hp) and cantilever rear springs. The springs proved so successful that all Tipo Bs were retrofitted. In April, Tipo Bs began appearing with Dubonnet independent front suspension and hydraulic brakes. Dreyfus contested the Turbie hill climb in April with the Dubonnet front suspension, and both Nuvolari's and Chiron's cars were similarly modified for the Monte Carlo race. It was in a Dubonnet-modified Tipo B that Nuvolari won his most famous race, the 1935 German Grand Prix. For the Grand Prix of France in June, the Nuvolari and Chiron cars carried a 3822-cc engine (78 x 100 mm) producing 330 hp. These cars also had a completely new chassis, incorporating a rear transaxle and IRS, and are referred to as Tipo C.

This is the ex-Scuderia Ferrari car 46, serial number 50006. From the Scuderia, the car was sold to Frank Ashby in England. The car was raced post-war by Ken Hutchinson, who sold it to J.J. Goodhew. From Goodhew, it traveled to Australia, where its new owner, John McMillan, campaigned it successfully. Its next owner, Leon Witte, restored the car, fitted telescopic shock absorbers at the rear to improve handling, and reunited it with its original engine.

The SCM *analysis: This car sold for $2,145,000, including buyer's premium, at the RM Classic Cars Auction at Amelia Island, FL, on March 11, 2000.*

Fusi shows six Tipo Bs produced in 1932 with three parts cars, seven produced in 1934 with four parts cars and six 1935 cars with spare engines and four parts cars, for a total of 19 cars and literally tons of parts. Two interchangeable four-cylinder castings made up the engine's top end: the center four cylinders were configured as a conventional four, with the outboard pair making up the other four. The two superchargers, however, fed each block exclusively, and I suspect that the resulting intake-path dynamics further assisted breathing. Along the same lines, the unique splayed rear drive (adopted from the Tipo A) worked by limiting wheel spin as the cars drifted through the corners. It's not clear that either feature was fully understood at the time, but the results were certainly fortunate.

Legend has it that the 43 road-going 8C 2900 passenger cars were assembled using spare engines built for the Tipo B. While the Tipo Bs never seemed to lack durability, the 8C 2900 was famous for cracking the large aluminum casting that comprised its cylinder block and head. Finally, in the 1980s, a batch of blocks was cast up in England and several cars, including at least one Tipo B near Chicago that had been immobilized by a cracked head, returned to service.

Two million dollars is a lot to pay for anything, even one of the most desirable vintage race cars in the world. However, two-seat Grand Prix cars from the same period (the P3 is a single-seater) will bring even more, as today's collectors want to bring someone along to enjoy the cacophony of whirs, grinds and shrieks that a blown 2.9 engine provides. A single-seat Mercedes W125 or a Maserati 8CM would cost about the same as this P3, and to get the extra seat a Monza provides, you may have to spend an additional $1m. So, in the context of similar race cars with the same types of heritage, this P3 should be considered fairly priced.

(Photo, historical and descriptive information courtesy of the auction company.)

From the May 2000 issue of SCM. ◆

Lord Ridley 6C/8C—Bitsa or Beauty?

Circumstances have conspired to put you in a position to build a neat 6C/8C hot rod, as the high road of preservation just doesn't make sense here

by Miles Collier

We recently received this letter, asking for advice about the restoration of a highly-modified Alfa Romeo 8C. We turned to preservation expert Miles Collier for his response. First, the query:

Dear *SCM:* I have found myself in an interesting situation, and am hoping for some input as to what to do. Through a variety of circumstances, I have become the owner of the Lord Ridley Alfa Romeo 6C/8C. This car was originally a 6C 1750 Gran Turismo (chassis #101014852), bodied as a Castagna drophead. In the 1950s, it was given the eight-cylinder engine and gearbox from 8C #2211136, as the original body was quite heavy and the blown six-cylinder 1750 motor was felt to be inadequate. The car was run in this configuration for many

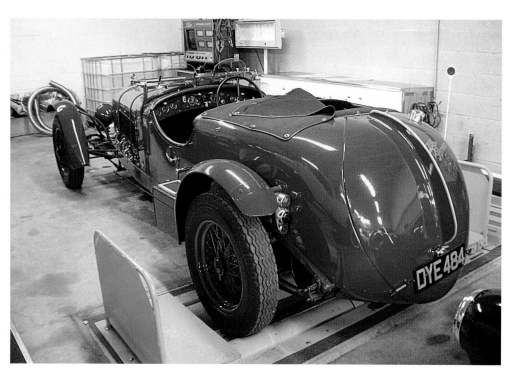

years, until re-bodied by Dick Brockman in the early 1980s as a long-chassis Le Mans car modeled after #2311204. Unfortunately, the original body was discarded at about that time.

The Ridley Special was then purchased at a Christie's auction in 1998 for $764,775. It was still complete with virtually all of the Monza drivetrain from 8C #2211136, which was then reunited with its original chassis by David George of Cochranville, PA. The remaining parts were then reassembled with another 8C engine and drivetrain, with none of the numbers matching. It is in this condition that it currently sits.

The body is of average quality and somewhat poorly proportioned compared to an original Touring-bodied Le Mans car. It has little inherent value, since it was not in this form when it was commonly known as the Lord Ridley car. The chassis, however, is perfect. The engine is a magnesium-block 8C engine with the engine bearers cut off, likely from #2211116 or #2211117 based on parts numbers, but further research is underway to try to pinpoint this engine number. The steering box is incorrect, as it needed to be mounted to the frame since the bearers are missing. The front axle is from the 6C chassis. In addition, I have an 8C gearbox and rear end, as well as a third-series 1750 engine and gearbox and a fourth-series block and blower.

So, the big question is what to do with the car? To restore or improve it in its current form would result in a well-built, non-original, and quite ugly car. I understand that this car will never be a proper numbers-matching Alfa 8C, but it could be built as a

recreation of a wonderful car. While it will be always be a re-bodied and re-powered 6C-based special, it could still be quite spectacular. It will have an original, numbered Alfa 6C chassis and most of an original 8C drivetrain and virtually the entire car will be constructed with proper Alfa bits.

My intent is to recreate and enjoy one of the world's great pre-war cars, with plans that would include vintage racing within the VSCCA, as well as tour events. As an aside, I have noticed that most of these Alfa 8C projects end up as short-chassis replicas in either Touring-bodied or Monza spec. I suspect that this is with future race involvement in mind, and also because Monzas have the most market value. (Perhaps people are hoping their values will rub off on their replicas.)

I have no intention of trying to pass this car off as a real car, although I suspect that other cars are floating around with even less provenance. Because of the value of the parts we have and the labor involved in completing this car, it is still going to be a very expensive automobile when completed. I consider myself to be quite fortunate to be in the position to do this project, but also recognize that I am never likely to purchase and race an original 8C.

I do appreciate your time in reviewing this letter and welcome your input in trying to put these parts to their best use.—*Bruce J. Rudin, M.D., via e-mail*

Miles Collier responds: To begin, let's take an inventory: You have an unmessed-about Alfa 6C 1750 long-wheelbase chassis, a full suite of 8C powerplant and drivetrain bits, and no body. (Or if you wish, a less-than-accurate '80s pastiche of a Touring-built Le Mans body.) This gives you plenty of options as you proceed.

Most restorations of important, high-value cars like an 8C Alfa hinge with profound solemnity on a get-it-right-at-all-costs approach to historic accuracy and the struggle to save every precious bit of historic fabric. While fascinating and intense, such projects generally do not offer the kind of creative fun that your 6C/8C presents.

As a first step in any restoration, I'd always want to consider the welfare of the car as an historic object, and consider what is right for the car and its place in automotive history. I recognize that this approach tends to fly in the face of much practice in the old car world, grounded as it is in its origins as a hobby. Unfortunately, hobbies tend to be about the hobbyist and his wants and desires, and as we know all too well, cars frequently pay for an owner's ego-driven restoration or modification program by having their authentic, historic lives erased and left to die on the floor of the restoration shop. I would hope that we now recognize that rare and special cars are deserving of a more thoughtful approach.

That said, does that mean you should try to return your chassis to its original incarnation as a 6C 1750 road car with its Castagna body? Despite the sermon above, I'd say no. My rationale is simple: For a collectible historic road car to be of the first quality, matching numbers are a crucial issue. As you probably won't be able to locate the original engine, gearbox and rear axle, you're left with only a type-correct drivetrain without the correct serial numbers. While this is not the end of the world, it's also a sacrifice not worth making when there are better and more usable options to explore.

ORIGINAL COACHWORK ISN'T THE ISSUE

Freed from the tyranny of matching numbers, you can probably also forget about the heavy, original Castagna coachwork, a less aesthetically pleasing wardrobe for such a potentially handsome car. (Though for daily use in-period it was much more practical than the sexy Touring or Zagato competition bodies that are so desirable today.) Unless the body was somehow kept or discarded in Arizona, the chance of it surviving in any usable form after 20 years of likely neglect and deterioration is mighty slim. Even if you like the styling and could obtain the body, I'm pretty sure once all the checks cleared you'd be upside down in a wholly unexceptional, non-numbers matching, street-bodied 6C 1750.

Since you do have all the 8C bits in hand, and a 6C chassis with 8C power makes a great and indistinguishable driving experience from a legitimate 8C, I think this is the way to go. I know of one such example that is driven with great competence and enjoyment at all the major U.S. tours, including the bi-annual Alfa 8C events, where its owner is having as much fun as anyone else.

Of course, the most important reason to take this route goes back to my initial point concerning the intrinsic integrity of the pieces you have to work with: You can do this swapping without major violence to any of the components, as the chassis has already been adapted by Lord Ridley when he installed the 8C engine. In other words, all this hot rodding is essentially benign to the parts, as it is now a bolt-in proposition. (And if for some reason the fit comes over you, you can decide to go back to 6C 1750 specification.)

The bottom line is that circumstances have conspired to put you in a position to build a really neat 6C/8C hot rod in good conscience, as the high road of preservation just doesn't make sense here. Therefore, unless you're desperate to recreate the "Lord Ridley" configuration

Cindy Lewis

Collier's 8C

(which without the Monza parts is a highly dubious undertaking at best), I would suggest you rebuild your car in the same vein as Mr. Brockman tried to, only I'd urge you to get the Le Mans coachwork fabrication dead-nuts correct.

YOU'VE GOT THE RIGHT CHASSIS

Why a Le Mans racer? Well, unless you're a gifted stylist, you won't possibly be able to come up with anything better looking on that long wheelbase you're stuck with. On this note, let me ascend to the pulpit again: Cutting up a proper chassis to turn it into a bastardized corto *is simply vandalism. Any argument that this practice was followed back in the period is pure sophistry, as that was then and this is now, and pre-war Alfas are no longer "just another used car" as they might have been considered then. Shortening a chassis is, for all intents and purposes, irreversible, and not only destroys an authentic original chassis, but makes nonsense of your serial number. To my mind, the practice is indefensible.*

You have a no-questions-asked, absolutely genuine 1750 lungo *chassis, that if kept un-modified, offers the prospect of some legitimacy to whatever you do next. While you will never have more than a modern hot rod built with period Alfa bits, you will have a car made of genuine, intact parts.*

Remember that the 8C lungo *Le Mans race cars were, like the Mille Miglia examples, competition cars from the ground up. Aside from a slight hint of wiener dog about them, they are just as spectacular and not significantly slower. Properly bodied, your car would have the virtue of preserving its chassis and avoiding the déjà vu, "boy-racer," Monza-look-alike syndrome that every 8C 2300 "bitsa" aspires to.*

The recreation of an 8C 2300 long-wheelbase Le Mans competition car with all the neat Le Mans trinkets is a pretty arresting sight. Better yet, this configuration will also allow you to pack your own luggage on all those tours like the California Mille that you're going to want to go on.

Various Alfa specialists can help you tune the motor with some minor but judicious modern tweaks to the blower and the Memini carburetor, which will give you some really good poke. I'll make sure I watch my mirrors and let you by when you come hauling up behind my 8C 2300 Corto on the next Alfa 8C tour.—M.C.

(Miles Collier is the owner of the Collier Automotive Museum in Naples, FL, and is regarded as one of the leading authorities on the art of preserving automobiles.)

From the July 2004 issue of SCM.◆

Crossing The Block

PREWAR 6C

#1164-1925 ALFA ROMEO 22/90 RLSS Boattail Roadster. Body by Thornton. S/N 9045. Maroon over black/black. RHD. Odo: 9,940 miles. V-pointed radiator and windshield are very characterful. Handsome torpedo coachwork installed in period.

Black headlamp bodies. Minor marks to paint. Suspension irons required repaint. Engine bay in need of TLC. Interior and trim refreshed in 1999. Cond: 2-. **SOLD AT $101,835.** *Much admired during viewing, which resulted in keen bidding and top-estimate valuation. Well worth it.* **Bonhams, Chichester, UK, 7/02.**

#293-1928 ALFA ROMEO 6C 1500 SS Spider. Body by Zagato. S/N 56134. Eng. #0211462. Red/black leather. Black cloth top. Odo: 9,317 miles. Jaeger gauges, Bosch headlights. Very good paint, chrome and leather. Older Michelin 5.50 x 18 tires

show first visual signs of dry rot. Hill and Vaughn restoration over 25 years ago. Cond: 3+. **SOLD AT $112,200.** *Very handsome, very slow. On the California Mille, leave first and arrive last. Poor car has been flogged on the "for sale" circuit for years. At last it gets a new owner, who paid full price.* **RM Auctions, Monterey, CA, 8/01.**

#51-1928 ALFA ROMEO 6C 1500 SPORT Spider. Body by Zagato. S/N 0231191. Red/black leather. Odo: 9,300 miles. Very well-preserved older restoration. A

genuine car. Hard to fault except the rear treatment on the body looks a little awkward compared to later Zagato efforts on Alfas. The progenitor of all the great Alfas of the '30s. Cond: 1. **NOT SOLD AT $140,000.** *Handsome car, but hugely lacking in the engine compartment, with just 1500 cc of naturally aspirated motor: Car has been for sale for years, at an ever declining price (that should send a message to the owner, yes?). We'll surely see it again.* **RM, Amelia Island, FL, 3/01.**

#86-1929 ALFA ROMEO 1750 SS 4-seat Sports Racing Car. Body by Carlton Carriage Co. S/N 03 12906. Eng. #6C 03 12906. Red/dark red leather. Black fabric top. RHD. Odo: 24,033 miles. Almost totally original car with a patina that won't

quit. Wonderful, successful racing history at Brooklands and other British venues. Super car and super provenance. Cond: 2-. **NOT SOLD AT $380,000.** *It would probably have done better at an English or Continental sale. Not all U.S. collectors appreciate honest wear and tear that can only be acquired through years of use.* **Christie's, Pebble Beach, CA, 8/01.**

#22-1930 ALFA ROMEO 6C 1750 GRAN TURISMO cabriolet. S/N 861336. Eng. #861336. Red/tan leather. RHD. Odo: 40,884 kilometers. 1.8-liter in-line 6, 4-sp. Very attractively restored in all areas except for odd-looking woodgrain sheets finishing rumble seat area. Thoroughbred chassis dressed with square-rigged styling, albeit the highest quality materials and workman-

ship. Cond: 1-. **NOT SOLD AT $190,935.** *Post-auction sale. Reached $191,000 in actual bidding, Last seen by SCM at Brooks' Amelia Island auction in 2000 where it no-saled at $162,000, then at RM Phoenix in January, 2002 where it was declared sold for $82,500(!). Bid here should have pleased the owner beyond measure, and car was fully valued.* **Christie's, Paris, France, 2/04.**

#306-1930 ALFA ROMEO 6C 1750 Cabriolet. Body by Castagna. S/N 6C-861336. Red/biscuit leather. RHD. Odo: 40,754 miles. Excellent top, upholstery, paint, ran very well with a delightful whir of gears coming from the engine. Correct throughout except for what looked like wood

grain Formica lining rumble seat area. Why? Rest of car was well done. Cond: 1-. **SOLD AT $162,000.** *Despite slightly square-rigged styling, this car was one worth stretching for—and someone did. Non-supercharged 1750s are not exactly tire-squealers, but still have their own appeal. And they're certainly a part of history.* **Brooks, Amelia Island, FL, 3/00.**

#1933-1930 ALFA ROMEO 6C 1750 Convertible. Body by James Young.

S/N 8613343. Red/black. RHD. Last restored in early 1970s. Converted from Autovac to 12-volt SU fuel pump. Paint just about okay, though in need of retrim and new top. Cond: 2-. **SOLD AT $76,869.** *With James Young drophead coachwork, this very characterful prewar Alfa transport for four with 6C 1750 twin-cam motor, albeit non-supercharged and only fed by single carb, just exceeded top guide price, going to private party.* **Bonhams & Brooks, Olympia, UK, 12/00.**

#108-1930 ALFA ROMEO 6C 1750 Convertible. Body by Castagna. S/N 6C861336. Red/gray leather. RHD. Odo: 40,772 miles. A well-restored, unsupercharged example with high-quality coachwork and well-detailed throughout. However, heavy

physically and visually, not characteristics well-heeled Alfa 6C collectors are looking for. Cond: 1-. **SOLD AT $82,500.** *Unsold at the Brooks Amelia Island auction in 2000 at a high bid of $162,000 (SCM Gold #14119). Nice car, but lacks the glamor and punch of the supercharged roadsters. Fair price here; bet that $162 large looks pretty good right now.* **RM, Phoenix, AZ, 1/02.**

#720-1930 ALFA ROMEO 6C 1750 3RD SERIES Drophead Coupe. Body by James Young & Co. Ltd. S/N 0412061. Eng.# 0412294. 6-cyl. Silver-gray/brown leather/black. RHD. Painted wires. Old repaint in

need of repeat. Original leather with much patina to fittings and dash. Power boosted by Series 3 Sport model's twin-cam motor. Cond: 2. **SOLD AT $105,300.** *Dull-looking coachwork in unexciting color did not hold back this flier which soared above top estimate until gavel fell—but then it was a pre-war Alfa twin cam.* **Brooks, London, UK, 4/00.**

#73-1931 ALFA ROMEO 6C 1750 SUPERCHARGED GRAN SPORT Spider. Body by Zagato. S/N 10814368. Eng. #10814368. Black/black leather. RHD.

Odo: 3,807 km. Stunning automobile in every respect and from every angle. Looks amazingly attractive in black. This color will show every body flaw, of which this car has none. As good as they get. Cond: 1+. **SOLD AT $447,500.** *The difference between a Spider and a tourer, a Gran Sport with supercharger vs. a straight 1750 with a changed engine? Consider Lot #39, a much-modified 8C 1750 Le Mans that didn't sell at $230,000, and you'll see immediately. This was market price.* **Christie's, Pebble Beach, 8/03.**

#72-1931 ALFA ROMEO 6C 1750 GRAN SPORT Spider. Body by Zagato. S/N 10814311. Eng.# 10814311. Black/burgundy leather. RHD. Supercharged car with 6th series gearbox (original box comes with car). Restored in late '80s with engine rebuild again in '98 for Mille Miglia revival, which it completed successfully. Also on Colorado

Grand, California Mille, etc. Cond: 1-. **NOT SOLD AT $300,000.** *6C 1750 Alfas seem to have hit a wall on price escalation. A few years ago they were climbing rapidly, but the 8C 2300s and 2900s appeared on the auction scene and overshadowed the 1750s. Should have brought at least low estimate of $400k.* **Christie's, Pebble Beach, CA, 8/00.**

#166-1931 ALFA ROMEO 6C 1750 GTC Coupe. S/N 10101423. Blue-gray, black/blue cloth. Odo: 2,510 km. Attractive color combo. Gorgeous wood trim interior. Huge doors were sagging, damaging paint in jambs. Driver's sill plate showed damage, otherwise car was near-perfect. Catalog cautioned there's a sister car in Italy with same S/N and indicated car may have been renumbered. Cond: 1. **NOT SOLD AT $160,000.** *Another car with stories. There are specialists in England and Italy who love to make one, two or six vintage Alfas out of one chassis,*

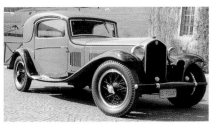

and the copies are turning up more frequently. Buyer beware. **Bonhams & Brooks, West Palm Beach, FL, 1/01.**

#379-1932 ALFA ROMEO 6C 1750GS GRAN SPORT Spider. Body by Zagato. S/N 10814402. Black/red leather. RHD. Correct but non-original supercharged engine. Very good upholstery and door fit, few paint chips on wheels, radiator plating fair. Actively

campaigned in classic rallies. Electric fuel pump added. Well-maintained older restoration. Cond: 2. **NOT SOLD AT $380,000.** *The popularity of the practical 1750 is exceeded only by the number available. Some Zagatos are really re-bodied sedans on cut chassis, but this was a legitimate example. High bid was within SCM's Price Guide and estimate offer should have resulted in a happy seller.*

#68-1933 ALFA ROMEO 6C 1750 Convertible. Body by Bernath. S/N 121215058. Burgundy metallic/cream. RHD. Odo: 85,000 kms. Wires. Completely original pre-war supercharged Alfa 6C 1750 with striking post-war alligator-nosed cabrio coach

work by Willy Bernath. Another original, though scabby and shabby, gem from Grell Collection preservation. Cond: 4+. **SOLD AT $145,559.** *Unrepeatable opportunity to acquire great rarity that offered enormous style. As with '49 Delahaye, should buyer, who had to pay 10% more than top forecast to win, leave it alone or destroy originality through restoration?* **Brooks, Monte Carlo, Monaco, 5/00.**

#98-**1933 ALFA ROMEO 6C 1750 GRAN SPORT Spider.** Body by Zagato. S/N 8513081. Red/red. RHD. Odo: 3,899 miles. Remarkably original, though the engine came from 6C S/N 8512865. Paint and brightwork good,

with only minor marks. Seat leather slightly dirty. Cond: 1-. **NOT SOLD AT $312,201.** *Definitely two bidders in the room for this one, and apparently a third player on the telephone. "Not quite enough," we were told! Worth just a tad more, although could really have been sold without major regret. Coys/Barrett-Jackson, Monaco, 5/02.*

#53-**1933 ALFA ROMEO 6C 1750 SUPERCHARGED GS Sport Spider.** Body by Zagato. S/N 121215062. 6-cyl. Red/black. RHD. Odo: 15,247 miles. Painted wires. Superbly presented. U.S. vendor. Maintained

under auspices of David George. Excelled in east coast Castle Hill Concours. Mint. Cond: 1. **SOLD AT $285,816.** *Hard to fault and made more than most optimistic forecast. With no-stories 1750 GS's going in the $350-400k range, unless we've missed something, this was a bargain. Coys/Barrett-Jackson, Monaco, 5/00.*

#702-**1933 ALFA ROMEO 6C 1750 GRAN SPORT Spider.** Body by Touring. S/N 121215050. Red/brown. RHD. Following a roll-over accident in the U.S. some years ago, extensive restoration by Paul Grist was recently completed. Cleverly, Old Master

patinated with slightly dulled finish. Floor unpainted. Leather actually new, but didn't look the part. Cond: 1-. **SOLD AT $392,630.** *Mid-estimate result was thoroughly deserved. While 1750s aren't showing the price appre-*

ciation of a few years back, they seem to be solidly in the $350,000 to $450,000 range. **Bonhams, Olympia, UK, 12/01.**

#37-**1933 ALFA ROMEO 6C 1750 Spider.** Body by Touring. S/N 12125048. Eng. #12125048. Red/black leather. RHD. Odo: 308 miles. Very fresh resto with Monza cowl and rear fin added after original manufacture for extra eye appeal, which the car

certainly had in spades despite the somewhat un-Alfa shade of red paint. Supercharged, of course, and ready for road, concours or race. Cond: 1. **SOLD AT $436,500.** *The right kind of money for this Gran Sport. Beautiful car but no racing history and, for some Alfisti, an important racing background is a car's raison d'etre. Christie's, New York, NY, 6/03.*

#65-**1934 ALFA ROMEO 6C 1750 GRAN SPORT Spider.** Body by Zagato. S/N 10814400. Eng. #10814400. Red/black leather. RHD. Odo: 289 km. Very fresh-looking, correct Roxas restoration. Class winner at Amelia Island concours, second in class at Pebble. Little use since restoration. Splendid

car. Cond: 1. **NOT SOLD AT $340,000.** *Worth another 50 grand and perhaps a bit more than that. 1750s have been a bit flat in the marketplace the last couple of years—perhaps everyone who had to have one got one. That happens, you know. Christie's, Tarrytown, NY, 4/01.*

#119-**1934 ALFA ROMEO 6C 1750 GRAN SPORT Spider.** Body by Zagato. S/N 10814400. Eng.# 10814400. Red/black leather. RHD. Odo: 7,828 kms. Fifth-series car

with Fran Roxas restoration. Supercharged. First in class at Amelia Concours in 1996. A stunner in all respects. Cond: 1. **NOT SOLD AT $319,000.** *Not nearly enough money for this one, folks. While the prices of 6C Zagatos have been flat the past couple of years, it still takes at least $350,000 to get into an outstanding car like this one. RM, Phoenix, AZ, 1/02.*

#235-**1934 ALFA ROMEO TIPO B (P3) Monoposto.** S/N 50006. Eng.# 50006. Red/black leather. Original Scuderia Ferrari car with dual superchargers. One of 3 P3s extant, but this one has the least exciting race history. Pushed across auction block. Restored

in Australia some years ago, now has nice patina. Appears race ready. Cond: 2. **SOLD AT $2,145,000.** *How much more might it have raised if those twin blowers had been screaming at the crowd? One of the immortals among racing cars and a fabulous piece of four-wheeled history. Price was in line with the current market. RM, Amelia Island, FL, 3/00.*

#90-**1937 ALFA ROMEO 6C 2300 B Spider.** Body by Touring. S/N 815022. Eng.# 823251. Red/red leather. RHD. Odo: 17 miles. Stunning "Torpedino Brescia" open bodywork, fresh engine by well-respected US specialist. However, provenance of this car very much in doubt. With no documentation,

we can only say that it has a nice visual appearance. Cond: 1. **SOLD AT $151,800.** *If this car had been presented with proof that it was an authentic, factory-built car, it could have brought more than twice this amount. Given the quality of the coachwork and mechanicals, this was a fair buy no matter what it was. RM, Phoenix, AZ, 1/02.*

#38-**1937 ALFA ROMEO 6C 2300 B Spider.** S/N 815022. Eng. #823251. Red/red leather. RHD. Odo: 172 kilometers. Lovely replica coachwork, engine uprated to Super Sport specs (110 hp), excellent doors and panels, correct interior and instruments and what appeared to be replica Model A Ford tail

lamps. Cond: 1. **NOT SOLD AT $165,474.** *So, what would a real one cost? Another $100k, at least. But it would be a real one, and this one will never be. Sold at RM Arizona, 1/02, for $151,800. Overall, decent bid given the visual presentation of the car and the high quality of the work that was done.* **Christie's, Paris, France, 2/04.**

#103-**1939 ALFA ROMEO 6C 2500 Cabriolet.** Body by Tuscher. S/N 913014. 6-cyl. 2443 cc. 95 hp. Two-tone gray/gray leather. Gray fabric top. RHD. Odo: 1,928 kms. Swiss coachwork on stodgy but bullet-

proof drivetrain. Hood fit a bit off, otherwise car looked very well in all areas. Older restoration still quite presentable. Cond: 2+. **SOLD AT $133,100.** *One-off example may well be the oldest 6C 2500 Cabrio extant. Full CCCA Classic and a handsome equipage. Price was right for buyer and seller.* **RM, Phoenix, AZ, 1/01.**

#100-**1939 ALFA ROMEO 6C 2500S Corsa Spider.** Body by Touring. S/N 915041. Dark red/light tan. RHD. Odo: 96,702 miles. Claimed to have employed many original components for1990s rebuild (or bitsa build?).

Body came from another 6C. Excellent paint and brightwork. Soiled seat leather. Cracked driver's mirror. Cond: 1-. **NOT SOLD AT $303,019.** *Even with jigsaw past, both the vendor and the auction houses thought it was worth more.* **Barrett-Jackson/Coys, Monte Carlo, Monaco, 5/02.**

#1034-**1939 ALFA ROMEO 6C 2500 SS CORSA Spider.** S/N 915006. Eng.# 923802. Burgundy/burgundy. RHD. Another Alfa shares this S/N. X-braced chassis likely to be manufactured c.1947. Bodied in he early

t1990s. Deliberately flattish paint, though with many marks. Interior only fair. Dull engine bay presentation. Sharp rear edge of cockpit must be painful. Cond: 3. **SOLD AT $64,527.** *Touring body replicated to Luigi Fusi design. Despite iffy-ness, certainly looked the part, and did generate mid-estimate money.* **Bonhams, Olympia, UK, 12/02.**

PREWAR 8C

#108-**1931 ALFA ROMEO 8C 2300 CORTO Spider**. S/N 2211080. Eng. #2211087. Dark red/black. RHD. Odo: 32,313 miles. Escaped Nazi invasion of Paris, post-WWII Swiss resident, exported to U.S. 1961. By 1970s chassis and engine in U.K.

where chassis shortened and made into complete car, acquired dismantled late 1980s by vendor Roger Saul of Mulberry, Paul Grist restoration. Cond: 2-. **SOLD AT $894,375.** *1997 Mille Miglia run. Paint marked (looking original!), gravel dented mudguards, driver's seat leather holed. Like so many pre-war Alfas, this 8C has complicated history. Even so, result was comfortably within forecast band.* **Bonhams, Sussex, UK, 9/03.**

#70-**1931 ALFA ROMEO 8C 2300 Le MANS LONG CHASSIS Spider.** Body a copy of Zagato. S/N 2111024. Black/dark red. RHD. Odo: 50,782 miles. Zipper, Harrah, Margulies, Hannen and Kato among former

big-name owners. Replicated bodywork very stone-chipped. Rear mudguards particularly

peppered. Brass showing through worn black paint on radiator surround. Worn and clearly very old seats. Engine bay unglossy but neat. Cond: 2-. **NOT SOLD AT $1,172,600.** *Following undistinguished period history, when carried Figoni coupe coachwork, this genuine works competition 8C chassis with Zagato replica body has become well known from belonging to several major collections and gaining much retro event exposure. Reserve was too ambitious for it to sell here, though.* **Christie's, London, UK, 3/01.**

#520-**1932 ALFA ROMEO 8C 2300 CORTO CORSA Spider.** S/N 2111027. Eng.#2111027. Red/tan. RHD. Odo: 384 miles. Confirmed to be ex-Scuderia Ferrari driven in 1932 Spa 24 Hours by Taruffi/ d'Ippolito when fitted with Zagato Spider coachwork. Rediscovered after 42 years in U.K. DIY part-resto with rear mudguards, running boards, radiator surround and grille missing. Interior stripped out, apart from door

trims. Buyer would most certainly throw body and interior away and start over. Cond: 3-. **SOLD AT $1,530,720.** *Sensational history and highly desirable spec. Much bidding in tent— and from four telephone players, too—from the opening bid of $1,123,200 until the gavel fell. This pre-9/11 result is unlikely to be bettered in U.K. for some time.* **Bonhams & Brooks, Silverstone, UK, 8/01.**

#46-**1932 ALFA ROMEO TIPO B P3 GP Monoposto.** S/N 5002. Eng. #50001. Red/brown leather. Ex-Scuderia Ferrari #38. Very fresh paint and detailing, slight wear on upholstery. Tremendous competition history on both sides of the Atlantic, crashes, engine

switches, etc. Now has proper Alfa racing engine, though not original unit. Substantially correct. Cond: 1. **NOT SOLD AT $1,400,000.** *Are P3s starting to soften? Two years ago, they were the flavor of the month, but then everyone who had to have one got one. Seller may have to lower his expectations to move* *this car on. Christie's, Pebble Beach, CA, 8/01.*

#58-1932 ALFA ROMEO 8C 2300 CORSA MONZA Spider. S/N 2211093. Eng. #2211240. Red/black leather. RHD. Older conversion to Monza-style coachwork, second engine, some lumpy bodywork and dulling paint gives the car great instant patina.

Veteran of numerous European vintage races and rallies. Cond: 2-. **SOLD AT $660,000.** *Bought for about 1/4 the price that a correct car with a famous competition history would bring. What do you think art collectors would say if people went around altering da Vinci's lesser works so they looked like the Mona Lisa? RM, Phoenix, AZ, 1/02*

#127-1933 ALFA ROMEO 8C 2300 2.6L MONZA CORSA Spider. S/N 2211095. Red/red. RHD. Odo: 2,765 miles. Discovered in Ethiopia by Freshman with a Chevy six-cylinder. Salvageable Alfa parts were sent to

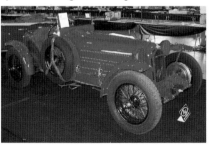

Italy where restoration/recreation was performed. Nicknamed "Nadine." An older restoration. Dead bugs in grille prove the car can get up to speed. Cond: 2-. **NOT SOLD AT $300,000.** *Soon to be the cover star of the yet-to-be-written book* How to Build a Car From a Fuel Tank, Firewall, Steering Wheel and Steering Column Box. *RM, Santa Monica, CA, 5/02.*

#90-1933 ALFA ROMEO 8C Long Chassis Spider. S/N 2111024. Black/burgundy. RHD. Odo: 50,782 miles. Ex-Chinetti and Harrah. Once Figoni coupe, then chopped and finally rebodied by U.K. specialist Paul Grist for Peter Hannen. Chipped paint. Black painted headlamp bodies and huge add-on tachometer red-lined at 5,000 to 7,000 rpm. Cond: 2-. **NOT SOLD AT $964,150.** *Run to exceed the magic 1,000,000 Euros level (to a phone bidder), but that still wasn't enough.*

Value now established in public. (Although brilliantly executed, we still feel there are a few too many faux-8C racers out there.—ED.) Coys/Barrett-Jackson, Monaco, 5/02.

#75-1933 ALFA ROMEO 8C 2300 MONZA Spider. S/N 2211125. Dark red/black leather. RHD. Odo: 35,060 miles. Fabulous racing history including winning first Bridgehampton road race. Owned and driven by numerous famous drivers. Partially

rebodied many years ago. Paul Grist restoration now nicely mellowed. Ready for race or road. Cond: 2. **SOLD AT $2,530,000.** *Matching-numbers car sounded wonderful, looked great, ran like a young bear and had more presence than Sophia Loren in an evening gown. A relative bargain, although the 8C market seems to have gone soft in the past few months. RM, Amelia Island, FL, 3/02.*

#60-1934 ALFA ROMEO 8C 2300 MONZA REPLICA Spider. S/N 2211133. Eng. #2211133. Red/black. RHD. Odo: 8,616 miles. Matching-numbers chassis and engine but carrying a new Monza-type body by master restorer Paul Grist to replace the original saloon. He also did the rest of the car up to

factory standards. 1996 Mille Miglia Storica participant. Lots of presence. Cond: 2. **NOT SOLD AT $850,000.** *Once owned by SCM Alfa guru Pat Braden, before it was "Gristed." If a real Monza is worth $3m, is $850k fair for a fakey-doo with authentic bits? Shame on the prestigious vintage events that let this car run—it devalues the real thing. RM, Amelia Island, FL, 3/01.*

#366-1936 ALFA ROMEO 8C 2900A Monoposto. Body by Botticella (1 of 4). S/N 412003. Eng.# 422012. Red/black. RHD. An 8-cylinder SC ex-Scuderia Ferrari team car that took 3rd place in the '36 Mille Miglia. Extensive post-war racing history in Argentina, where it was converted to a

single-seater and acquired an Alfa Tipo 308 crankcase. Returned to original 2-seater configuration in '80s restoration. Cond: 2. **NOT SOLD AT $2,900,000.** *Neither the original body nor motor, but very convincing with a patina that included exhaust soot on the rear body panel. Provenance and rarity failed to attract the low estimate of $3m. Rumored to have been sold after the auction. Brooks, Carmel, CA, 8/00.*

#336-1938 ALFA ROMEO 8C 2900B Coupe. Body by Touring. S/N 412036. Eng.# 422041. Red/red leather. RHD. This 1938 Paris Salon car was also the 1947 Mille Miglia winner (carbureted); now supercharged as original. It was campaigned extensively in Argentina and disappeared for a while, but was rescued from oblivion and restored by

Lucio Bollaert. Berlinetta styling a triumph of esthetics and light weight. Missing headlamp lens, otherwise hard to fault. Known history from day one. Totally legit car. Cond: 1-. **SOLD AT $3,082,500.** *One of the great cars of all time. Mere ownership, though expensive, assures your name in automotive history. The price was fair enough in the current market; it would take an open car, or one with even better history, to bring more. Brooks, Carmel, CA, 8/00.*

POSTWAR 6C

#24-1943 ALFA ROMEO 6C 2500 Spider. S/N 915134. Red/red leather. RHD. Odo: 7,301 kilometers. Recent replica coachwork by Diomante in the style of the ex-Pintacuda "Corsa Spyder". Impeccably

presented; a car with great presence but body's not the real thing. Cond: 1. **SOLD AT $228,410.** *After-auction sale. Actual top bid during the auction was $203,664. Didn't cost as much as an authentic example but it will never be worth as much, either.* **Christie's, Paris, France, 2/04.**

#119-**1946 ALFA ROMEO 6C 2500SS Cabriolet.** Body by Pininfarina. S/N 915535. Eng. #926871. Red/tan. RHD. Odo: 38 miles. Aluminum body, year of manufacture corrected during viewing. Chile restoration in

1995, repainted more recently, some bubbling. Badges, wipers and battery missing, trafficator slots empty, oil and water leaks declared. Cond: 3. **NOT SOLD AT $71,550.** *Too much to do, too much to undo—$118,500 ambition unachievable.* **Bonhams, Sussex, UK, 9/03.**

#52-**1947 ALFA ROMEO 6C 2500 coupe.** S/N 916.015. Eng. #926332. Red/fawn. RHD. Odo: 13,889 kilometers. 2443-cc I6, 4-sp. Genuine mileage from new. Incredibly undisturbed with well-charted history. Chassis and panels good, paint somewhat flat with minor

marks. Brightwork fair. Original fawn interior. Cond: 2. **SOLD AT $69,230.** *A special car, and really the buy of the auction. These big 6Cs trade in a thin market, but they are eligible for nearly every event, and, so long as*

you have very strong arms for the ponderous low-speed steering, can be pleasant to drive. **H&H Auctions, Buxton, UK, 4/04.**

#54-**1948 ALFA ROMEO 6C 2500 SUPER SPORT Cabriolet.** Body by Pinin Farina. S/N 915716. Eng. #AR928020. French Blue/black leather. RHD. Odo: 50,315 kms. Clean, straight, show-ready inside

and out. Bright blue finish not to everyone's taste. Ex-Eric Clapton. Right-drive. Cond: 1. **SOLD AT $88,000.** *6C 2500s trade in a very thin market. The Cabriolets are all right-hand drive, and they have a ponderous feel to those accustomed to the lithe 1900s and Giuliettas that followed. The bid was low by perhaps $10,000.* **RM, Phoenix, AZ, 1/02.**

#43-**1948 ALFA ROMEO 6C 2500 SS Cabriolet.** Body by Farina. S/N 915716. French blue/black leather. RHD. Odo: 50,306 km. Sharp car all around, new top, electric fan added, unusual color. Four-speed with synchromesh, triple dual-choked Weber carburetors. Non-factory but period door pulls,

steering wheel and window winders. Cond: 1-. **NOT SOLD AT $102,001.** *Purchased by Eric Clapton in 1991 for $104,500 (he sold in '99), sold at 2002 RM Phoenix for $88,000. Very legit-looking car estimated at correct money for an SS. Came close to the low estimate of $110,000 but not enough to move it.* **Christie's, Paris, France, 2/03.**

#18-**1949 ALFA ROMEO 6C 2500 SS Cabriolet.** Body by Pininfarina. S/N 915810. Green and silver/tan leather. RHD. Odo: 85,503 kms. Door fit off, few chips on older

repaint, excellent interior, very clean engine compartment. Cond: 2. **SOLD AT $129,375.** *Selling price includes 2.5% import duty. Price was market-correct for all concerned. Not very pleasant to drive, these cars really belong on the show field. And it will take a lot of money to make this one a prize-winner.* **RM, Monterey, CA, 8/02.**

#30-**1949 ALFA ROMEO 6C 2500 SS Cabriolet.** Body by Pinin Farina. S/N 915797. Dark blue/red leather. Tan canvas top. RHD. Odo: 23,774 miles. A few swirl marks in paint, otherwise very good appearance

throughout with excellent door fit. Side body panels a little wavy. Nice interior and dash. A car to own for style rather than speed. Cond: 2+. **SOLD AT $126,500.** *Visually nicer car sold at B-J in January for $18k less, and was a bargain in retrospect. This car was fully, but fairly, priced. Owned by an SCM subscriber who actually drove the car with some frequency.* **RM, Amelia Island, FL, 3/01.**

#74-**1950 ALFA ROMEO 6C 2500 SS "COMPETIZIONE" GT Coupe.** Body by Ghia. S/N 64251. Eng. #924866. Blue/light blue leather. RHD. Odo: 4,505 km. Alleged to have been owned by Fangio but provenance

is fuzzy. Has Gilco *tubolare* chassis. Interior looks very American in style. Excellent appearance throughout, but styling elicited adverse comments from some Alfisti at auction. Cond: 1-. **NOT SOLD AT $160,000.** *One of four built. Hard to value accurately, but we'd reckon market level is somewhere between the high bid and the low estimate of $220,000.* **Christie's, Pebble Beach, CA, 8/01.**◆

Section II
The Glorious Years

The Italian economy was ravaged by World War II, and securing basic transportation of any kind was a struggle—hence the emergence of Lambretta scooters and Isetta micro-cars. While the first post-war Alfa Romeos were large, luxurious 6C models assembled from bits that had survived the Allied B-17 strikes, clearly the market needed something simpler and less costly.

This led to the four-cylinder 1900s, but "downmarket" for Alfa still meant twin-camshafts, huge brakes and often multiple carburetors. In fact, the four-door Berlinas were marketed with the slogan, "the family car that wins races."

Continuing to look for the sweet spot in the market, in 1954 Alfa unveiled its smallest car ever, the Giulietta Sprint. Along with its open sister, the Giulietta Spider, these two cars redefined the notion of what a small sports car should be. They had copious performance, albeit in a high-strung rev range, along with creature comforts that were superb for the era, including roll-up windows—something MGs didn't get until 1963.

Capitalizing on the success of the Giulietta, Alfa then introduced the upscale six-cylinder 2600, perhaps the most competent high-speed cruising cars of their era.

I've lived a lot of my Alfa life behind the wheels of 1900s, 2600s and Giulietta Sprints and Spiders, and can't say that I've ever had a bad time. Well, other than when my 1962 Giulietta Spider Veloce threw a rod out the side of the block, causing me to be very late to my junior quals at Reed College and putting my budding career as an intellectual historian at risk. But my hands, grease-stained from picking up pieces of connecting rod and alloy block from the road, provided a convincing excuse to the proctor.

I recently had the chance to spend a weekend driving a 1957 Giulietta Normale, owned by *SCM*'s legal analyst John Draneas, through the Oregon high desert. As we left the town of Condon one morning, driving towards the rising sun, bundled against the cold with the top down, I remembered all the miles I've spent peering through Alfa windshields at challenging roads, all the times I've hit redline and upshifted with a flourish, all the times I've waited until an impossibly late moment to mash on the brake pedal and used the wash-tub sized aluminum drums to slow the car and set me up for the next turn.

These are joyous Alfas, full of youth and vigor and excitement. If you've never owned one, you are missing a crucial part of the sports car experience. If you have owned one, you know exactly what I mean.—*Keith Martin*◆

1953 1900 CS Farina

It is impressive that you can get such a nicely restored 1900 for so little. Their instrumentation is a joy, and roadholding is beyond reproach

by Pat Braden

Chassis number: CO 1534

With its unitary construction—the first on an Alfa Romeo—the 1900 was Alfa's first mass-produced car, introduced in 1950. It was assembled on a new production line at Alfa's original Portello works, which was funded in part by the Marshall Plan.

Initially powered by a 1844-cc, 90-hp twin overhead camshaft four-cylinder engine and offering fine handling, the four-door sedan quickly became popular with sporting drivers and racers.

In 1951, Alfa introduced the short-wheelbase 1900 C chassis, which served as the basis for many special bodies by the major Italian body builders. The most popular series came from Touring, and the most sporting from Zagato. In 1953, the Super series was introduced with a larger engine.

This fastback coupe bears typical Pininfarina hallmarks that can also be seen in similar bodies on other Italian chassis of the era. One of the more conservative of the bodybuilders, Giovanbattista (Pinin) Farina gave this car an understated elegance of line, while the large fastback window suggests speed and potency.

Chassis 1534 (the bodybuilder's number) is one of eleven of the Corto-based Pininfarina fastback coupes known to exist. It has undergone a full ground-up restoration, and has been hardly used since. Consequently, it appears in excellent condition and features nonstandard Zagato seats trimmed in black leather (the original seats are available with the car, but in poor condition), a Nardi wood-trimmed steering wheel and Borrani wire wheels.

This car would make a perfect entry for the retrospective Mille Miglia, the Tour de France, Carrera Panamericana, or any of the many other historic events for which it is eligible.

The SCM analysis: This Alfa sold at the Coys of Kensington London Auction for $37,338 on May 10, 1999. The 1900 Corto (literally, "short," but called Sprint) chassis is especially significant because it was a favorite of Italian bodybuilders in the era that defined the shape of modern automobiles. Designs on Alfa's 2.5-meter chassis ranged from the understated elegance of Touring to the grotesque excesses of Ghia. As a result, the 1900 buyer has quite a variety of body styles from which to choose, including the other-worldly Bertone BAT trio.

Pininfarina was one of the more conservative of the Italian stylists, and his cars are always in excellent taste. However, of all the body styles draped over the 1900 chassis, I think this Pininfarina fastback is one of the less successful. Compared to the similarly conservative three- and five-window Touring coupes, it's heavy amidships and awkward from behind. In this case, the short wheelbase does not serve well the overall design of the car. Even on his own terms, this is not one of Pinin's best: If you're after a fastback design that suggests power, his 1953 Ferrari 342 coupe, with its gaping egg-crate grille, oozes it.

The price of this fully-restored car is further evidence of its mid-range character. A fastback Zagato body on the same chassis shows an almost-identical front end, but its more-aggressive design will bring double the price of this car. The three BATs, unarguably the most expensive and flamboyant of all 1900s, were once offered at $9 million for the trio. Reading between the lines of the auctioneer's description, this appears to be a car prepared for the auctions and unused except to drive across the runways. It is presentable, but clearly not the best of the breed.

Further, this is not a high-performance 1900. With an 1884-cc engine, single downdraft carburetor and four-speed column shift, it offers less punch than other 1900s. The TI version of 1952 produced 115 hp, as did the updated Super version, introduced in 1954. The 1954 Super Sprint added dual downdraft carburetors and a five-speed gearbox to the larger engine.

It is impressive that you can get such a nicely restored 1900 for so little. These cars were durable to a degree that shames modern Alfas. Many 1900 sedans spent long, productive lives as taxi cabs and patrol cars for the police. Their instrumentation is a joy and roadholding is beyond reproach for an early '50s chassis. Maintenance costs are low: points, plugs, condenser, and valves you can adjust with just a big screwdriver. In spite of the car's negatives, if there are no surprises lurking under the hood, the lucky buyer is likely to find that this Pininfarina fastback is the most satisfying car he's ever owned. Indeed, it will probably whet his appetite for a 1900 CSS or even a 1900 Zagato.

(Photo, historical and descriptive information courtesy of the auction company.)

From the February 2000 issue of SCM.◆

1954 1900 Super Sprint

The Super Sprint is a sleeper in the sub-exotic category of vintage cars

by Craig Morningstar

Chassis number: 1900C01822
Engine number: 10200110051

Its factory devastated by wartime bombing, Alfa Romeo did not resume car production until 1947, and the firm's first all-new offering of the post-war period arrived in 1950. Designed by Dr. Orazio Satta Puliga, and intended for volume production, the 1900 was the first Alfa to employ unitary construction and, in keeping with the company's sporting heritage, was powered by a twin-overhead-camshaft engine. A four-cylinder unit, the latter displaced 1884 cc and produced 90 hp, an output sufficient to propel the four-door sedan to 93 mph.

Although ostensibly a family conveyance, the 1900 was endowed with sporting credentials like wishbone and coil spring independent front suspension, and an exceptionally well-located live rear axle. It should have surprised nobody therefore, when the 1900's potential was realized in the form of two high-performance derivatives. Launched in 1951, the 1900 Sprint featured bodywork by Pinin Farina (cabriolet) and Touring (coupe), both models using the 100-hp engine of the 1900TI sports sedan. The model was upgraded for 1954, gaining a 1975-cc engine and five-speed gearbox.

This Series II Sprint features five-window Superleggera coachwork crafted in aluminum by Touring. The engine is a later 2-liter unit dating from 1957, mated to a five-speed gearbox with floor-mounted shifter. We are advised that approximately $70,000 was spent on restoration in the US, including mechanical work and a bare-metal repaint in burgundy. The brake system was overhauled, and a new wiring harness and new Michelin tires were fitted. The car features original Carello driving lights, Connolly leather upholstery, Alfin brake drums and Borrani wire wheels. After importation into the U.K. in 1998, further work was carried out, including attention to the brakes, electrics, fuel pumps and gearbox. The car was purchased by the present owner at Brooks' Geneva sale in March 2000 and has not been used since. It is accompanied by a large history/restoration file and U.K. registration document.

The SCM analysis: This car sold for $54,959, including buyer's premium, at the Bonhams Monte Carlo auction May 26, 2003. At their March 2000 Geneva sale, it sold for $62,121, so while this car may be a good value in terms of machinery for dollars spent, one would be hard-pressed to call the earlier purchase a good investment.

A ward of the Italian government, Alfa Romeo was struggling to get back on its feet after Allied B-17s devastated the factory in October 1944. The 1900 series was a pivotal model, as it was developed at the end of the custom coach-built era and was the first series of mass-produced Alfa Romeo cars.

Although built primarily as a sedan by the manufacturer, virtually all major Italian carrozzerie offered coupe or cabriolet versions based on the 1900 chassis. During its ten-year production run, just over 20,000 units of the 1900 series were built; approximately 80% were sedans, 10% were Jeep-like vehicles called matta *(Italian for crazy) that were built for the Italian Army, and the other 10% were* corto *or short versions for the coachbuilders.*

On the short chassis, there were three series of Super Sprints, all with coachwork by Carrozzeria Touring. Production numbers were around 965, but an exact figure is not known. Touring built bodies for a number of manufacturers including Alfa Romeo, Ferrari, Pegaso and, of course, Hudson. (You remember the Hudson Italia, don't you?) The first and second series Super Sprints, popularly referred to as "five-window" coupes, were quite similar to each other. The tipo III, the "three-window" coupe, resembled a large Giulietta Sprint, and shared few exterior trim parts and no sheet metal with the earlier bodies.

These Super Sprints were built one at a time as special-order vehicles, so paint and trim detail decisions were left to the stocking dealer or specific customer. There are numerous differences between specific cars of the same type and model year, which makes them more or less difficult to restore, depending on your point of view. The exteriors of these cars are relatively clean, with little trim other than bumpers, grilles and light bezels.

The example pictured here is a type I Super Sprint equipped with a post-1958 2-liter, 1975-cc engine (or at least cylinder head) with side-draft carburetors. This is a problem with regard to authenticity but a plus for someone who wants a nice driver. Parts for these later engines are more plentiful, and the modern carburetors are much easier to service. Both the 1884-cc and 1975-cc engines were built with a cast-iron block and aluminum-alloy cylinder head and were quite sound powerplants that would happily rev past 6,000 rpm. The five-speed transmission, however, was somewhat fragile.

There are a number of Alfa Romeo 1900s running European and North American vintage tours with great regularity and dependability. There are always a few in the Mille Miglia, being driven "con brio." The Super Sprint is a sleeper in the sub-exotic category of vintage cars that represents an expensive restoration but an easy ownership experience. Despite the fact that the previous owner took a $7,000 loss on this car, I still believe that there is room for these cars to appreciate. Without question, a properly set-up one offers a pleasurable and surprisingly sophisticated driving experience.

(Photo, historical and descriptive information courtesy of the auction company.)

From the November 2003 issue of SCM. ◆

1954 1900 Sprint

This 1900 has been to more European auctions than most SCMers. But this time around, the seller really timed it right

by Craig Morningstar

Chassis number: AR1900C01822

The 1900 debuted with mechanical specifications worthy of the marque's history. Fitted with a double-overhead-cam four-cylinder engine, it was a modern car that was easy to maintain. It was the first Alfa Romeo to have unibody construction, and the cooling system was one of the best of the era. Despite its rigid rear axle, it had an efficient and well-guided suspension with excellent road-holding in all circumstances.

The 1900 C Sprint (for *corto*, or short) was built on a shortened chassis with a 2,500-mm wheelbase, and fitted with a 100-hp version of Alfa's 1975-cc four-cylinder and a five-speed gearbox. Most of the 1900 C Sprints were bodied by Touring, but some cabriolets and coupes would also come from other coachbuilders.

The car presented here is Touring coupe #01822, painted in the emblematic color for post-war Alfa Romeos, dark Bordeaux. It is an ideal mount for all historic competitions, from the Mille Miglia to the Tour Auto and the Carrera Panamericana.

The SCM analysis: This car sold for $79,554, including buyer's premium, at the Artcurial Briest Poulain Le Fur auction held in Paris on February 15, 2004. It was sold previously at Bonhams' Monte Carlo auction on May 23, 2003, bringing $54,959, and at the 2000 Brooks Geneva sale, where it made $62,121. It was also profiled in the November 2003 issue.

By now, most SCMers know the 1900 drill backwards and forwards. But in case you're new to the fold, the 1900 was the product of the post-World War II reorganization of Europe, designed by a new generation of engineers and stylists that knew their efforts needed to succeed if Alfa Romeo was to appeal to a broader base than it had with the 6C. As such, the 1900 marked the beginning of the high-volume production era at the venerable marque. Many of the lessons Alfa would learn in producing this series would pave the way to the successful launch of the classic post-war Alfa, the Bertone-designed Giulietta Sprint of 1954.

Initial 1900 production began in 1951 at the Portello factory in Milan and at first the car was built only as a sedan. In time, the short version of the chassis was developed to support more sporting versions of the 1900. The chassis was certainly stiff enough for such applications and the twin-cam engine offered high specific power output on the low-octane fuel available at the time.

Series one and series two Sprints were "five-window" coupes, while the series three cars were "three-windows," with wider, window-less C-pillars that made the cars look like big Giuliettas. While 1900s were indeed a significant step toward mass production for Alfa, all three series of Sprints were still "made-to-order" and there's not a lot of commonality among specifications for any of the cars.

The car pictured here is equipped with a later 2000-cc head and induction system, which includes side-draft carburetors instead of the proper twin-choke Solex downdraft units. If you're counting rivets, this is a minus, but if you're in want of a driver, it's quite nice. The car does not have bumpers, which could have been the way it was built, but not likely.

If those are the negatives, the positives are in its appearance. Finished in an attractive combination of Bordeaux with natural color hides and contrasting dark beading, this should be a very easy car to live with—or at least admire in the garage.

Ah yes, the garage. This car has been spending a lot of time there, racking up only 82 km of use since first spotted at that auction four years ago—a demonstration of one of the reasons SCM asks its analysts to record odometer readings. Frankly, whether the mileage on a collectible car is "authentic" is something we don't strive to prove. Rather, the simple difference in readings between each time we see a car tells a tale of its own.

The lack of use for this car is really a shame, as 1900s were capable performers for the era, solid and dependable cars that ask little of their drivers. Many serve well for collectors who enjoy vintage tours, especially high-profile ones like the Mille Miglia Storica, for which this car is eligible. Further, when properly set up (and it really takes an Italian speed shop to get the suspension right), they handle well even while their excessive body lean makes them look something like a Buick Roadmaster that's been put on the Atkins diet.

Despite this usability, prices have been stagnant. Perhaps the previous owners were speculators who simply got tired of seeing no appreciation in their investment and dumped the car. Clearly, owner number three timed the market, or at least the one in Paris in February, correctly.

In its recent auction appearances this 1900 has seen more of Europe than most Let's Go-toting backpackers, so the only thing we can safely discern from its auction record is that the auction companies pocketing the commissions are quite fond of the car. As far as the market at large is concerned, before we judge this last nearly $80k sale to be signs of a new pricing trend, it's worth noting that adjusting for the French auction's 15% commission means the "huge profit" this last seller reaped is smaller than it initially appears, about five grand, give or take. Even so, it sure beats the nearly $10k loss a previous owner took.

That said, I'd still be willing to call this sale a positive trend for the wallflower 1900. This is a car that really deserves to "come into its own" and realize higher prices. If this car is truly as represented, with solid mechanicals (a question unto itself, given the number of times it has changed hands), this may be all the money (plus about $20,000, according to the SCM Price Guide), but a not-unfair price for a car with this heritage. There are a number of far less attractive cars, built in far higher numbers, that sell for quite a bit more money. Further, being a 1900 owner myself, I guarantee that the more the new owner drives his car, and the harder he pushes it, the more it will reward him.

(Photo, historical and descriptive information courtesy of the auction company.)

From the June 2004 issue of SCM.◆

1955 1900 SS Cabriolet

Ghia was certainly among the most daring of the Italian bodybuilders; styling efforts ranged from the sublime to the unarguably ugly

by Pat Braden

Chassis number: 01959

This unique 1900 was bodied by the Swiss coach-building company, Ghia Aigle, specifically for the 1955 Geneva Salon.

This is the earliest of eight Alfas bodied by Ghia Aigle known to survive, and as such, in many respects the most interesting and most important. After the Geneva show, the car appears to have remained in Switzerland before being acquired by a Dutch Alfa enthusiast earlier last year. Today the car is remarkably well preserved and apparently unmodified from its appearance 45 years ago.

During the 1980s, S/N 01959 underwent a restoration by its then-owner, Pierre Le Grand. The car then passed unto the hands of Claud Fresard and was featured prominently in the "Musée de l'Automobile Muriaux" near Saignelegieer in Switzerland. The collection had a strong tendency towards vehicles with a Swiss coachbuilt history.

On finally leaving the museum, and Switzerland for apparently the first time, the car was acquired by an enthusiastic Dutch classic car collector, and he has maintained, used and displayed it for the past eighteen months. Finished in traditional Italian racing red, with tan leather upholstery, this beautiful sports car benefits from the successful, well-proven mechanics of the popular, sporting 1900 model allied to the handsome work of one of Europe's most respected and stylish coachbuilders.

The SCM *analysis: This car sold for $64,390 at the Barrett-Jackson/Coys of Kensington Auction in Monaco on May 27, 2000. That is a handsome price for a 1900, reflecting the car's custom coachwork. The competition 1900 Zagato coupe can bring $20,000 to $50,000 more, while we've seen average Touring coupes sell for under $40,000.*

In the first half of the 1950s, car designers made the transition from pre- to post-war design. Ghia was certainly among the most daring and experimental of the Italian bodybuilders. Their styling efforts ranged from the sublime to the unarguably ugly. By exploring both boundaries, they clarified for everyone else what worked and what did not. As a result, and certainly because of some of their most outlandish efforts, they had a major impact on the shape of the modern automobile. Ghia's international respect is reflected in the fact that they worked for American manufacturers at a time when it was politically correct to sneer at European cars. The Chrysler Dual Ghia, of Rat Pack fame, is one example.

Ghia Aigle was an attempted expansion of Ghia by Mario Felice Boano and his son Gian Paolo, owners of Ghia at the time. They purchased the Swiss company De Secheron and renamed it, but only a few cars were built in Aigle, Switzerland. Towards the end of the company's short life, many of its bodies were actually formed at Ghia's facility in Italy, then installed on chassis in Aigle. It's notable that, according to Peter Marshall, two Ghia Aigle coupes and one Spider still remain in Switzerland.

This cabriolet embodies styling elements of both Ghia's successes and failures. The finely drawn front end on this car, with its delicate heart-shaped grille, hints of the elegance that characterized the origi-

nal Volkswagen Karmann-Ghia. The scoop on the rear fender suggests the gaping grilles that adorned some of Ghia's most ridiculous creations, rear fender scoops being a popular area for experimentation as designers searched for ways to create an attractive rear fender line on otherwise slab-sided efforts.

Touring included rear fender scoops in a much more restrained way on its Tipo 55 prototype 1900 C cabriolet, and they were seen on several other marques on both sides of the Atlantic. The wrap-around windshield on this 1900 is another signature of '50s cars, and it works nicely in this instance.

Virtually all the Italian bodybuilders used the 1900 platform. The most notable experiments were undoubtedly the three Bertone BAT coupes. The majority of custom bodies on the 1900 floor pan were coupes, and only a small percentage had convertible tops. It is likely that the 1900 pan was simply not strong enough for a topless car, and reinforcements to the floorpan were required for the few that were made by Zagato, Touring, Farina, Boneschi and Pininfarina.

The chassis number of this car is for an early 1955 second-series Sprint, indicating a 2.5-meter wheelbase with dual carburetors on an engine producing 115 hp.

Its provenance goes back to its first appearance at the Geneva Salon for 1955, but there is a significant gap in ownership between that date and Le Grand's restoration sometime in the early 1980s. The new owner will surely want to fill this information gap, but the effort may be difficult because the car seems to have remained in very private hands.

The 1900 driveline is very sturdy and even though this car has sat idle for much of its life, it should still give strong service to its lucky new owner. The price seems more than reasonable for an attractive open Alfa with an interesting history. Let's hope we see the car on some European touring events in the near future.

(Historical and descriptive information courtesy of the auction company.)

From the September 2000 issue of SCM. ◆

1955 "Super" Sprint

The buzz in the room after the sale was, "the East Coast dealer who stole this car will pocket a quick $20K" —and perhaps he did

by Carl Bomstead

Chassis number: AR1900C02186

The 1900 Alfa Romeo of 1950 marked a turning point for the marque. Gone were the straight-eight and supercharged projectiles that had written so much motor racing history. Now Alfa replaced them with a modest four-cylinder engine housed in a modern-style steel saloon body. But still the engine possessed twin overhead camshafts and the suspension was ranked with the best. Even in those austere days, there was room in Italy for glamour and excitement in automobiles. In the following year the 1900C appeared with a platform slightly shorter in wheelbase than the original saloon. The 1900C provided the dynamic new school of Italian designers with the perfect base on which to create coupe bodies of unsurpassed elegance, and the stylists at Ghia, Touring, Pinifarina and Vignale eagerly took up the challenge. This example is the work of one of Italy's most illustrious coachbuilders, Carrozzeria Ghia.

Apparently, this Ghia-bodied Alfa was sold new at the Paris Salon in 1955 to a member of the Spanish Royal family. Painted in gray with a black roof and a black and white interior, the car is presented in original condition and is said to have only 50,000 miles from new. It is still fitted with the original 16-inch Nardi steering wheel and polished Borrani wire wheels. Following the car's import into the United States in 1990, it has been preserved in original condition, and in 1999 it won Best Unrestored Car at the Concorso Italiano at Quail Lodge. Offered with copies of Italian registration documents dated from 1957 and a California title, this Alfa has an interesting history and should make a welcome addition at any Alfa meet.

The SCM analysis: This car sold for $35,200, including buyer's premium, at Christie's Pebble Beach auction, held August 18, 2002.

Alfa 1900s continue to be an acquired taste. They fall somewhere in between the ground-pounding eight-cylinder, supercharged cars of the '30s and the high-revving, small-displacement Giuliettas and Giulias of the '50s and '60s.

The first completely new postwar Alfa, the 1900 was of monocoque construction, a first for Alfa, and was powered by a new in-line four-cylinder engine with a cast iron block and aluminum head. In the four-door 1900 Berlina, the single-carb 1884-cc engine produced 90 hp, and it took 18.4 seconds to go from 0 to 60, but still managed to be a factor in competitive road events including the Carrera Panamericana. The 1900 Berlina became known as "the family car that wins road races."

The 1900 evolved through its nine-year production run, with a larger, 1975-cc engine introduced in 1953. Dual-carbureted versions of this engine produced as much as 115 bhp. At the same time

the mechanicals were developing, chassis were made available to various Italian coachbuilders, including Vignale, Zagato, Touring and Ghia.

The most striking examples of Italian coachwork on the 1900 chassis were the C52 Disco Volante or Flying Saucer, and the BAT series of aerodynamic prototypes built by Bertone.

Ghia was producing some attractive coupes as early as 1953, and by 1955 their involvement with the Chrysler Corporation was apparent in their designs for the 1900C. The Chrysler "dream cars" of the early 1950s were designed by a team under the direction of Virgil Exner and built by Ghia. The influence of this relationship is obvious when the car pictured here is compared to the Chrysler Dual Ghias.

There is some controversy about this particular 1900, as noted on page 10 of the December issue of SCM. According to Alfa guru Peter Zobian, S/N 2186 was actually a Super Sprint that was ordered with a single-carb, lower-performance Sprint engine (kind of like ordering a Hemi 'Cuda and then specifying a slant-six engine). Zobian argues that the car should be priced as a Super Sprint; I would disagree.

This Alfa 1900C was offered with a pre-sale estimate of $50,000 to $70,000, which, given its generally unrestored condition (euphemistically referred to as "patina"), was optimistic. Our own Dave Brownell described the car as having "Good door fit; some paint chips and cracks, especially to nose; paint worn on trunk lid; fair to good plating. Another time-warp car preserved in near original condition," and rated it a #2-. So clearly it was a sound car, but just as clearly would need a full restoration before being trotted out onto a national concours field.

This same car was offered at the 2000 Brooks auction in Monterey, and was unsold at a reported high bid of $55,000. However, this bid may have been the result of an overexcited chandelier.

Especially in the rarefied Monterey atmosphere, buyers will step up for perfect cars, but generally turn up their wallets at cars with needs, especially when they are fringe models like this 1900C.

The buzz in the room after the sale was, "the East Coast dealer who stole this car will pocket a quick $20k," and perhaps he did. From my perspective, $70,000 is what this car would be worth when completely restored, and perhaps even uprated to a Super Sprint engine. As it sat, the $35,200 it brought should be considered a bargain, but certainly not the deal of a lifetime.

(Historical and descriptive information courtesy of the auction company.)

From the February 2003 issue of SCM. ◆

1955 1900 SS Zagato

Many find the distinctive body style pleasing, even exciting, while others are turned off by its novelty

by Pat Braden

Chassis number: AR1900C02056

One of the most respected of automotive design firms, Zagato was founded in Milan by Ugo Zagato, who used techniques learned in the wartime aeronautics industry to create a series of lightweight competition cars. Alfa Romeo immediately realized the potential of Zagato's designs, and thus commenced a fruitful collaboration that has lasted to this day. Legendary racing Alfas, from the P2, the 6C 1500 and 1750 to the 8C 2300, were joined by lightweight coupes on the Giulietta and Milano chassis.

Immediately after WWII, Zagato got back into business by producing bodies for the Fiat Balilla. They also built a few factory team cars for the new GT racing category, and catered to the growing privateer scene with true dual-purpose cars that provided daily transportation and weekend trophies with equal ease. Zagato's own history records that "avant-garde styling, together with light weight and wind-cheating lines were a trademark that distinguished Zagato's cars of that era."

The 1900 series was introduced in 1950 as the first Alfa designed for mass production. Owners enjoyed the benefits of the twin-cam, 1875-cc, 100-hp engine, wishbone and coil-spring independent front suspension and an exceptionally well-located live rear axle. The ultimate 1900 was the 1900 Zagato (SSZ), with its dual-carbureted, 115-hp engine.

This particular SSZ was restored by Epifani Restorations of Berkeley, California, and is described as "pristine" both inside and out. Painted Rosso Cordoba red with a red-piped gray leather interior, it achieved third in class at the 1990 Pebble Beach Concours d'Elegance, and has only been shown at concours events since.

Although this car has only been used for display, it has the high-compression race engine so would be suitable for the Mille Miglia and California Mille. The addition of a fuel cell and roll-cage would make a worthy addition to any grid of 1950s GT race cars.

The SCM *analysis: This car sold for $217,000, including buyer's premium, at the Bonhams & Brooks auction at the Cavallino Classic in West Palm Beach, FL, January 20, 2001. The price, near the high end of the auctioneer's estimate and well above SCM's high Price Guide figure of $125,000, reflects the pristine condition of the car and its essential desirability.*

Avant-garde styling from Zagato occasionally means striking, sometimes bordering on ugly. In that sense, the 1900 Zagato can be considered a forerunner of the ES30: Many enthusiasts find the distinctive body style pleasing, even exciting, while others are turned off by its novelty. Contemporary Zagato bodies on the A6G Maserati, the 8V Fiat and even the Giulietta seem smaller, lower and more tasteful, while the same styling applied to the 1900 chassis comes off looking narrower and awkward. That may be because the 1900's tall,

twin-cam engine prompts a high nose, which is further emphasized by the twin scoops that run along the top of the hood, and slab sides that are interrupted only by a delicate styling line.

Since Zagato built these cars on order to the owner's specifications, no two 1900 Zagatos are alike. A few "double-bubble" 1900 Zagatos were built, giving the car a notable similarity to the Fiat Abarth Zagato. (Interestingly, I believe that there are far more "double bubble" 1900s in existence today than were originally created. Funny how that happens.) Similarly, interiors on these cars show interesting variations, including the arrangement of the attractive three-dimensional instruments on the dash. One of the most appealing features of this series is the use of Zagato seats, which are well-ventilated with outstanding side support from bolsters that resemble flying buttresses.

The car here is much sleeker than others because of its longer tail section, which tapers aerodynamically while other Zagatos abruptly drop off. Though this car has been used only for show, it is inherently capable of extremely high average speeds over difficult terrain. In the 1950s, 1900 Zagatos were the cars to beat at European hillclimbs.

While the 2-liter engine and large frontal area limit its top-speed potential, getting there is all the fun. At speed, the Alfa's cast-iron powerplant emits a hollow wail. Engine and road noise resonate inside the aluminum body, which carries minimal sound-absorbing material. The car is much more spacious inside than it appears, with plenty of room between the driver's and passenger's seats and ample elbow room outboard.

As noted above, this car sold for a remarkably high price, appropriate for its remarkable condition. The new owner faces a classic question: Whether to use the car as it was meant to be used, thereby risking injury to it, or to retain it as a showpiece and conserve a considerable investment. It will be very interesting to note the price of the next 1900 SS Zagato to cross the block and see if this price was an aberration, or a harbinger of value increases to come.

(Photo, historical and descriptive information courtesy of the auction company.)

From the April 2001 issue of SCM. ◆

1957 Spider Veloce

The Giulietta Spider was a delightful automobile, redefining the essence of Alfa Romeo as a beautiful, responsive and brilliant-driving open car

by Donald Osborne

Chassis number: 149502103
Engine number: 131530751

Introduced in 1956, the Giulietta Spider Veloce featured hotter cams, higher compression and a pair of Weber dual-choke carburetors, which boosted output to 90 hp at 6,500 rpm—well more than one horsepower per cubic inch. Alfa's unit-body chassis also addressed the age-old problem of managing a live rear axle by incorporating alloy components to reduce weight and stabilizing axle location with trailing arms and a differential-mounted triangular trailing link. The Giulietta was one of the best-handling cars of the 1950s and so good that its basic design persisted in the Alfa Spider into the early 1990s.

Like most models, the Giulietta "grew" during its history, eventually evolving into the 101 series in 1959, with a two-inch-longer wheelbase. Many aficionados, however, prefer the original 750 series and its 220-mm wheelbase for quick, precise handling. The longer wheelbase of the later Giuliettas and Giulias may give a more relaxed ride, but there is no substitute for a 750 series Giulietta Veloce's nearly telepathic reaction to its driver's input.

The car on offer is an original Giulietta Spider Veloce with correct and matching numbers throughout. Restored some time ago, it is still in fresh condition and has recently been treated to several sympathetic performance modifications including new, stiffer Centerline coil

springs, a thicker front stabilizer bar and period-correct Koni Classic Red shocks.

Finished in white with correct black vinyl interior, the car has a black cloth convertible top in good condition. It comes with a factory tool roll, spare and jack. There is no radio, only a factory blanking plate, but the sound of the Alfa twin-cam four's assertive exhaust note through its dual Webers creates its own tunes which no radio can match.

The SCM *analysis: This car sold for $41,800, including buyer's premium, at the Gooding & Company auction held in Pebble Beach, CA, on August 15, 2004.*

The Giulietta will always be regarded as one of the most significant cars of the 20th century, not in the least because it saved Alfa Romeo after World War II. As a maker of expensive, limited-production high-performance touring and racing cars since the '20s, Alfa needed a new plan to survive in a changed, post-war economic environment. The first step was the introduction of the 1900, a unit-bodied sedan that spawned coachbuilt coupes and a convertible. But this was just a warm-up for Alfa's first real volume car, the 750 series Giulietta.

The main Giulietta model was always intended to be the berlina, or sedan, but when production was delayed the Sprint coupe wound up being introduced first. How this came to pass is a quintessentially Italian story, as the coupe was actually created as a prize for a lottery. Ironically enough, this was being held by the Italian government—also Alfa's owner—for buyers who were on the waiting list for the belated sedan. The response to the Sprint coupe was so overwhelming that Alfa commissioned Pinin Farina and Bertone to design a Spider too. Pinin Farina won the contract with this simple and elegant design that immediately became an icon.

The Giulietta Spider was indeed a delightful automobile, redefining the essence of Alfa Romeo as a beautiful, responsive and brilliant-driving open car. This new, modern Alfa was also more comfortable and refined than its British competition (namely the MGA and Triumph TR3), featuring roll-up windows, a top that kept out most of the weather, and a fairly functional heater.

Alfa's attempt to try to control a live rear axle also paid dividends when compared to its contemporaries, but in reality, the better-balanced Sprint always offered superior handling to the Spider, which can surprise the unwary driver with a fair amount of axle hop in the middle of a turn.

The major areas of concern for any prospective Giulietta owner are the condition of the rocker panel and rear suspension mounting points. Given the unit-body construction, major corrosion in these places can severely compromise the whole deal. This can be a big problem in a car that should be driven hard.

Body panels, trim and interior pieces have become widely available, and should not present a problem for someone looking to restore one of these models. While mechanical parts for the 750-series cars are harder to find than those for the later 101 series, growing interest in the earlier cars—and rising values—are causing many parts to become more readily available than in the past.

Giuliettas came in both Normale and Veloce versions. While the added performance and personality of the Veloce models make them a must-have for some buyers, it is important to know that their more "nervous" character will not suit all drivers. These cars have a tendency to foul plugs if not driven enthusiastically, and their alloy sump can fail to heat the oil adequately under easy driving or cool weather conditions. These same traits do make the Veloces superb cars on vintage events, where their performance can be exploited to maximum advantage. Of course, if you're just looking for an antique to putter around town in, Normales sell for about half the price of Veloces.

Be aware as well of the proliferation of "abnormales," standard Normales fitted with the Veloce's dual Weber carbs. There's more to a Veloce than its carbs, though few people will go to the trouble of replicating all the details so it's usually not too hard to pick out a clone.

A proper and original Veloce will have a tachometer that reads from 2,000 to 8,000 rpm, rather than the 1,000 to 7,000 of the Normale. The Veloce speedometer goes to 140 mph, while the Normale's reads only to 120. Veloces have a chrome plug on the dashboard blanking the choke knob of the Normale, as the Veloce's Weber DCO3s do not

have chokes. A fresh air scoop is welded into the grille opening on the driver's side of the Veloce, with two duct holes on the driver's inside fender, one leading to the air cleaner and the other to the passenger compartment. The Normale only has the one going to the passenger compartment. Finally, Veloces have a rubber stop mounted on a welded point on the driver's-side frame rail, directly below the motor mount, to arrest the engine from moving under full acceleration.

The car on offer here, a genuine Giulietta Spider Veloce, presents itself well. The restoration looks fresh, with good paint, panel fit and chrome. The interior is correct, with proper rubber floor mats and vinyl seat trim. The performance modifications show that the car has clearly been prepared for driving, although the aftermarket Technomagnesio alloy wheels are somewhat jarring in appearance. Fortunately, the owners have chosen not to slam in a later-model five-speed gearbox, which destroys part of the original driving experience of the car, using the more primitive tunnel-case four-speed. Further, the five-speed modification also requires that the rear axle ratio be changed for the best performance, another alteration of the car's basic nature. As it sits, with a four-speed and the correct 4.1 rear axle, the car is a perfect mount for any of the 1,000-mile vintage rallies.

Though on first glance $42k might seem like a lot for a Giulietta, this isn't just any Giulietta and the price paid here falls right in the middle of the $33,700-$45,000 SCM Price Guide range. 1956 and 1957 Veloces are valued at about 50 percent above the later models, simply because of their eligibility for the Mille Miglia and other such vintage events—something this '57 would be well suited for. Well bought and well sold.

(Photo, historical and descriptive information courtesy of the auction company.)

From the November 2003 issue of SCM. ◆

1958 750 Spider Veloce

I remember when I first saw a Veloce engine in 1968; with its twin-overhead cams and dual Weber carburetors, I felt I was looking at a Formula One car

by Keith Martin

Chassis number: AR149505411

It only took delivery of a few Giulietta Sprints to their new owners in 1954 for word to spread that Alfa Romeo had built something exceptional. Alfa Romeo, caught by surprise, had to quickly figure out how to increase production to meet the demand that far exceeded its expectations. In 1955, it introduced a Pininfarina-bodied roadster called Spider, and, in 1956, a higher-performance model, Veloce.

The list of performance modifications on the Veloce is lengthy and resulted in a more responsive, faster car. Higher compression, more aggressive cams, twin Weber carburetors replacing the single Solex, tubular headers, and a finned cast-aluminum sump featuring a built-in oil cooler were standard on the Veloce model of Sprint and Spider.

One of only 835 Spider Veloces built in 1958, this car has benefited from a frame-up restoration. The owner reports that the entire tub was media-blasted, zinc-chromated and primer-etched, then finished in Alfa Romeo white. The engine was completely rebuilt in Italy using all-original Weber DCOE-3 carburetors, valued at $2,000. The car is also outfitted with its original Zagato air cleaner—a rare item—valued at $10,000. It has a set of original Borrani wheels with original decals. Other original components consist of original steering wheel with horn ring and horn button, and Alfa Romeo radio blanking plate.

The owner reports that this example was a rust-free Californian car showing no damage, found in Ventura in 1989 and fully restored this year. Fresh restoration included new carpets, rubber mats, paint, seats, windshield, tires, hubcaps and hardware, all done to the highest standards. This is an excellent example of a very important car that is sure to bring its next owner miles of pleasure and reliability.

The SCM *analysis: This car sold for $28,600 on August 16, 2002, at RM's Monterey Sports Car auction.*

Slowly but surely, Alfa prices have been climbing over the past three years. And unlike in the past, when Veloces and Normales would bring about the same money when they crossed the block, buyers have finally figured out that the Veloce is the one to have.

I remember when I first saw a Veloce engine, in 1968. At the time, the twin SUs of my MGA—and its crude cast-iron headers—were my idea of exotic. When I looked at the Alfa's all-alloy engine, with its twin-overhead cams and dual Weber carburetors, I felt like I was looking at a Formula One car.

The '60s and '70s were the era when we turned our Solex-carbureted Normales into "Abnormales" or "almost-Veloces" by throwing on a pair of Webers, like replacing the Autolite two-barrel carb on a 260-ci Mustang with a Holley four-barrel and hoping for the best.

But a true Veloce is a completely re-engineered beast. From a different rear-axle ratio to thicker front brake shoes, the Veloce was a true café racer, designed to be revved to 8,000 rpm over and over again without complaint. In fact, the tachometer on the 1300-cc Veloce didn't start until 2,000—after all, who would bother to run one below that level?

This car appears to be complete and correct, although I would take issue with the auction company's description of the $10,000 Zagato air cleaner. If it means the air filter canister that bolts to the firewall, that's a difficult but not impossible piece to find, and shouldn't set you back more than $1,000. If it means the cold air box, I once had one made of magnesium that was stamped Zagato. If that's a $10,000 piece, the fellow I gave it to as a gift for buying six Alfa gearboxes from me will be one happy customer when he reads this.

(As an aside, the Borrani stickers for the wheels touted in the description are as far away as your nearest bicycle shop.)

Alfas have always been known for being far more sophisticated than nearly any other comparable sports car of their era. And yet, their values have lagged behind those of MGs, Triumphs and Austin-Healeys. Perhaps it's because their installed base of fans is smaller, perhaps because their engines can be more difficult to tune, perhaps because Americans prefer tractor-sourced powerplants with lots of torque in their small-displacement sports cars.

In any event, it appears that Alfas are finally having their moment in the market sun. I would expect to see properly restored Veloces, both Spiders and Sprints, bringing $30,000 with some regularity during the next couple of years.

Alfas are much easier to restore now than they were in the late '80s. Whereas today you can order up nearly every piece of rubber trim imaginable—from the trunk mat to the rubber around the windshield—from firms such as Matt Jones' Re-Originals, back then we would buy entire cars just to get a set of original floormats.

Further, the amount of enthusiast knowledge concerning what goes into a proper restoration is much larger, and, with the Internet, much easier to access, than it was 15 years ago.

So, other than lack of funds, there's no excuse for restoring a Giulietta improperly. If you don't have the money to do one right, please just pass it on to someone who does. We certainly don't need any more botched Spiders floating around out there.

This car should be considered fully priced at the current time, but it represents a curve that is moving upwards. So let's call it both bought and sold well.

(Photo, historic and descriptive information courtesy of the auction company.)

From the April 2003 issue of SCM. ◆

1958 750 Giulietta Sprint Veloce

I don't think the word "ergonomics" existed at that time, but the car was a delight to drive

by Raymond Milo

Chassis number: 149306552
Engine number: 131530984

It only took delivery of a few Giulietta Sprints to their new owners in 1954 for word to spread that Alfa Romeo had built something exceptional. Alfa Romeo, caught by surprise, had to quickly figure out how to increase production in order to meet demand. Alfa's previous best-seller had been the 2600 Sprint, with 6,999 produced; by the time the 1300/1600 Sprint went out of production in 1964, more than 45,000 had been delivered.

In 1956 they introduced a high-performance model, the Veloce. The list of modifications was lengthy and resulted in a more responsive and much faster car. A higher compression, hotter cams, an 8,000-rpm tachometer, twin Webers replacing the single Solex carburetors, tubular headers, and a finned cast-aluminum sump featuring a built-in oil cooler were included on the Veloce model, offered in Sprint and Spider bodies.

The example shown here is from a prominent collection. It has benefited from no-expense-spared ownership, having recently been taken back down to its bare metal and repainted because of one single flaw. The front seats were recently redone in the correct blue-gray corduroy and leatherette combination.

Originally delivered with the Veloce package, this car reportedly performs very well. In a further effort to bring the car to near-perfect condition, the clutch and throw-out bearing were replaced. As a testament to its pristine condition, this example recently won Best Alfa at a concours.

The SCM analysis: This car sold at RM's Monterey auction, August 16, 2002, for $36,300, including buyer's premium.

As with most successful designs, there is a legend about the birth of the Giulietta. In 1952 Alfa sold bonds to finance production of the new car. To enhance the sale of the bonds, Alfa offered a lottery to the bondholders, promising a number of winners free Giulietta Berlina four-door coupes. Four-door cars are more complex to make and the Berlina was way behind schedule, so management went to Bertone, asking him to quickly knock off a bunch of two-door Sprints. According to the story, there were four cars ready after ten days, and the winners of the lottery were satisfied. I don't recall any of them complaining about getting a Sprint instead of a four-door Berlina.

Whatever the truth is, Franco Scaglione, Bertone's designer, produced a masterpiece. Visibility was excellent, with thin A-pillars and large windows all around. The engine was a jewel, made completely of alloy, and with a pair of chain-driven overhead cams at a time when American manufacturers were trying to wean themselves from the Jurassic-era flathead.

I don't think the word "ergonomics" existed at that time, but the car was a delight to drive. All the controls were easy to reach and labeled with symbols, rather than words, that described their function.

The original gearbox was a work in progress, the early "tunnel-case" four-speed being replaced with a far superior "split-case" model sometime in 1958. While the electricals on the Normale models were trouble-plagued Lucas, the Veloces had a more reliable Marelli system. Overall, the Sprint was a resounding success, and was embraced by Europe, where it was extensively raced. Americans, still discovering European sports cars, fell in love with the Giulietta Spider.

By the end of 1956 a slightly more powerful version of the engine was offered, called the Veloce, with the usual hop-up bits (twin Webers, etc.). The European Sprints morphed into racing versions, first called SVZ (modified by Zagato) and eventually into the full-blown, purpose-built SZ. Period photographs often show a grid composed completely of Giulietta Sprint Veloces and their variants. But Americans, in love with wind-blown hair and tolerating pigeon droppings on their seats, continued to prefer the Spider. Here in the States, the Sprint was a rare bird, and the Sprint Veloce even rarer.

I glanced at this particular car in Monterey, and was disturbed by one thing—the level of the restoration. It was a near-perfect car, but so near-perfect that running it on the California Mille could be a 1,000-mile exercise in rock-chip terror if the new owner is as compulsive as the old one must have been.

Less disturbing, but incorrect, was the five-speed gearbox, sourced from a later model. While this is a frequently seen upgrade, purists prefer these early Veloces with their archaic, but period-correct and now almost charming tunnel-case gearboxes. One would hope that the attention applied to the cosmetics was repeated with the car's mechanicals, including often-overlooked items like the steering box and suspension bushings.

Like so many fully restored cars we see, it sold well above the Price Guide, while at the same time probably below the amount involved in the restoration. No, I don't think we are coming back to the market of '89. One swallow does not make a summer, and properly presented cars at Monterey often bring prices that drive statisticians crazy. Sprint Veloces in #2 condition are still in the $20,000 range on a very good day.

I hope the next time I see this Sprint Veloce, it's on a mountain road, body heeled far over in the typical Sprint attitude, engine buzzing easily to 7,000 rpm and the new owner smiling grandly while collecting a few nicks to the paint. All this Alfa really needs is a little patina, and a quick drive through the coast range would be a good start.

(Photo, historical and descriptive information courtesy of the auction company.)

From the January 2003 issue of SCM.◆

1958 Giulietta Sprint Veloce

Notoriously difficult to restore, with very fussy interiors

by Keith Martin

Chassis number: 149306552
Engine number: 131530984

Dear **SCM:** *Thank you for the glowing review and for raising the bar on Alfa Giulietta Sprint Veloces in the January 2003 issue of* SCM. *This recent eBay result (item #2421596395, ending July 2, 2003) will help substantiate the elevated pricepoint that* SCM *supports. These fine cars are finally getting their appropriate respect in the market.—**Santo Spadaro, via e-mail***

I clicked on the attached link, and found the car that had sold was in fact the exact car that we had profiled in our January issue. Giulietta Sprint Veloces are important, and indeed undervalued cars. Finding one that made a strong price at both a land auction (RM, Monterey, August 2002, sold at $36,300) and on eBay just eleven months later for nearly the same amount, $34,300, caused me to revisit this Sprint.

But there's more. On checking back through my own records, I found that I had sold this car to a Florida Alfa fanatic (and a cheapskate, as well, over a decade ago). But more on that later.

Here's an excerpt of what the seller had to say in his eBay listing:

"I bought this car in August of 2002 at the RM auction in Monterey, where it had been consigned from a prominent Southern California collection. It has benefited from a no-expense-spared ownership, having recently been taken back down to its bare metal and repainted because of a single flaw. The resulting silver repaint is stunning. The front seats were recently redone in the correct, period, blue-gray corduroy leatherette combination.

"Originally delivered with the Veloce package, this special car performs exceptionally well. In a further effort to bring the Alfa to near-perfect condition, the clutch and throw-out bearing were replaced. As a testament to its pristine condition, this example recently won Best Alfa at a concours.

"It is an expertly restored car that started from an original Sprint Veloce and returned to better-than-new standards both visually and mechanically. The Giulietta series was the linchpin of Alfa Romeo's success, and upon inspection of this example it is easy to understand why."

For those not familiar with Alfa lore, Alfa was best-known before WWII for its thunderous, supercharged six- and eight-cylinder cars, the 6C 1750s and 8C 2300s and 2900s. The Ferraris of their era, they simply outclassed everything else on the road.

After the war, Alfa struggled along, building at first pre-war six-cylinder designs, and then the more sporty four-cylinder 1900s. But it wasn't until the lithe Giulietta Sprint was launched in 1954 that Alfa began to achieve, once again, worldwide acclaim.

While the Spider was more popular in the U.S., in Europe the Sprint, especially the factory hot-rod Veloce version, became the consummate café-racer. Pulling 90 hp out of its dual-cam 1300-cc all-alloy engine, the Veloce came factory equipped with dual Weber DC03 carburetors, forced cold-air induction, a two-piece finned aluminum sump, high-lift cams, mechanical advance distributor, a larger gas tank, larger front brakes and more.

The tach didn't even start until 2,000 rpm—after all, who would let his Veloce engine, with its 8,000-rpm redline, stay below 2,000 for long?

Giulietta Sprints are notoriously difficult to restore, cosmetically, as their interior and door panels are filled with fussy, hard-to-source bits. The mechanicals are a bit easier, as they are relatively robust, and a comprehensive supply of parts exists both here and in Italy.

When I first saw this car, it was still with its original owner in Berkeley, CA. I don't recall how I heard about it, but I went to see it and was impressed by how non-mucked-with it was. Although it had been repainted once, sometime in the late '80s, it was in its original shade of robin's-egg blue. It still had the original, and slightly goofy-looking, mattress-tacking interior. All of the chrome was intact and the engine sounded good and pulled strongly. There were no dents, and no evidence that the car had ever been rusty. The seller wanted $15,000.

A subscriber to *SCM* who lived in Florida was looking for a Veloce in this condition and asked me to buy the car for him. I did, somewhat to my regret. Since the money was wired to my aging grandmother's account in San Francisco, I asked if he would sent her a check for $250, as a thoughtful gift to compensate her for the hassle of going to the bank, withdrawing the money, etc.

He refused and I sent her some money instead, but I've never forgotten the fellow. He never thanked me, or her, for helping him get the car.

In any event, he restored the car, and my understanding is that he then sold it along with some other cars he had. It was restored when he sold it, and the new owner had it restored again, to even higher standards.

For too long, Sprint Veloces have been undervalued and under-appreciated by collectors at large. Our own *Price Guide* lists them at $18,000-$22,500, a number that now needs to be revised upwards. Granted, this car was a #1, rather than a #2 car that our guides value, but nonetheless, I would think that $22,500-$28,000 would be a fair market valuation for a #2 Giulietta Sprint Veloce in today's market.

Further, I find it to be most interesting that this car would sell, for nearly identical prices, at two quite dissimilar venues. It bodes well for both land auctions and electronic ones that a good car, properly presented, can make the same money at both.

From the September 2003 issue of SCM.◆

1959 Spider Veloce

Finding a real Veloce can be a challenge. An 8,000-rpm, no-redline tach, dual DCO3s and a cast-alloy sump do not a real Veloce make

by Pat Braden

Chassis number: 1495F05317

In the early 1950s, youthful sports car enthusiasts could choose between the MG-TD or the XK Jaguar. The performance and price gap between those two models was only partially filled by the Triumph and Austin-Healey. Only the more affluent could enjoy the superior weather protection and comfort of a Porsche or Aston Martin. The Alfa Romeo Giulietta Spider, introduced in Italy in 1955, offered weather protection equal to the most expensive sports cars and a very comfortable ride for only about $900 more than an MG. Its styling was fresh and aerodynamic, its handling light and responsive and its dramatic 80-hp, all-alloy twin-cam engine set it apart from the majority of pushrod sporting engines of the era.

The 1290-cc displacement of the Alfa gave it somewhat leisurely performance compared to American cars and the Jaguar, and the supple suspension, though wonderfully comfortable, was initially regarded as suspect by enthusiasts schooled on harsh-riding MGs. In competition, however, the Alfa quickly proved itself against cars of significantly higher displacement. Typically, enthusiasts wondered how to improve the car's performance even more.

They did not need to wait long for the authoritative answer. One year after the Giulietta appeared, the factory offered its own hot-rodded version, the Giulietta Veloce. If the twin-cam Giulietta engine was attractive, it became absolutely irresistible when fitted with dual DCO3 Weber side-draft carburetors. The visual impact of the Giulietta Veloce's engine is immediate: Its dual Webers occupy almost as much real estate as the engine itself, which is canted slightly to make room for the huge carburetors. The Veloce carried other important features that helped assure a reliable 90-hp engine. Hotter camshafts, a shaved head, forged pistons, a cast-alloy sump and electric fuel pump were some of the added features contributing to its performance. The Veloce came with a 10/41 ring and pinion (compared to the 9/41 setup of the Giulietta) and could reach 112 mph. *Road & Track's* test of a Veloce in 1958 reported a 0-60 time of 14.1 seconds.

The car pictured here is red with a black interior, with red piping to the seats. It has original dual Weber DCO3 carburetors and tubular headers in a slightly over-detailed engine compartment. The body is straight, with no evidence of rust. A later four-speed transmission has been installed. Upon close inspection, all the hallmarks of a "true" Veloce, including a special rubber mount on the frame on the exhaust side of the engine, are present.

The SCM *analysis: This car sold for $20,140, including commission, at the January 2000 Barrett-Jackson Auction. This is at the high end of* SCM's *Price Guide, and a top price for a non-concours car.*

In 1959 Alfa made an unannounced transition from the 750 to the 101 series Giulietta mechanicals. As a result, it's possible to find a combination of new and old components in 1959 cars, so the "later" four-speed gearbox may in fact have been original for the car. It's fortunate that the owner stayed true to the essential character of the car and did not opt for the easy conversion to a fifth speed.

Following several decades of enthusiast conversions, finding a real Veloce can be a challenge. An 8,000-rpm, no-redline tach, dual DCO3s and a cast-alloy sump do not a real Veloce make. Converted Giuliettas lack the forged Borgo pistons and additional valve shims that help make the engine bullet-proof, even over 7,000 rpm. The easiest way to identify a Veloce is the 750F designation on the bulkhead plaque. And if you think that's a "conversion" too, then check for the electric fuel pump lead coming out of the wiring harness amidships beneath the car, and the separate carburetor intake duct on the driver's side of the horizontal grille.

As desirable as the Veloce is, it has some drawbacks as an around-town driver. Just as the Veloce is Alfa's textbook on how to modify an engine, it is a demonstration of the difference between horsepower and torque. The Veloce offers gobs of the former and precious little of the latter. As a result, getting underway from a stop requires considerable throttle and a sensitive application of the clutch. About 3,000 rpm and some clutch slippage are required to pull away without stalling. Veloces are also notorious for being hard to start in the cold. The standard response is to subtract the ambient temperature from 100 to get the number of times to pump the accelerator pedal before starting. Another aid to easy cold starts is to run a very large ground wire between the battery (in the trunk) and a starter mounting bolt.

Today, a straight, rust-free body on a Giulietta simply means that its inevitable rust has been cleansed and the nose straightened after countless parking-lot and curbside encounters. Though the overall impression of the Giulietta Veloce is one of delicacy bordering on the fragile, they have proved to be very durable, both as cars and investments. The new owner of this car may not be able to resell it at an immediate profit but, if the car is as sound as it appeared to be, should be able to enjoy numerous weekends and vintage rallies, tach whipping to 8,000 rpm and engine making glorious, Italian small-displacement twin-cam sounds. If properly maintained, this car should never go down in value, and may even hit the $25,000 mark in a couple of years.

(Historical and descriptive information provided courtesy of the auction company.)

From the April 2000 issue of SCM. ◆

1959 Giulietta Sprint Zagato

The lack of pre-1978 history, besides a photograph, is troubling. Even today, one can order a replica SZ body from Galbiati's shop

by Pat Braden

Chassis number: AR-10126*00082*

The Giulietta Sprint Zagato echoes the severe tumble-home roofline of the fabulous Bertone BATs and the slanted tail of the same bodybuilder's Sprint Speciale. The BATs, however, were strictly styling exercises and the Sprint Speciales were too heavy to be race cars. It was Zagato that finally filled Alfa's need for an aerodynamic Giulietta coupe that would win races.

Two series of the Sprint Zagato were produced between 1959 and 1961. The first series featured a smooth, flowing body that ended in a short, curved trunk. It was markedly different from the second series, which was redesigned to feature a longer but more abruptly-ending tail.

Weighing in at slightly more than 1,700 pounds, both iterations of the SZ were excellent performers, given their 1300-cc, 100-hp DOHC alloy engine. Sporting all of the best features of the Giulietta, including large, finned drum brakes and lightweight solid rear axle, the aluminum-bodied SZ brought an impressive series of podium finishes to both factory teams and privateers.

A photograph of the SZ described here, wearing Italian plates, was taken in England in the 1960s. Recent traceable history, however, dates back to 1978, when the car was found in storage south of Milan. At that time, it was missing both doors and its rear bodywork was slightly damaged. In that condition, the car was sold at the Imola autojumble to a Swiss dentist who restored and then campaigned it at club rallies and races. In 1994, the dentist sold the car to Italian auto broker Franco Manetti, who imported it to the US in 1999. The car comes with its original racing seats, rollbar, engine and transmission.

The SCM *analysis: This car was sold for $49,500 at the RM Monterey Auction on August 19, 2000. The sale price of this car is double the low auction estimate and reflects both the good condition of the car and its essential desirability.*

Before the war, the combination of an Alfa Romeo chassis and a Zagato body set the standard for high-performance, lightweight sport cars. After the war, that relationship changed. While Alfa was busy assembling 6C 2500s from pre-war parts, Zagato was busy building Fiat Topolino bodies. The 1900 SSZ Alfa Zagato coupe was a consistent hillclimb winner in the mid-'50s, but it failed to rekindle the strong bond between the two firms that characterized the pre-war relationship.

The potential big break for Zagato came when the Priolo brothers came to them and asked for a lightweight body on a recently wrecked Giulietta Sprint Veloce. The substantially lightened Zagato-bodied Giulietta proved a potent contender for the brothers, and it was not long before customers began to line up for duplicate lightweight Giulietta Zagatos.

Alfa wouldn't supply the pan and driveline, so Zagato was reduced to buying new Giulietta Sprint Veloces at full price, then cutting the bodies off and fitting their own lightweight creations. In spite of the necessarily exorbitant cost, the Giulietta Zagato coupes continued to sell. Finally, the Zagato brothers made their point to Alfa management, and they were allowed to buy just the pan and running gear
from the factory at a considerably reduced cost. The Giulietta Sprint Zagato was the result.

The original version, sometimes referred to as "the football," had a rounded-off tail that was symmetric with the car's front bodywork. This was an era of aerodynamic experimentation, however, and the second style of Zagato bodywork on the Giulietta followed the theories of the German aerodynamicist Kamm: the "coda tronca" (truncated tail). Before Kamm, the laminar flow of air over a body was maintained as long as possible, resulting in an extended tail which tapers to almost a point. Kamm's theory was that the extended tail simply prolonged aerodynamic drag, and it would be more efficient to end the laminar flow as early and abruptly as possible. The coda tronca design of the Giulietta Sprint Zagato was carried over to the Giulia TZ and TZ2 cars, as well as the later Type 33 racers.

Normal Giulietta Veloces need at least 3,000 rpm for getting underway from a stop. Because of its light weight, the Zagato version requires much less throttle. Though most of the Zagato Giuliettas have had a racing history, they are actually quite capable of everyday transport if the owner is so inclined. Unlike the later IRS Giulia TZ, very little fiddling with suspension settings is required to produce a very competitive car. And, since the driveline is virtually stock 101 Giulietta Veloce, replacement parts are not a real problem. In many ways, the Giulietta Sprint Veloce Zagato is the best of all possible worlds.

This car was bid considerably over the auction estimate, which was too low to begin with. Pricing balances the car's positive appeal against the fact that it was not completely original, though most of the pieces to make it so came with the car. The lack of pre-1978 history besides a photograph (how do they know it is the same car?) is troubling; one can even today order a replica SZ body from Galbiati's shop. At nearly $50,000, however, this was a fair enough deal for everyone involved. It's hard to name another car that combines such performance, practicality, rarity and charm.

(Photo, historical and descriptive information courtesy of the auction company.)

From the November 2000 issue of SCM.◆

1959 2000 Spider

The cast-iron 2-liter is either the best bargain in the business or a car the collector can safely ignore

by Pat Braden

Chassis number: AR 10204016371637
Engine number: AR 0020401974

A replacement for the 1900 line, the 102-series 2000 cars first appeared in 1958 and were unusual insofar as production of the Touring-bodied Spider version outstripped that of the four-door Berlina. A Bertone-bodied Sprint coupe followed in 1960. Nowadays referred to as the "Cast-Iron 2-liter," the twin-cam 2000 engine combined elements of the superseded 1900 and new Giulietta, retaining the former's cast-iron block and separate cam covers but featuring the latter's bucket-and-shim method of valve adjustment. Spider and Sprint versions came with 115 bhp on tap, good enough for a top speed in excess of 110 mph. Beneath the skin the 2000 remained much as the last of the 1900s, with independent front suspension, live rear axle, five-speed gearbox and drum brakes all round. Despite a relaxed high-speed cruising ability and excellent smoothness, the 2000 in its day tended to be overshadowed by the smaller and cheaper Giulietta, and only now is the model beginning to receive the attention it deserves.

Imported to England in 1991 from the USA by its former owner, the late Robert Charibi, this Touring Spider underwent extensive restoration work culminating in a class win (against strong opposition) at the National Alfa Day in 1993 and was placed runner up (by a single point) in the Master Class category the following year. Regarded as one of the finest examples of its type anywhere, the car has been kept in de-humidified storage since October 1994 and remains in excellent condition throughout.

The SCM *analysis: This car sold for $18,400 (including 15% buyer's premium) at the Brooks Goodwood auction on June 23, 2000.*

The cast-iron 2-liter is either the best bargain in the business or a car the collector can safely ignore. Both positions present strong arguments.

On behalf of the car, its styling and spacious interior are the equal of Ferrari and Maserati convertibles costing at least three times as much as this Alfa. The car's elegant Touring body accurately reflects the best of contemporary design, and the detailing of the car is excellent. Maintenance of this Alfa is absolutely bargain-basement when compared to the more illustrious marques. The only real challenge during a tune-up is having the small cups used to adjust valve clearances on hand. Otherwise, all the necessary parts are easily—and inexpensively—available. If you want a beautiful Spider that can be run regularly and maintained economically, this is the car for you. Charibi was clearly of this persuasion.

On the other hand, this is neither a Ferrari nor Maserati. Elegant styling aside, the 2-liter, four-cylinder engine offers only 115 hp to a car weighing in at 2,770 pounds. The top speed of 111.3 mph comes slowly: a Road & Track *road test of the model in July, 1959 gave a 0-60 time of 14.2 seconds and a 0-100 time of 50 seconds.*

Leisurely performance, however, was not the car's greatest drawback. At the time the model was introduced, all indicators were positive. As a follow-up to the fabulously popular 1900 sedan, the new 2-liter offered fresh new styling and the option of regular-production Spider and coupe versions.

The new 2-liter Berlina, however, was certainly one of the ugliest Alfas ever produced, and the svelte Spider and Sprint were completely overshadowed by the Giulietta, which had been introduced in a dramatic 1954 lottery that remains one of the great marketing triumphs of the industry. Moreover, the Giulietta Veloce Spider, introduced in 1956, was nimbler than the 2-liter, and was actually faster by a small margin. Simply put, the 2-liter didn't stand a chance against its smaller stablemate.

The 2000 was again overshadowed by its replacement, the 2600, which offered near-identical styling plus a 145-hp, 2.6-liter, six-cylinder, twin-cam engine and a top speed of just over 120 mph. It's the kind of story that gives product planners nightmares.

Forty years have passed since its introduction, and the 2-liter has yet to emerge from the shadow of the Giulietta or the 2600. Interesting—even attractive—it's still a slug in the minds of most collectors, and hardly more than a footnote in the literature of the marque.

At the same time, this also explains its appeal to certain collectors: If you are willing to ignore the car's context and focus on what the 2-liter really offers, it's a fantastic bargain. You could buy a good one for what it costs to give a Ferrari of similar configuration a thorough tune-up. The sale price of this car, just over SCM *Price Guide range, is probably a fraction of the money invested in its restoration. Owning "one of the finest examples of its type anywhere" is a calculated choice. The only real challenge of 2-liter ownership will come after a decision to sell the car: finding another enthusiast of similar persuasion, which might take quite some time.*

(Photo, historical and descriptive information courtesy of the auction company.)

From the January 2001 issue of SCM. ◆

1960 Giulietta Sprint "Veloce" Coupe

Believing that this car is unrestored requires an astounding suspension of disbelief: It is a mixture of the very impressive and the very terrifying

by Pat Braden

(Note: The following grammatically challenged description of the Sprint appears exactly as found on the eBay posting, edited only for brevity.—ED.)

Chassis number: 10105 1493-21167
Engine number: AR 1315 011460

Red exterior with the original red and gray leather interior & red carpets. The panel fit on the Bertone coachwork and over-all aesthetics are excellent. Interior, although original, shows very minimal wear, no rips or tears. The odometer indicates 96,000 but not convinced if they are miles or kilometers. The Arizona title shows the mileage to be actual. The car is powered by an alloy 1300 cc double overhead cam, 4 cylinder engine, coupled to a four-speed transmission. Equipped with factory Weber carburetors, and the rare, original cast aluminum intake plenum and air filter canister. The engine has enjoyed a recent "freshening" and runs and drives beautifully.

Also present is the original Nardi trademark wooden steering wheel. New Michelin radial tires on original wheels in the correct size and type. This Alfa was imported 4 years ago from Italy to Northern California to participate in annual Italian automobile festivities in and around the Monterey and Laguna Seca area, and also to take part in the California Mille. It has also participated in the Arizona Governors Cup (Hospice) Rally. This is a private-party sale, you are not dealing with a dealer. The value guide indicates by VIN that this car may be, indeed a '59, but it is registered and was imported as a '60. The Alfa can remain in secure, indoor storage for up to 30 days, after payment in full, while the new owner arranges for shipping or transportation. I will gladly answer any and all questions relating to this rare, Alfa Veloce coupe. Thanks for looking and Good Luck!

Corrections: This Alfa is fitted with a five-speed transmission, not a four-speed as listed in the above text. Also the numbers stamped into the factory ID plate are 10105 1493-21167 Motore AR-1315. The actual number stamped on the alloy engine block are: AR 1315 011460. Inspection also shows the car is fitted with Koni shock absorbers at all four corners. Thanks!

The SCM *analysis:* In 1954, with the introduction of the Giulietta Sprint, Alfa joined Jaguar, Aston Martin, Porsche, Maserati and Ferrari in offering a lightweight twin-cam engine in an aerodynamic grand-touring body. Originally equipped with a dual-throat, downdraft Solex carburetor, it was only two years later that the factory hot rod version, the Veloce, made its debut. With twin Weber side-draft carburetors and a host of internal improvements, the Giulietta Veloce was Alfa Romeo's tutorial on how to wrest 90 durable horsepower from a 1.3-liter engine that could maintain 7,000 rpm all day long.

This Giulietta is a mixture of the very impressive and the terrifying. Someone spent a lot of money on the restoration, and, according to the nine photographs posted on eBay, it appears to be in #1 condition. The body panels are straight and the doors don't show the typical Sprint droop, which occurs as a result of their considerable weight. The chrome is unmarked and all the trim pieces, including the hubcaps, are correct. The interior has been redone in red and

gray leather or leatherette, and the red carpeting is all new. The trunk fabric lining is correct and the battery area is undamaged. The engine bay is both correct and spotless.

This car sold for $16,500 on eBay on March 21, 2002. The sum—$1,500 over SCM's high Price Guide price—probably represents a loss over the amount of time spent on getting the car to its current condition. Moreover, whoever did the restoration, presumably an Italian, knew what original Giulietta Sprint Veloces looked like, and maintained that appearance meticulously. Shiny paint, sparkling chrome, a spotless interior and pristine engine bay add up to a no-objections car. Perfection invites picking nits: The only fault is that the original radio blanking plate (a very rare item) is missing and the holes for the radio have been filled in, so the surface is perfectly smooth. So far, so good.

In fact, perhaps too good to be true. The car, by itself, is utterly captivating, but the owner's description shouts "caution!" Despite the seller's continued insistence that the car is "original," there are many things wrong here. In the first place, the Nardi wheel was not an original item on the Veloce, and the car cannot possibly be as original as the owner claims. This is a 42-year-old car, with 96,000 miles (the speedo reads to 140, and cannot be in kilometers), yet there is no visible wear on the seats, carpet or pedals. A four-speed transmission was original equipment, but this car carries a five-speed. Along the same lines, the Koni shocks were not original equipment. Finally, a Giulietta engine at 96,000 miles probably deserves a thorough overhaul, not a refreshment.

Believing that this car is original and unrestored requires an astounding suspension of disbelief. A more credible claim for this car would have been that it underwent a cost-no-object restoration and has been compulsively cared for ever since.

But there's more to this story. A check of serial numbers reveals that this car began life as a Solex-carbureted Sprint Normale, not a Sprint Veloce. The seller, who expressed surprise when supplied with this information, was still able to find a buyer who was willing to purchase a make-believe Veloce. The new owner is an automotive enthusiast/journalist who states that he is completely happy with the car.

Slowly, fakey-doo or clone cars are being accepted for what they are, and they are being purchased by those to whom originality is not paramount. In fact, SCM's Price Guide listing of $15,000 for a #2 Sprint Veloce should probably be revisited in light of this sale. True Sprint Veloces are hard to come by, which makes properly done clones like this desirable. And so long as someone is not fabricating a famous race history or other provenance to go with the car, what's the harm? It's really not much different than putting a set of triple two-barrel carbs on a 1965 GTO that was originally equipped with a four barrel, or converting a 260-ci Mustang to a high-performance 289. So long as buyer and seller both are clear about exactly what the car is, at the end of the day everyone should be happy.

The increasing acceptance of well-done clones is evidence of the birth of a whole new market segment.

From the July 2002 issue of SCM. ◆

1960 2000 Spider

Maintaining the Solex PH44 carburetors, with their prone-to-malfunction secondaries, is enough to drive almost any technician to heavy drink

by Craig Morningstar

Chassis number: AR1020401698

In 1950, Alfa Romeo turned away from the costly and complicated, hand-built, eight- and six-cylinder high performance sports and racing cars that had made their name before World War II. The new 1900 was intended for a very different market, to take the company into the second half of the 20th Century. It had a lusty four-cylinder engine boasting twin overhead camshafts like all Alfas before and since, but intended for mass production.

In 1958 the four-door 2000 Berlina arrived to supersede the 1900. The 2000 was also offered in coupe and spider form. The spider's Touring body was delectable, beautifully finished and equipped, a classic grand tourer for two fortunate occupants.

The Alfa pictured here is immaculately presented, having formerly been the subject of a thorough restoration. The paintwork, interior and mechanics are all reported to be in perfect condition. The car is also sold with its rare additional factory hard top, which has also been restored, and it retains its original period radio.

In the former ownership for 13 years, it was recently purchased from Italy by the current owner.

The SCM analysis: This car sold for $31,189 at the Christie's Holland auction on Aug. 31, 2003.

The mid-1950s was a prosperous period at Alfa Romeo. The company was embarking on a major expansion at the behest of its holding company, Finmeccanica. The mass-produced (by Alfa standards anyway) 1900 had brought the company from postwar uncertainty to an enviable position as a European sport and luxury producer. The Giulietta model range that followed was a huge commercial success.

The 102-series 2000 model range was a somewhat simplified evolution of the 1900, including a Berlina (sedan) built by Alfa Romeo, a Sprint (coupe) with a Bertone body penned by a young Giorgetto Giugiaro, and the Spider from Touring. A handful of special-bodied cars by Vignale and Frua were also built.

A total of 7,089 102-series cars were built and almost half were Spiders. This was a strange model mix for Alfa Romeo, as usually the sedan was built in the largest volume, followed by coupes and then a much smaller number of Spiders. Of the series production brought to the U.S., the Spider made up approximately 95%.

The coupe and Spider had 115 hp, and the Berlina, 105. They all had a much-improved five-speed transmission, column-mounted on the Berlina and on the floor in the coupe and Spider.

The 2000 is a comfortable cruiser that offers a lot in the way of creature comforts, like roll-up windows and a top with decent weather sealing. This is offset by underwhelming performance, as the 2000 is barely able to outrun the 1300-cc Giulietta. In fact, Editor Martin has compared the acceleration of the 2000 to "driving a Giulietta Normale with a telephone pole tied to its rear bumper."

The vastly superior 2600 model, with a magnificent all-alloy 2.6-liter six-cylinder engine, was to be launched in 1962.

Our example has spent a good portion of its life in Italy, which is not reassuring. Italy is notorious for rusty cars, and Alfas are not noted for their resistance to harsh weather. Nor are Italians noted for babying their cars. An Italian restoration is often average paint, okay interior, and great mechanicals.

More recently the car has lived in the Netherlands, which is mostly below sea level, not a terrific recommendation either. Although the car has undergone a thorough restoration and appears to be in perfect order, I would still bring a magnet when looking at this or any vintage Alfa.

The 2000 engines are quite stout and under-stressed, putting out moderate power at moderate revs. The design is based on sound architecture, as is the rest of the drivetrain. The basic transmission was used through the last Spiders produced in the '90s and the rear axle is bulletproof as well. The suspension has a lot of travel for its era and offers a smooth ride and competent handling. The aluminum-finned drum brakes are quite able to haul the rather heavy car down with aplomb. However, maintaining the Solex PH44 carburetors, with their prone-to-malfunction vacuum-operated secondaries, is enough to drive almost any technician to heavy drink. Be aware that most parts for these cars are difficult to find and quite expensive.

A great number of 2000s have been scrapped in order to facilitate the plentiful and more attractive 1900 restoration projects, so the supply of good ones is limited. This car sold at a huge price, easily 50% above what we might have expected it to bring. If in fact the body is straight, rust-free and without Bondo, and the mechanicals check out, the new owner should simply refuse to open the Alfa section of the SCM Price Guide and just enjoy his car. However, it will be at least five years before he can expect to see market values in general catch up with his expenditure.

(Historical and descriptive information courtesy of the auction company.)

From the January 2004 issue of SCM.◆

1963 Giulia Sprint GT

It would not be out of line for the new owner to face a $3,500-$5,000 repair bill to put his new toy back on the road, not including an engine rebuild

by O. Delmas Greene

Chassis number: AR605503

With the introduction of the Giulietta in 1954, Alfa Romeo established the "small car, big performance" formula which would characterize the Milanese marque's finest offerings from then on. Alfa's classic 1900-cc twin-cam four was downsized to 1290 cc for the series 750 Giulietta, gaining an alloy cylinder block in the process. The debutante Sprint Coupe was soon joined by Berlina and Spider versions, and then in 1959 came the special-bodied Sprint Speciale.

The Giulietta Sprint coupe eventually evolved into the Alfa most familiar to Americans, the 1600-cc Giulia Sprint GT—often called the GTV. Later variants were equipped with 1750-cc and 2000-cc engines. They are regarded as a nearly perfect small-displacement GT car, with a five-speed gearbox, four-wheel disc brakes and superb interior ergonomics—that is if you have short legs and long arms.

We are advised that this example underwent extensive restoration circa 1994, while in the hands of its previous, second owner. It was acquired by the vendor that same year. A new clutch and gearbox were fitted in 1995, and just 4,000 km have been covered since, out of a total of 10,000 since the restoration. Kept in a heated garage, the vehicle has not been used since 1996.

Finished in grey with red interior, this handsome and desirable Italian GT is presented in excellent condition throughout.

The SCM *analysis:* This car sold for $7,842 at the Bonhams auction held in Geneva, Switzerland, on March 8, 2004.

Among non-Alfisti, the differences between the 101 series and the 105 series Giulias are confusing at best, not least because production overlapped in 1963 and 1964, and the name of the car changed only by the addition of the "GT" moniker. That considered, it is not surprising that the car pictured here was described as a Giulia Sprint by Bonhams, when in fact it is a Giulia Sprint GT. However, the two cars have completely different sheetmetal, the 101 Sprint being the final derivative of the Giulietta Sprint platform, while the 105 Sprint GT was an entirely new chassis.

Alfa Romeo built a new plant at Arese to assemble the 105 series, while the 101 series was still winding down at its old Portello site.

The 105-series Sprint GT body, by Bertone, provided a larger interior than in the 101-series Sprint, with a more functional back seat (though one only useful for small passengers or short trips) and a larger greenhouse. On the outside, the GT can be distinguished by its more modern looking front end, with headlamps set into a wide grille and vertically positioned parking/turn signal lights on the outside front edge of the fenders.

An offset was designed into the front edge of the hood, where it contacts the front valence. At first glance, this "step-nose" may appear to be just a large horizontal shadow, but it is actually a rather interesting design element—the cognoscenti lamented its disappearance on the 1969 GTV.

The 105-series chassis received several updates over the 101 series. The front double wishbone design was replaced by a single lower A-arm and two separate upper links, which allowed for better adjustability. At the same time, almost all the front suspension grease fittings disappeared in favor of sealed joints. (These "lifetime lubricated" seals go dry after about ten years. One way to renew them is to use a horse-hypodermic to inject a lubricating fluid directly into the rubber bushings.) Lateral support of the rear axle was accomplished by using a pivoting T-arm instead of the triangular-shaped piece found on the earlier 101 series.

A little internal tuning to the twin-Weber equipped 1570-cc engine brought the power of the 105-series Giulia up to 106 hp, a significant increase over the 92 of the 101-series Sprint, which was only offered by the factory in single, two-barrel Solex configuration.

Alfa's 105 Sprint GT series included a number of other interesting models, including:

• The 1300-cc GT Junior, which was offered primarily for the European market, where a smaller engine displacement was desirable for tax reasons. (See page 62.)

• The GTC, a convertible version with essentially the same drivetrain. (See page 58.)

• The twin plugged, lightened and race prepped GTA. (See Alfa Romeo Profile, SCM issue August 2001.)

Purchasing any Alfa from this era requires close inspection of sheet-metal rust in the rocker panel and floor pan areas. Luckily, replacement parts for nearly everything that is prone to rust are available. Unluckily, it takes a skilled craftsman to weld them in so that the repairs are invisible, which is the reason so many GTs are heavily undercoated. Think of it as Italian floorpan pancake makeup.

Replacing weather-stripping and window seals is usually necessary to eliminate rattles and leaks, and runs about $500. Dash tops crack with age, but covers are available.

The car pictured here was bought at the low end of its market value, and could be a deal for the buyer if the mechanicals are in order. However, this a dicey proposition given that the car has been stored for eight years, even in a heated garage. It would not be out of line for the new owner to face a $3,500-$5,000 repair bill just to put his new toy back on the road, dealing with brakes, clutch, suspension and engine disassembly and check over—and that doesn't include rebuilding any major components.

Even so, the new owner does have some room for reconditioning without losing his shirt, as Alfa's generally robust mechanicals are much easier to make right than a rusted body. Assuming the body is as sound as it looked to be, this could turn out to be a good buy. Even better, if the new owner is handy with a wrench, this car could even be called a bargain.

There's a reason that the Sprint GT/GTV series has such a large following: It's handsome, easy to live with, handles well and has enough scoot to be entertaining on twisting roads. When all is said and done, the 105-series Giulia offers a whole lot of collector car fun for not a lot of money. I call this well bought.

(Photo, historical and descriptive information courtesy of the auction company.)

From the August 2004 issue of SCM.◆

1963 Giulia Spider

Sometimes the key to understanding auction catalog descriptions is not in what they say, but what they don't say

by Giuseppe Tomasetti

Chassis number: 375514

After World War II Alfa Romeo could no longer afford to produce purely the bespoke motor cars that had made the marque famous on both road and track. It was not until 1954 that Alfa found its savior in the Giulietta Sprint, Nuccio Bertone being commissioned to design this small coupe just weeks before its debut at the Turin Show. The resultant shape pleased the eye from any angle, but Bertone's styling for the convertible model was less appealing and the design was passed to Pinin Farina; using a chassis seven inches shorter than the Bertone coupe, the Spider was equally graceful.

The initial 750 Series Giulietta chassis featured independent front suspension with a coil-sprung live rear axle and drum brakes all round. The engine, like the suspension, owed much to Alfa's racing experience, hence the ability of the twin-cam four cylinder to produce 65 bhp from just 1290 cc.

Major changes appeared in 1959 with the 101 Series. Though outwardly similar, the 1290-cc engine was strengthened while the bodies received minor detail alterations. The final change came in 1962 when the renamed Giulia models appeared with five-speed gearboxes and a 92-bhp, 1570-cc version of the twin-cam engine.

This smart Giulia Spider has been prepared for competition and features modified suspension and brakes to provide a firmer ride and more effective stopping capabilities. The car is believed to have resided in Italy from new, and now carries FIA papers allowing it to compete in such events as the Coppa d'Italia in which the vendor informs us the car has recently competed. It has a strong engine, which we are reliably informed produces in the region of 110 bhp.

Finished in red and white, this exciting racing car should provide an effective and enjoyable entry into historic motorsport.

The SCM *analysis: This car sold at Coys' True Greats auction held December 11, 2000 at the Business Design Center in London for $8,508, including buyer's premium.*

Sometimes the key to understanding auction catalog descriptions is not in what they say, but what they don't say. For example, the references to "modified suspension and brakes to produce a firmer ride" and to an "engine which we are reliably informed produces in the region of 110 bhp" really means, "We are told this is a race car, but who knows?"

Nonetheless, a race car purchased at auction can often be a good buy. In this case, the race preparation alone probably equaled the selling price, thereby making the car free. Why was the car thrown into the deal for nothing? Because auctions pander primarily to three groups—high-end ultra-exotic buyers, shiny chrome groupies, and tightwad bottom-feeders. Series production cars fitted out to FIA race specs don't appeal to any of these audiences. This "right

product in the wrong sales environment" can lead to good deals if you know what you are doing and if the car is properly inspected.

This Alfa Spider adds an interesting twist to our analysis. Spiders are viewed in Europe as touring cars. In the U.S., with a tip of the hat to Max Hoffman, they are viewed as sports cars. In fact, the Europeans have it right. The Alfa Giulietta/Giulia made its name as a coupe, not as a Spider. (See Alfa Romeo Giulietta da Corsa, Hughes & da Prato, Haynes Publishing, Great Britain, 1989.) Except for Consalvo Sanesi's Spider in the 1956 Mille Miglia, all of Alfa's factory racing cars (such as the SV, SVZ, SS, SZ, TZ and GTA) were closed cars. The same is true for Ferrari (250 series through GTO) and Porsche (356 through 910).

In today's Euro historic racing world, however, organizers are looking for a varied mix of cars in each grid. Who wants to look at 36 real and/or fake Shelby Mustangs filling up a Tour Auto grid? In Europe, Alfa racing Spiders are uncommon. Thus, for many events over here, a Spider may be more likely to be accepted than a GTA. Further, an Alfa Spider like the one described here should qualify for the highly competitive, not to mention fun, Giulietta/Giulia historic race series—a case in which the organizers do want to see a grid full of the same types of cars.

If you know what you are doing, a properly prepared race car can be a very good buy at auction. This is especially true if, before you bid, you factor in the cost of the engine, transmission and suspension rebuild you will probably have to go through before you are satisfied with the car's performance. After all, what you are really buying is a racing shell that hopefully has a lot of safety and go-fast parts bolted on to it. If the car here was prepared, even minimally, to a decent standard and had been raced enough to begin the sorting-out process, then this competitive and easy-to-maintain Spider was a good buy.

(Photo, historical and descriptive information courtesy of the auction company.)

From the March 2001 issue of SCM. ◆

1964 Giulia Spider Normale

While their engines are rugged when properly set up, they don't gladly suffer fools with tools

by Keith Martin

Chassis number: AR372440

As described by the seller on eBay Motors: This is a 1964 Giulia Spider that has been in the same family since new and underwent a complete restoration in 1984. All of the mechanical systems were renewed during this time. The engine was totally rebuilt with all original Alfa parts including a new-stage two-head by Sperry Valve Works. A Weber 36 DCD carburetor and a Crane ignition system were installed. The front brakes were upgraded to series 105 discs.

The body was stripped to bare medal and repainted an authentic red lacquer finish with matching paint codes to the original. The top and interior have worn with time and do need to be restored. Overall, this is one of the finest Spiders around and is a very comfortable driver.

It is in need of some cosmetic restoration but very dependable and mechanically solid.

The SCM *analysis: This car sold on eBay Motors (#2424457587), on July 26, 2003, for $10,300.*

My first Alfa was a 1963 Giulia Spider, in red with a black vinyl interior. I was 17 years old at the time, living in San Francisco, and had already owned a '59 Bugeye Sprite and a '58 MGA roadster. The Alfa was listed in the San Francisco Chronicle, with an asking price of $1,000.

My good friend and fellow Alfa fanatic Bjarne Holm and I drove over to see the car in his '57 Alfa Giulietta Spider Normale. The red car was straight, with no rust (after all, it was only five years old at the time), and had its motor upgraded through the installation of a 1700-cc piston and liner kit. The Porsche gang would probably call that a big-bore kit. I bought it for $920.

Compared to the MGA, the Giulia Spider was a luxury car. It had, among other wonders, roll-up windows. Its alloy mechanicals included a five-speed, split-case gearbox, a chain-driven dual-overhead cam engine and a finned sump.

There may be no better vintage sports car in its price range than an Alfa Giulia Spider. A first-rate Normale (generally identified by its Solex carburetor-equipped engine) will set you back $18,000-$22,000, and a Veloce (dual Weber carbs) $22,000-$26,000. True, that's a lot more than an MGB, but you get a lot more car in return.

The knock on Alfas was the lack of qualified mechanics. While

their engines are rugged when properly set up, they don't suffer fools with tools gladly. Having no money, I tried every shortcut in the book while rebuilding my Alfa engine and gearbox. I got to the point where I could change out a head gasket in under two hours.

I drove my car to Reed College, in Portland, OR, for my sophomore year, and learned that straight 50-weight racing oil doesn't do well in 25-degree weather. I fabricated a ski rack for the car, drove it to the nearby Mt. Hood Meadows ski area at least three times a week and discovered that stock, narrow-profile Pirelli Cinturatos were damned good in the snow.

Because I was driving back and forth to San Francisco several times a year (my best time was just a hair over nine hours for the 650-mile trip), I changed out the rear-end gear ratio from the buzzy 5.12 stock ratio to the more relaxed 4.56 that came standard on the Veloce model.

The car that was sold on eBay looks like a decent one. Unfortunately, the seller didn't provide any pictures of the undercarriage and said nothing about corrosion. By now, unrestored Spiders often have rust in the footwells, in the rockers and, most dangerously, around the front attachment points of the traction arms.

This car is missing its bumperettes in the front, and there is no picture of the rear. The camshaft cover is incorrect, coming from a later car that had some emissions equipment on it. The upgrade to a Weber 36 DCD is a good one; the Solex had a vacuum-operated secondary, while the Weber opens both barrels at once. However, the stock air filter can be made to work with the DCD and allows for a minor cold-air ram effect. In this case, a cheesy Pep Boys filter has been installed instead.

The interior is tidy, with all the correct switches and gauges in place.

However, as with any eBay Motors listing where the seller is vague and the photos are non-specific, you're really buying a pig in a poke (or, in this case, pasta in a basket). The car could be full of Bondo, with bad panel gaps, horrible compression, trashed synchros and a derelict suspension.

But if this car is as solid as the seller claims it to be, then this price was quite fair. The new owner can spend $5,000 or so attending to various things that need attention and still not find himself underwater.

From the October 2003 issue of SCM. ◆

1965 Giulia TZ

Some dubious Zagato-bodied Alfas are available today; the extra money paid for this particular TZ may prove to be cheap insurance

by Pat Braden

Chassis number: AR10511 750085
Engine number: AR00502A 18638

The Giulia Tubolare Zagato, or TZ, emerged victorious from its racing debut at Monza in November 1963, and from then on proved a competent competitor. Of the 112 TZs made, approximately two thirds survive.

Chassis number 085 was completed on March 9, 1965, but was not officially sold to Autodelta until December 31 of that year. The car was probably raced by French ace Jean Rolland in the interim, substantiated by the second owner's testimony and small details on the car that are peculiar to TZs raced in France.

In April 1966 the car was sold to Tuscan racing driver Aldo Bardelli. Earlier that month, during the Colline Pistoiesi event in another TZ, his car had caught fire. Bardelli was invited by *Ing.* Chiti to Autodelta's new Milan works to inspect two potential replacements. Bardelli says he chose this car, recently returned from the Tour de Corse, because he knew Autodelta had installed all the latest tweaks for Rolland.

Arguably the most successful of all TZ-owning privateers, Bardelli went on to win countless races in 085 over the next few years. He points out that not once, in all his races with this car, did he crash it.

Bardelli recalls: "Alfa Romeo asked me to drive under contract, but I declined, preferring an open arrangement where I received 500,000 lire (a considerable sum then) per race and car preparation carried out by Autodelta." In total, he competed in 300-350 events with this and other cars, but he remembers the European Championship hill climb at Ollon-Villars in Switzerland in particular: "I was with this TZ and the race was run in two heats. Having won the first, I returned to my car in the Parc Ferme to find all four tires slashed. It was a public holiday but Ferrari kindly lent me a spare set which Scarfiotti helped me change, and I won the second heat and my class overall."

In 1971, 085 was sold to Florentine driver Armando Ciuffi and was entered in a handful of events before finally being retired. It has been in the present ownership since acquisition from Ciuffi in 1989. This car has the twin-plug ignition system as fitted to the later TZ2s and incorporates a host of other Autodelta features: flared wheel arches for wider, team-specification wheels; extra bodywork, air scoops and retaining straps; larger valves; "duck-bill" exhaust system and a special sump stamped Coppa Speciale. The deep red paint has a charming patina of age, while the original-specification black vinyl/cloth interior retains the correct steering wheel, instruments and switches, the latter including a fake brake light switch. Lead seals on the steering column and scrutineers' stickers on the original Plexiglass side windows bear witness to a lengthy and illustrious competition career.

The vendor states that this car has never been restored, but was thoroughly checked over and received an engine rebuild. A recent test drive revealed that the car starts readily and idles well, the suspension is firm, the brakes good and the transmission excellent, all gears engaging smoothly. In short, the car is a delight to drive and surprisingly rapid.

TZ 085 features both works and privateer history, is offered in full period race specification and comes with original Italian logbook, ASI homologation and comprehensive history file.

The SCM *analysis: This car sold at the August 5, 2000 Brooks auction at the Nürburgring, Germany for $246,985, including buyer's premium. This is significantly over the SCM Price Guide's high figure of $200,000 and is due, no doubt, to the car's fully documented provenance. Few well-documented or well-equipped TZs can bring as much as 085, but it's clear that buyers continue to be willing to pay a significant premium for a "no-questions" car. Some dubious Zagato-bodied Alfas are available today, and the extra money paid for this particular TZ may prove to be cheap insurance.*

Alfa's TZ was a challenging car to sort out, its independent rear suspension being the most critical element in obtaining decent handling. Hopefully, a few chisel marks remain to indicate optimum alignment settings for the rear suspension. Otherwise, the new owner is likely to discover he owns a mount that can only be tamed over a number of races.

Once sorted out, however, the TZ is a very competitive and comfortable race car. The "Sebring" exhaust is deafening both outside and inside the car, but the protection of a helmet and the excitement of a race are enough to make a high-speed experience thoroughly enjoyable. The easy availability of Alfa parts also helps make this car a practical and regular weekend competitor.

The price paid for this TZ proves once again that a car can be restored many times, but is only original once, and it is in that state, if useable, that the car retains its highest value.

(Photo, historical and descriptive information courtesy of the auction company.)

From the February 2001 issue of SCM. ◆

1965 Giulia Sprint Speciale

When considering an SS, the first concern must be fit—not of the body panels, but of the driver

by Donald Osborne

Chassis number: 381350

The Bertone-penned Sprint Speciale version of the Giulietta first appeared in the Alfa Romeo catalogue in 1957. With super-streamlined bodywork, it was reckoned to be absolutely sensational looking, bearing a marked resemblance to some of the legendary Italian marque's earlier competition designs, particularly the Disco Volante sports-racer and the still futuristic *Berlina Aerodinamica Tecnica* show car.

The Giulietta's successor, the Giulia, appeared in 1962. It featured a larger 1570-cc engine and five-speed gearbox, and was fitted with front disc brakes. A Sprint Speciale version of the Giulia again became the road going Alfa model to have, the extra engine capacity, coupled with the slippery aerodynamic shape, providing effortless high-speed cruising.

A letter on file from the secretary of the Alfa Romeo Owners Club confirms that Giulia SS chassis number 381350 pictured here was manufactured in Italy in 1965. The vendor tells us that the left-hand-drive coupe was restored to a very high standard, some four years ago by XK Engineering. The aerodynamically efficient bodywork has been finished in silver and the interior trimmed in black. With legendary Alfa 1.6-liter, twin-cam four-cylinder engine and well-spaced five-speed manual gearbox, this is one of the prettiest Grand Tourers from the 1960s.

The SCM *analysis: This car sold for $21,999, including buyer's premium, at H&H's Buxton auction, October 7-8, 2003. The price, at the mid-range of the* SCM *Price Guide, represents good value for this limited-production, special-bodied Alfa.*

The Alfa Sprint Speciales are as close as you can get to a "show car for the street." Originally conceived as a competition variant of the Giulietta, Bertone's steel body made the car heavy and thus uncompetitive, compared with the alloy Zagato-bodied Alfa race cars. Nevertheless, it certainly made for a stunning style statement for the road.

Blessed with the competent mechanicals of first the 1300-cc Giulietta and then the uprated 1.6-liter and five-speed of the Giulia, Sprint Speciales are cars that are as enjoyable to drive as they are to look at. The aerodynamic Bertone body allowed the SS to have a higher top speed than the standard-bodied cars, an assured highway cruiser that topped out at 120 mph.

Mechanically, there's little difference between a stock Giulia Veloce and an SS, as both have dual Weber carbs, tubular headers, a two-piece oil sump for enhanced cooling and other Alfa go-fast parts of the era.

Giulia engines and gearboxes are reliable and long-lived, provided they have been serviced by knowledgeable hands, with accurate and timely valve-adjustments being of utmost importance. This makes service records and ownership history a definite plus, as these cars suffered through a time when they were inexpensive enough to be considered just used cars.

When considering an SS, the first concern must be fit—not of the body panels, but of the driver. These cars have fairly flat floors and low seats, which combined with the traditional Italian "legs up, arms out" driving position, can make these cars uncomfortable for six-footers or people with long legs.

As with all low-production cars, body condition is an area of concern. Sprint Speciales are expensive to restore properly, as they were hand-finished cars with body panels that do not easily swap from one car to another. Shut lines are particularly important, especially the door-to-fender contour on the sharply rounded sides. These should look quite even, which is difficult to achieve in a car that does not carry its original bodywork.

Special attention must also be paid to ensure that the unobtainable trim pieces such as bumpers, grille bars and window surrounds are present and in good or restorable condition. Badges and wheel covers, however, have been reproduced and are readily available.

A good Sprint Speciale should feel quite solid, with few rattles or clunks. In spite of the reputation for poor build quality that Italian cars of this era have, limited-production models like these were carefully assembled. After all, when new these cars were more expensive than the six-cylinder Alfa 2600, and at nearly $6,000 in 1965, we are talking Jaguar E-type money.

Speaking of Jags, the car pictured here has been restored by XK Engineering. Given their first-rate reputation for paint, it may be assumed that the bodywork on this SS was properly done, something to be careful about on a car as prone to rust as an Alfa.

Giulia SS values have not moved much recently, remaining stuck in the $20,000 range since reaching a high of $50,000 during the speculator's market in the late 1980s. There's certainly potential for these cars to appreciate again.

With the stylistic inspirations for the SS, the fabulous Alfa BAT 5, 7, and 9 show cars, trading in the seven-figure range, the Sprint Speciale is a far more practical and inexpensive way to put some of this kind of style in your garage, in a car that offers considerable driving fun as well. Considering this combination of visual flamboyance and driving practicality, this Sprint Speciale, and indeed any properly-restored SS in this price range, should be considered well bought.

(Photo, historical and descriptive information courtesy of the auction company.)

From the April 2004 issue of SCM. ◆

1965 Giulia Sprint GTA

This is arguably one of the most successful dual-purpose sports cars ever produced

by Pat Braden

Chassis number: AR613096
Engine number: AR00532/A19783

The official build record states that this GTA was completed on December 16, 1965. It was the 54th car of the model to be produced and the 14th given over to Alfa's competition partner, Autodelta. Its works racing career ended in 1970, when it was returned to Alfa Romeo and used for testing. In 1988, the car was sold by Alfa Romeo to a new owner in Italy.

With the intent of retaining the Group 4 competition features, the new owner commissioned a major professional restoration to return the car to 1965-67 Autodelta specifications, which would enable it to be used on the road. This work included a complete rebuild of the bodywork, detachment and restoration of the lightweight Speralum 25 panels, anti-corrosion treatment and a repaint to the correct Alfa Red 501 livery. While the bodywork was attended to, the engine was also rebuilt with a balanced crankshaft, flywheel and clutch. New cams and a special head gasket were fitted to bring the compression ratio down to a level suitable for road use. The rear axle was also replaced since it had a short differential more suited to hill-climbing than road use.

In 1968, the front brakes had been changed from Dunlop to the more reliable ATE. These were retained, using GTA 1300 Junior steering connectors, as were the original Dunlop rear brakes. The restored bodywork, with its smaller wheel arches, required a return to the correct 7 x 14-inch Campagnolo wheels all around. In order not to preclude road use, the original roll bar has not been fitted, but the interior has been refurbished in vinyl to the correct pattern. The Autodelta driving seat is fabricated from aluminum over a light steel frame.

The car is not currently road registered, but is offered with a letter from the Alfa Romeo Register confirming its date of manufacture, which should aid this process. In addition, a detailed file contains photographs of the restoration, photographs of the 1967 GTA team in action, the Alfa Romeo build sheet and FIA specification details for the GTA, together with a copy of an original GTA parts list.

The completed car will require running-in prior to active use. It should make an excellent entry for a number of events from saloon car racing and track days to road rallies such as the Tour de France.

The SCM *analysis: This car sold for $58,750, including buyer's premium, at the Christie's Pebble Beach auction on August 20, 2000.*

True dual-purpose cars are rare, as performance is typically sacrificed for drivability, or vice-versa. Alfa Romeo's GTA is arguably one of the most successful dual-purpose sports cars ever produced, keeping company with the Ferrari TdF and SWB.

To spark interest in its Bertone-bodied GT Sprint, Alfa introduced a lightweight version in 1965, the GTA, which was identical to the production car at casual glance. Exterior differences were limited to a mesh grille, a row of rivets in the rain gutters, a fabricated loop that functioned as the door handle, lightweight Campagnolo wheels and a unique trunk badge. Inside, lightweight seats and a lack of sound-deadening material were almost the only sacrifice to performance. The result was a Q-ship that weighed 1,642 lbs. compared to 1,984 lbs. for the production Sprint. Power increased from the stock 106 hp (at 6,000 rpm) to 115 hp, thanks in part to twin-plug ignition, a compression ratio of 9.7:1 (compared to the stock 9:1) and higher-performance camshafts. By virtue of its rear seat, the GTA qualified to run as a sedan in the U.S. and it contested many memorable races against Pete Brock's potent Datsun 510s. The GTA could truly bring home trophies as well as loaves of bread. Especially in this price range, it's hard to imagine a more perfect dual-purpose machine.

Subsequent models improved the GTA's competitiveness but ended its dual-purpose nature. The fire-breathing 2-liter GT-Am was a true Trans-Am car notable for its large fender flares, while the GTA-SA used an oil-driven turbocharger to wring 220 hp from the GTA's 1570-cc powerplant.

The decision to return this car to its original configuration is laudable, as well as a good business decision. The sales price, at the high end of SCM*'s guide, reflects an Autodelta association, recent restoration and documented racing history. However, the auctioneer's text glosses over the fact that this GTA has endured a very hard life, having served 18 years as a test mule for the factory. Its serial number is missing from Tony Adriaensens' definitive work,* Alleggerita, *and the auctioneer's references to documentation seem to refer to the model type rather than this particular car. We assume that papers accompanying the car must have established this GTA's provenance to both Christie's (one of the advantages to purchasing a car from an auction company with a first-rate, researched catalog) and the buyer's satisfaction.*

Even with a strenuous racing history taken into consideration, there simply isn't a more versatile automobile for the money.

(Photo, historical and descriptive information courtesy of the auction company.)

From the July 2001 issue of SCM. ◆

1965 Giulia Spider Veloce

You can either regard this car as a starter kit for a 100-point concours winner or an untouched piece of automotive history

by Pat Braden

Chassis number: AR390615
Engine number: 21-02355

Introduced in 1963, Alfa Romeo's Giulia was a much-appreciated improvement on the already superb Giulietta, which itself had been upgraded in 1959 to the 101 series. Comprising mostly detail improvements, the Giulia's major change was the increase in the engine size to 1570 cc (nominally 1600 cc), accomplished by increases of 5 mm in bore and 13 mm in stroke. The 21.7% increase in displacement, and particularly the longer stroke, gave the Giulia solid and relaxed performance that its Giulietta predecessor had lacked. In 1964, the high-performance Giulia Veloce was introduced to the U.S. market. With dual twin-choke Weber carburetors, hotter camshafts and distributors with only mechanical advance, the Veloces delivered 129 hp at 6,500 rpm with great reliability and driveability.

The Giulia's solid rear axle suspension gave a high level of handling and responsiveness, totally free of the peculiar, even evil, handling characteristics that plagued independent rear suspension cars of the period. The precisely controlled suspension responded instantly to drivers' inputs and did exactly what its driver expected. The Veloce was one of the period's most rewarding sports cars and a natural for SCCA road racing competition.

Many Giulia Spider Veloces found their way directly from the showroom floor to the race track. In those days it was common, indeed, expected, for production class cars to be raced as they came from the showroom with little more in the way of preparation than removing some accoutrements like the spare tire and tool kit.

This is one such production racer. It was the 1966 E-Production winner in the SCCA's Northwest Region, driven by Wayne Whittington, and has sat for 15 years before being discovered and lovingly recommissioned to completely original condition. Even most of the car's paint is original, and has the patina that only a good life and cosseted mellowing can confer.

This Giulia Spider Veloce is replete with a full complement of factory details, including the correct Spider Veloce insignia, Pininfarina-badged radio blank plate, original steering wheel and all its exterior chrome trim. Even more important, it is fitted with a number of period performance parts, including Autodelta-badged gauges, cold air intake, competition seat belts, camshafts and Koni shock absorbers. Included with the car are its original owner's manual and fully-stocked tool roll. The top was new in June of this year.

This Spider Veloce has never been restored. Instead, it has been meticulously prepared to retain as much of its originality as possible. Few correct Giulia Spider Veloces survive. Fewer survive in this car's excellent condition. It won third place in the "Retired Race Car" class at the Forest Grove, OR, Concours d'Elegance in July, 2000.

The SCM analysis: Stripping away the fluff of the auction description, this is a retired race car that has had, according to the catalog, all its stock parts re-installed after an engine rebuild. Well-preserved, unrestored cars are the new darlings of the auctions and this car's desirability is directly related to its condition, provenance and rare period hardware from Alfa and Autodelta. You can either regard it as a starter kit for a 100-point concours winner or an untouched piece of automotive history. The healthy sale price of $23,100 (including buyer's premium) at RM's Monterey auction on August 18, 2001, suggests that it crossed the block as a historic object.

In the Giulietta and Giulia era, Don Black, parts manager for Alfa's distributor in the U.S., actively promoted amateur racing. He offered cash prizes to winning Alfa teams, and cooperated with Chiti and Autodelta to bring factory race cars and parts to the U.S. He even created a line of high-performance items (with part numbers ending in ZZ) that were exclusive to the distributorship. Many of the ZZ parts were never intended for anything but out-and-out competition on the track. Hopefully, the new owner will be able to find a copy of Black's Competition Advisory Service, a thick manual that gives ZZ parts specifications and detailed technical information about preparing Alfas for racing.

However, as this car has been seen regularly on the street and in vintage events in the Pacific Northwest, it is reasonable to assume that few, if any, of the ZZ parts remain. Instead, they seem to have been replaced by a bewildering array of faux-Speed Racer decals and badges, perhaps visual evidence of the seller's unfulfilled race track fantasies. Fortunately, these are easily removed.

The Giulia-series cars are the pinnacle of post-war Alfadom, unfettered by the federal safety and emissions regulations that eventually degraded the marque from true dual-purpose sporters to quasi-luxury wannabes. There are more dramatic Giulias: The basic drivetrain also powers the TI Super sedan, the GTA and the Zagato-bodied TZ and TZ2 competition cars. None of these models, however, are more satisfying overall than the Giulia Spider Veloce, which retained the delicious bodywork of the Giulietta Spiders but eliminated the poor driveability of the Giulietta Veloces. This particular car, because of its provenance and unrestored status, deserves to be at the top of the SCM Price Guide, and should prove a wise and satisfying investment.

(Photo, historical and descriptive information courtesy of the auction company.)

From the November 2001 issue of SCM.◆

1965 Giulia GTC

When you're speaking of an Alfa, the terms "usable" and "collectible" are not mutually exclusive

by Pat Braden

Chassis number: N/A

With a total production run of 1,000 units between 1965, when it was launched at the Geneva Salon, and 1966, the Giulia GTC Alfa was an exclusive 2+2 convertible derivative of the Bertone Giulia Sprint GT coupe.

Visiting the new Arese plant when the Giulia GTC was introduced, the British magazine *Autocar* commented that "despite the high rates of manufacture, all Alfas are still largely hand-built, and every engine is stripped for examination when it has been run at the factory before being passed to the assembly lines."

The convertible conversion was carried out by Carrozzeria Touring, with reinforcement applied to the floor pan to ensure that there was no loss of rigidity. Features of this disarmingly pretty convertible include a disappearing top and rear quarter windows winding fully into the body sides to give the appearance of a roadster.

The GTC was one of the last cars to be built by Touring, which was in receivership when this model was launched, and was finally wound up on March 1, 1965, though it continued to fulfill outstanding orders until 1967, when the factory was converted to make soap powder and boot polish.

Powered by a 1570 cc twin-cam, all-alloy, four-cylinder engine, the Giulia GTC had a top speed in fifth gear approaching 112 mph with the top up. Disc brakes were fitted to all four wheels.

This car has had only two owners since new, and has been in its current ownership for the past 31 years. The odometer reading of 125,000 miles is said to be genuine.

In 1997-98 it was the subject of a six-month total body restoration, in which the body shell was stripped to bare metal and all dents and rust were eliminated before the body was refinished in red. It has been fitted with new taillights and lenses, door glass and bumpers, and the rubber gaskets have been replaced. Interior trim is in tan. Additionally, the engine has been completely rebuilt at a cost of almost $5,400. This included a cylinder head rebuild, new crank, pistons and sleeves. Since the completion of the rebuild, the vendor stated that the car has covered approximately 100 miles.

The SCM *analysis: This car sold for $11,500 at Brooks' Quail Lodge Auction in Carmel, CA, on August 19, 2000.*

This price is at the low end of the auctioneer's estimate, reflecting the unfinished condition of the car. The engine rebuild and body work probably emptied the bank for this restoration, leaving some very visible but easily correctable faults to rectify: the center tunnel carpeting behind the front seats is worn bare and the decorative metal flashing across the top of the windshield is badly damaged.

The faults are especially unfortunate because Alfas are relatively inexpensive cars to maintain and restore. For many collectible cars, $5,400 would hardly buy a ring job, let alone a new crankshaft, pistons and liners. Moreover, it is probable that the preceding 124,900 miles on this GTC were covered with its original engine and only regular maintenance. When you're speaking of an Alfa, the terms "usable"

and "collectible" are not mutually exclusive.

The appeal and utility of a four-place Alfa convertible may set owners of Alfa GTV coupes dreaming about "chop-top" conversions. Several Giulia Sprint GT coupes have been converted to GTCs. It is not a simple conversion, requiring careful engineering to provide a good fit and finish for the top, and inventiveness in designing roll-up rear quarter windows. Most importantly, the steel top of the Giulia coupe is a structural member of its unit body. Touring's conversion added cruciform strengthening to the floor pan to offset the loss of the structural top. Aftermarket conversions that have not been similarly reinforced will have unacceptable cowl shake and may eventually sag so much that the doors cannot open.

This GTC is powered by a later 1750 engine. Though the 1750 is considered even more reliable than the Giulia engine, an original engine would have made this collectible car a more attractive investment.

There's a lot to like about a GTC Alfa: a short production run when the car was still mostly hand-built, open-air motoring with room for four, an easily maintained powertrain and a distinctive body. The new owner got a solid driver at a good price.

The danger is that, if it remains just a driver, this GTC will eventually disappear. At this point in its life, the non-original engine and lack of detailing give cause for concern. A little more money invested now will elevate this car to a condition that makes it truly worthy of conservation, and much less liable to being driven into oblivion by a subsequent owner.

GTCs in brilliant condition can bring nearly $20,000, but they are far and few between. Assuming that there was no rust under the carpets, in the rockers or the structural crossmembers added by Touring, at $11,500 the new owner can do a little freshening up and have a nice car at a fair price. And unless you're thinking about cutting the top off of your 164 (wouldn't that be an interesting project), the GTC is the only way you can take the family with you and simultaneously enjoy an open Alfa sports car.

(Photo, historical and descriptive information courtesy of the auction company.)

From the December 2000 issue of SCM. ◆

1965 Giulia TI

Those in the know will tell you the blandly styled "square-rigged" sedans are the most fun to drive

by Donald Osborne

As described by the seller on eBay Motors:
This '65 Alfa Romeo Giulia TI is very original and unmolested. For a 40-year-old car, it is in great condition. It idles, runs and drives well. It also looks very nice.

It's lived its whole life in California and Arizona and it is rust-free. There appears to be no large body damage or repairs. The paint is in the original color, but has been re-sprayed sometime in the past and is getting rather thin in several places. Also, the rear bumper has some pitting and should be re-chromed. It looks fine for a driver, but the paint and chrome could be improved.

It has a 1,600-cc engine, single carburetor, as original. The engine had a rebuild in the last few years and is healthy. The five-speed tranny shifts smoothly with no grinding and stays in gear. The brakes are good and the engine runs cool. Tires are period correct for the car and in good condition with lots of tread left.

The car is reliable enough to use as a daily driver, though the speedo does not work. I have an NOS replacement that goes with the car. Actual mileage is unknown.

The SCM *analysis: This car was sold for $6,500 on eBay Motors on July 18, 2004, when the auction (#2484982020) was ended using the "Buy It Now" option.*

The Giulia TI berlina (TI for Tourismo International, and berlina for four-door sedan) was introduced in 1962, replacing the Giulietta-based, 101 series Giulia as the first model on Alfa Romeo's new 105 series chassis. This platform would provide the basis of the superb line of small Alfas for the following 13 years, most notably the Duetto and the GTV.

While the sleek spiders and elegant coupes of this era are undoubtedly the best known and most desirable to collectors, those in the know will tell you the blandly styled "square-rigged" sedans are the Alfas that are the most fun to drive. Why? Because you get the legendary twin-cam four and slick five-speed gearbox, but in a package that's better balanced than either of the sportier body styles. The additional weight over the rear end of the berlina plants its live axle better during cornering, and neither the coupe nor spider can beat it for pure "tossability" on a winding road.

However, looks are not a strong point of any Alfa sedan of the period, and this one is no exception. Beauty may be in the eye of the beholder, but it's hard to imagine anyone calling the Giulia TI "attractive." The best that can be said here is that the car is brutally functional, and unlike its stablemates, the berlina does provide room for four real adults and their luggage. While it may have looked like a brick on wheels, scientific measurement of the aerodynamics told a different story. Careful attention to the shaping of the fenders, wheel openings, windows, roof, and trunk lid resulted in an impressive drag coefficient of 0.33. This was not only better than the shapelier Alfas of the period, but it wasn't matched by a production sedan until the Audi 5000 of the late 1970s.

The wind-cheating lines of the berlina contributed greatly to the success of the TI's racing variant, the legendary TI Super. Just 501 of these factory hot rods were built between 1963-14, with a 155-hp, dual-carb engine and four-wheel disc brakes. They were potent racing weapons and spawned the most desirable regular production variant of the Giulia sedans, the twin-cam Giulia Super of 1965-72, a cult car if there ever was one.

The car pictured here, however, is the initial and basic single-carb version, with just 104 hp. Its ribbon speedometer and steering wheel horn ring are dowdy compared to round instruments of the later Super. Originally built with its five-speed shifter on the column, our feature car has at least been converted to the later floor shift.

As in every Italian car of this period, the amount of rust in the floor panels, trunk, suspension and rear axle mounting points are the key to its viability. Since these cars will rust anywhere that's not a desert, and there is no economic sense in "restoring" a berlina (unless it is one of the TI Supers, and even then you'd best start with a darn nice car), it is likely that you will find either poorly executed patch panels or just the typical large holes in many cars.

Mechanically, the twin-cam engine is robust, with its only bad habit a tendency toward having weak head gaskets. Pre-1967 cars are equipped with corrosion-prone Dunlop brakes, though many of these have already been converted to the better, later ATE braking system. The gearbox, while slick, can suffer from worn second-gear synchros (you quickly get used to skipping the one-two shift when the transmission is cold) and in more severe situations this can even cause the gear lever to pop out of engagement.

Interior trim is difficult to obtain, with most of the reproduction kits being made for the more popular coupes and spiders. The quality of the original vinyl was quite good, and generally the weakest part of the seats is the stitching and foam padding, which dries out. (Both of these problems are easily rectified.) Alfa sedans suffer from the same dash top cracking as their more sporting siblings, and often from the indignities of extra holes cut into the doors and kick panels for aftermarket stereo speakers.

This car looks to be in good condition, and the seller has specifically addressed the two biggest potential issues in the description, overheating from a blown head gasket and a worn gearbox. I would have liked to see the seller fix the speedometer before unloading the car, especially considering that he already had the part.

Even so, the price paid here seems about right, with the more potent Giulia Super listed in the SCM *Price Guide at $8,000-10,000 and the ultimate TI Super at $15,000-20,000. For about half the cost of a new Honda Civic sedan, this Alfa's new owner gets a similarly practical, vintage four-door and the right to say he drives a sporting Italian automobile from a legendary automaker. Not a bad deal in my book.*

(Photo, historical and descriptive information courtesy of the auction company.)

From the October 2004 issue of SCM. ◆

1966 Giulia GTC

By the time you made this car into a driver, you'd be so far underwater that Hurricane Isabel would seem like a spring shower

by Donald Osborne

Chassis number: AR755050

As described by the seller on eBay Motors: This car is a true rarity, one of only 25 imported into the U.S. in 1966, and one of only 1,000 produced. Bertone designed this classic cabriolet, powered by a 1570-cc, DOHC four-cylinder engine, with maximum power of 105 hp at 6,000 rpm. Top speed is 112 mph.

The GTC is much more highly valued than the fixed-head Giulia Sprint or Junior, and is listed in *Classic & Sportscar 1996-1997 Classic Car Buyers Guide* as valued at £9,000 (or about $16,000) in "basket case" condition. This example is much, much better than a basket case.

The vehicle is nearly complete, with only a small piece of trim missing. The door handles and windshield wipers have been stashed in the trunk. The body and frame of the car are in excellent condition. According to the owner, there is very little, to almost no rust on the frame. The body also has virtually no rust. The traditional tough spots on an Alfa, such as the rocker panels, have no sign of rust. The car is painted entirely in gray primer.

The engine was inspected and found to only have 30,000 original miles. It has not been started since about 1994, and will need a set of carburetor kits in order to get it running. It may even need to be flushed, or at the worst rebuilt. The disc brakes will also need work. The tires are dry-rotted and flat, and it is currently sitting on rollers. The convertible top frame is in serviceable condition, however the cloth top itself will need to be replaced. This car has never been hit, the frame is straight and the body has had very little work done to it.

This car was driven sparingly during the 1980s but has not had contact with a road in a decade. It has been stored in a bone-dry storage garage in the interim, though Hurricane Isabel caused the water to rise in our area (Maryland) and the garage where this classic car has been kept since 1982 was briefly flooded for about an hour.

The SCM *analysis:* This car sold for $12,321.20 on eBay Motors on November 2, 2004.

The GTC had its genesis when Bertone tried to interest Alfa in an open version of the "cast-iron" 2000 Sprint coupe. This was a four-place convertible that was shown in 1960, but Alfa chose not to produce it, instead opting for a convertible version of the higher volume Giulia Sprint. This Bertone-designed coupe was launched in 1963 and quickly established itself as a new benchmark in small performance cars (see page 51). Surprisingly, when it came to actually building the cut-coupe GTC, another Italian design house, Carrozzeria Touring, did both the engineering and construction.

Considerable strengthening was carried out to make up for the loss of the coupe's roof and C pillars. This included extra bracing in the foot wells behind the front wheel arches, a reinforced floor pan, and thicker door frames and sills. In addition, the rear seat backrest was narrowed to accommodate the lowered soft top, which disappeared completely behind the seats. This led to reduced shoulder room in the back seat and a smaller trunk, though Alfa did enlarge the trunk lid. The GTC also acquired roll-down rear quarter windows in the process.

In spite of Touring's best efforts, contemporary testers found that there was a fair amount of scuttle shake in the GTC—not the best thing for a car whose performance reputation was built on its handling and tossability. Nevertheless, the GTC still retained much of the dynamic character of its sibling, and its free-revving DOHC four and superb five-speed gearbox made it a joy to drive. The GTC was marketed for just two years, 1965 and 1966, and discontinued when the Pininfarina-designed Duetto Spider was brought to market in late 1966.

Touring built the GTC to a good standard, but rust is even more of a plague in these cars than in the coupes, due to the vulnerability of the additional structural bracing. Seals between the rear edge of the convertible top and the body can fail, allowing water to find its way into the top well and sills. This can exacerbate issues with corrosion that even coupes have in the double-skinned rocker panels, trunk floor and floor under the pedal box. It is equally important to check the drain holes in the bottoms of the doors.

As on any convertible, interior trim in a GTC can take a beating due to exposure. Most of the interior pieces are available, except for the smaller rear seat and rear side panels, which are unique to the cabriolet. Replacements for the soft top are available from specialists, but are a very expensive item as the market is obviously tiny.

This brings us to the car pictured here. Where to even begin? Let's start with the seller. This is another case of a car being sold "on behalf" of the owner, which is seldom a good thing. That said, there were a number of questions and answers that followed the listing and provided additional information about the car. Of course, the photos are worth all the description in the world, confirming that the car has been idle for more than twenty years.

If that's not bad enough, photos of this GTC from "circa 1982" seem to show the car already in primer, with rather suspect looking sills. Other photos showed the underside of the car, but mainly the suspension (which revealed a great deal of surface rust on the shocks, springs, and brake rotors, as well as corrosion on the alloy differential), but there were no detailed shots of the all-important sills.

The interior shots reveal rusted pedal arms as well as rust on the turn signal switch and mold on the front kick panels. This is important to note, as these panels cover the vital front chassis reinforcements—and if they are damp enough to grow mold, what lies underneath could be truly scary. Add in the confusing claims of a car kept in a "bone dry storage garage" that was also "briefly flooded," and I would be suspicious that this car is one step removed from a pile of iron oxide.

Even if the total effects of water damage aren't irreversible, at the very least this car will need a complete mechanical and electrical rebuild, in addition to a comprehensive structural check and likely rust repairs. The eight-year-old English magazine price guide is also rather optimistic, as the value for one of these cars, in very good condition, is closer to $20k, and the best in the world might only be worth $35k. Certainly $16,000 for a "basket case," which this car is likely only a close inspection away from being, is far too much.

So too is the $12k spent here, an extremely hopeful purchase, as there is little chance this car could become anything more than a driver. Even to bring it up to that level you'd certainly be so far underwater that Hurricane Isabel would seem like a spring shower. Perhaps the eBay ID of the winning bidder, "Idiot7," may tell us all we need to know here. Count this as a great triumph for the seller.

From the March 2005 issue of SCM.◆

1967 Giulia Sprint GT Veloce

Porsche enthusiasts sneered at Alfa's solid rear axle, but it is one of the last of the Alfas that can be maintained with a standard set of hand tools

by Pat Braden

Chassis number: AR 243657

As described by the seller on eBay Motors: This rare Alfa is a complete car. All bits and pieces are intact. No alterations or modifications have been made, inside or out. It has been well kept and always garaged. It is in daily-driving condition, and is rarely driven except in dry weather. The car has an excellent interior with new rugs. Both front seats have been restored, not just recovered. All gauges are functional. Overall, the car is in very nice shape.

A former California car, it is currently in Portland, Oregon. As the car is mechanically tip-top, the next step is paint. Known issues include rust at the right fender bottom (two very small bubbles), five body dings and a fixable crease in the rear bumper. Mechanically, the car has no problems and will require regular maintenance only. This second-owner car is a cherry and way neat. Treat yourself to a fine Italian car with a historic racing lineage.

The SCM *analysis: This car, item 1837631059 on eBay Motors, sold for $7,300. The sale received 32 bids from 15 individuals, and ended on June 27, 2002.*

A classically simple and durable design that can be maintained with easily available and inexpensive parts is an almost irresistible combination. And that describes the 1600-cc Alfa GTV.

There's a lot to like about the GTV. First, it is ultimately simple—it is one of the last of the Alfas that can be maintained with a standard set of hand tools. The alloy dual overhead-cam engine is a classic design, and the dual Weber carburetors make an impressive visual and performance statement. The fully synchronized five-speed gearbox was considered the benchmark of its time. And though Porsche enthusiasts sneered at Alfa's solid rear axle, it nevertheless provided more predictable and forgiving performance than the independent rear suspension of the German car.

In spite of its compact exterior dimensions, the interior of the GTV is surprisingly roomy and its front bucket seats provide excellent lateral support during heavy cornering. There are small rear seats, a feature that allowed the cars to run as sedans in the U.S., where the competition in the Trans-Am between GTVs and Pete Brock's Datsun 510s was fierce.

Virtually every Alfa advertisement mentions the marque's racing history. In the case of the GTV, the link is not overblown, since the hugely successful GTA competition cars are based on this model.

The GTV was introduced in 1966 as a slightly revised version of the Sprint GT. The world had fallen in love with the hatchback styling of the Giulietta and Giulia 1600 Sprints, and initial reaction to the new notchback was lukewarm. Alfa came up with the competition GTA to promote the new body style. There is no doubt that the outstanding success of the GTA ensured the popularity of the GTV.

The selling price of $7,300, slightly below SCM *Price Guide range of $8,500 to $12,000, probably reflects the fact that some repairs are still needed by this car, including a paint job. Thirty-two bids are a lot, but the fact that the bidding competition failed to push the final price into* SCM's *price range is evidence of the essentially penurious nature of most Alfa owners. Bidding started at $100, and it took 13 more bids to break $2,000. A serious bidder entered at $5,250, and kept bidding to $7,200. With a minute left in the auction, the new owner entered his only bid. The action revealed a good e-bidding strategy: Stay out until the last moment so as not to drive up the price needlessly, then just top the high bid. This presumes you know what you're willing to pay and have enough discipline not to "bid with your heart" as the auctioneers love to urge.*

However, you have to wonder some when this GTV is described as "rare"—more than 14,000 were made—and its most appealing feature is that it is "complete." Admittedly, the car is going on 35 years of age, but there are plenty of examples of this model still around.

In any event, for the money, the new owner got a potentially trouble-free, supposedly two-owner car with only 100,000 claimed miles. The blown head gaskets that plagued later 1750 and 2000 Alfa models are almost unknown on the 1600-cc Giulia, and the car's mostly California history has managed to stave off serious rust. The corrosion mentioned on this car is nominal and common. This was an era when rustproofing was in its infancy, but Alfa had not yet begun buying the rust-prone steel from Eastern European countries that led to tin-worm disaster with later models. Even if the new owner is confronted with an unexpected mechanical drama, a good used engine and transmission can be had for about $1,500, keeping the overall investment still within SCM *Price Guide range.*

If there are no mechanical surprises lurking, the rust is as minimal as described, and the car is in decent driving condition, this should be considered a fair deal for seller and buyer both.

From the August 2002 issue of SCM. ◆

1968 and 1970 GT Juniors

A well-sorted, rust-free GT Junior can make any daily commute into a mini-Targa Florio, as you run up and down through the gears

by Keith Martin

"You'll never have more fun than when you're driving a car with a motor that's too small, with a great five-speed gearbox, on a mountain road." That's what Bob Lutz, GM Vice Chairman of Development and long-time friend of SCM, told me on the California Mille some years ago. I had just spent a good 30 minutes harassing his 300-hp, 1955 Chrysler 300C with my 1300-cc 1958 Alfa Romeo Giulietta Spider Veloce.

The Alfa GTV two-door coupe, part of the 1600-cc Giulia lineup that followed the Giulietta, is acknowledged as one of the great GT cars of all time. But less well known is its 1300-cc, five-speed variant, the GT Junior. This car was never officially imported to the U.S. The base model of the line, they came with rubber floormats rather than carpets, and simple stamped hubcaps. They had an ultra-close ratio fifth gear. Even in our land of superhighways, they could hold their own at 80 mph, and return over 30 mpg as well.

While trolling eBay, I came across a pair of GT Juniors that sold.

Here is the seller's description of item # 1875252752:

This 1960 Alfa GT Junior is a very original car. It has not been changed from the original factory specification. The car drives like new and handles well. The paint seems original, in that it is the same throughout the entire body (no respray). Interior is like new and original. The dash has one small crack in it. Window glass is all in good condition with only one scratch on passenger side.

The car was imported from San Remo, Italy, so it has no heater connected, but is in the car. The motor is in good running condition with no oil leaks or burning. All cylinders have good compression and leakdown is minimal.

The car comes with new Yokohama YK420 tires and new performance drilled and grooved disc brakes for all four wheels.

Minimal rust in the right door, I was told it is not bad and can be fixed easily. The paint is in great shape and shines well. Only one small dent on right hand quarter panel and would be easily fixed using the paintless dent removal method.

The SCM analysis: There was only one picture, which was nearly useless, in the listing. The car did have incorrect 1750 hubcaps, and there were some panel fit issues evident. It was light gray with a red interior. There was no VIN listed.

Located in Lancaster, CA, after four bids, it sold on December 31, 2002, for $6,800. The seller, whitebuffaloracing, had a feedback rating of one.

And the second description, of item # 1876788424:

This 1968 Alfa GT Jr. 1300 is a very clean, two owner car with records from 1974. It has a 100% rust free body and no accident

damage. It has always been maintained by Alfa of Tacoma. It comes equipped with its original tool kit and manuals.

The paint is in very nice condition. It has been repainted once in the original color. All of the glass is good including the rubber seals. The interior has been redone.

The mechanicals on this car are very sound including the clutch and transmission (5-speed). The brakes and tires are in good condition and it is equipped with stock wheels and hubcaps. All of the gauges and the electricals are in good working order. The panel fit is excellent.

The floors are rust free along with the trunk floor and jacking points. The chrome is in excellent shape including the grill. This is a very nice original car in good working order.

The SCM analysis: The VIN was listed as AR1227011, and the car was green with a tan interior. The listing included eleven photos, including the engine bay and the spare trunk well, always a rust-prone area.

Located in Seattle, WA, after ten bids, it sold on January 18, 2003, for $5,800. The seller, classyclassics, had a feedback rating of 20.

In my opinion, the second car was a much better buy than the first. The seller had extensive documentation, it had been cared for by Alfa Tacoma, a firm with a first-rate reputation, and they offered many photos for potential bidders.

And yet it sold for $1,000 less than the white Junior from Lancaster.

In any event, a well-sorted, rust-free GT Junior can make any daily commute into a mini-Targa Florio, as you run up and down through the gears just to keep up with traffic. The engines are robust and easily maintained. While not truly built for four adults, Juniors have more rear seat room than the equivalent 911.

And each time you drive a GT 1300 Junior, you get a small taste of Alfa Romeo in its salad days, when its chain-driven overhead cams were definitive, its styling state of the art, and its position as one of the great sports car manufacturers on the planet was secure.

Sadly, those days are all now long past. But by buying the green Junior here, for less than $6,000, you could be experiencing Alfa at its very best.

From the March 2003 issue of SCM. ◆

Affordable Classic: 1962-65 2600

If you wanted to take a cross-country trip, no car would be a better choice than the 2600; you might even be able to enjoy its 124-mph top speed

by Pat Braden

There are collectibles that play to the crowd, leaving us all in awe of their technical and artistic mastery—and the amount of money invested in them. Other collectibles, more affordable, strike purely personal chords: a first car; the car I was married in; or the one I've wanted forever.

Generally Alfa 2600 coupes and Spiders, as reasonably-priced classics, fall into the second category, along with Austin limousines and Lloyds. On the other hand, think of the other all-alloy twin-cam straight sixes, and the value we set on them: Maserati, Aston Martin and Jaguar.

The disparity in value is not due to any styling deficiency on the part of the Alfas. The 2600 coupe has a svelte Bertone body, and the famed Carrozzeria Touring was responsible for the Spider. Both had spacious, comfortable interiors, often in

The 2600 Spider coachwork was by Touring

leather. You get a superb five-speed gearbox, full instrumentation, excellent outward vision, optional power windows and front seats that are the equal of BMW or Mercedes sedans. With the exception of a solid rear axle, the 2600 gives away nothing in the areas of technical sophistication, styling, or even rarity.

The 2600's limited following is due exclusively to the fact that it is an almost-3,000 lb. car, powered by a 2584-cc, 145-hp engine, which gasps through three twin-throat, progressive Solex sidedraft carburetors. As an offsetting virtue to this guaranteed leisurely performance, none of the other marques can match the 2600's maintainability and reliability. If you wanted to take a cross-country trip, no car would be a better choice than the 2600, and you might even be able to enjoy its 124-mph top speed on a long stretch of road. If you're willing to indulge a private pleasure, the 2600's a sure bet, then. It is not rust-prone, nor does it blow head gaskets like its smaller siblings.

Early cars had rear drum brakes; the later four-wheel-disc cars are preferred. The only unobtainable part is the windshield, and the most problematic are the 400-mm Michelin X tires which are proper for the series. Wire wheels are a rare and desirable option, and a factory hardtop is a handsome addition to the Spider, if somewhat superfluous for today's sunny-day drives. Conversion to 40 DCOE Weber carburetors with a modified intake manifold and reground camshafts can improve the performance of the car, but those modifications also dilute its main appeal, which is its rock-solid dependability. ◆

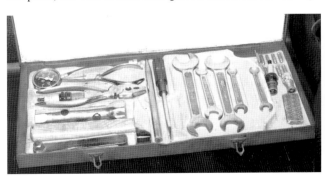

With a full set of tools, your're ready to travel cross country

Admire the interior; just don't crack the windsheild

1965 2600 SZ

By far the cheapest of any large-displacement Zagatos

by Michael Duffey

Chassis number: AR856057

After years of four-cylinder power, Alfa Romeo switched to a six-cylinder engine late in 1962. This new model, known as the 2600, had the familiar dual overhead camshaft configuration which put out 145 hp at 5,900 rpm. Top speed was 120 mph. Models included a four-door Berlina with factory bodywork, a Sprint coupe with bodywork by Bertone, a Spider convertible by Touring and the rarest model, the SZ coupe with bodywork by Zagato, pictured here. Equipped with its original 2.6-liter engine and five-speed transmission, this very original California car had less than 60k original miles, with just one repaint and retaining its very nice original black interior. This car received the "La Dolce Vita" award at Concours Italiano in 1996.

The SCM *analysis: The car described here sold for $27,500 (including 10% commission) at the RM Classic car auction held in Monterey August 27-28, 1999. It is hard to put your finger on exactly what features of the standard Bertone 2600 Sprint make collectors overlook it. The 2600 is often described as heavy or ponderous, and indeed the impression while driving one of these cars is exactly that—if you use the Giulietta as the base line. If put in the perspective of a mid-'60s, six-cylinder coupe and compared to say, a Mercedes-Benz 220SEb, the Alfa suddenly comes off as a much sportier package. Factor in the lighter SZ at 2,500 pounds coupled with a wheelbase that is 80 mm shorter than a standard Bertone 2600, and we have what is clearly the sportiest of all 2600 models. With a production of a little over 100 examples, we also have the rarest of all the 2600s.*

All of these attributes, with the added sizzle of Zagato bodywork, should be the recipe for a six-figure car. This was in fact the case during the grand days of the late '80s when TZ-1s were fetching $500k.

Factor in the lighter SZ at 2,500 pounds coupled with a wheelbase that is 80-mm shorter than a standard Bertone 2600, and we have what is **clearly the sportiest of all 2600 models.** With a production of a little over 100 examples, we also have **the rarest of all the 2600s.**

Lesser Zagatos like this 2600 were "dragged up" by the skyrocketing value of their more desirable brethren.

Just like everything else, the 2600 has fallen to a fraction of its old value and today's collectors have learned a few lessons since those days and won't pay big money for anything simply because it is rare or similar to another, more valuable car.

Still, the 2600 is by far the cheapest of any large-displacement Zagato, and thousands cheaper than its nearest Zagato competitor, the Lancia Flaminia. These factors, and the buying public's comfort level with Alfas (compared to Lancias at least) make the 2600 SZ a car with a certain following and an established value. Not all buyers, particularly ones at auctions, are familiar with the values of not-so-well-known models like this one, and I wonder how much SCM's price guide influenced the final purchase price. Right in the middle of the $25k-$30k range, the price just might show that this was an educated buy, and that both seller and buyer are accepting the reality of today's marketplace. Still, for a rare Zagato, this was a good buy.

(Photo, historical and descriptive information courtesy of the auction company.)

From the January 2001 issue of SCM.◆

Another SZ, handsome in silver.

1966 2600 Sprint

Any project car is a risky buy, but this one raises more red flags than a May Day parade in Beijing

by Donald Osborne

Chassis number: AR825472

As described by the seller on eBay Motors: This rare automobile has been in the body shop for six years. The exterior has been slowly and carefully rebuilt. All the bondo has been removed and replaced with body sections taken mainly from other vintage Alfas.

I purchased the car in San Francisco, where the car still sits. I moved to Hawaii several years ago and have been unable to follow the project through to its completion. It was moved out of the shop last week and needs a new home as soon as possible.

The interior leather is in good condition. The front seats were completely redone recently in good quality, matching black leather. Enrico Tenni at Valtellina Automobili, an Alfa Romeo specialist, re-built the engine. He planned to modify the manifold to fit dual Webers and can still undertake this project if desired. The original manifold and Stromberg carbs are not included. Otherwise, it is mechanically complete.

All the pieces (headlights, door panels, door handles, etc.) are in storage and are included. At present all it requires is a professional coat of paint and some time to put it all back together, and it will be truly beautiful.

The SCM *analysis: This car sold for $5,402 on eBay Motors (#2449764206), December 30, 2003.*

The Bertone-bodied 2600 Sprint was Alfa's top-of-the-line offering in the 1960s, with 6,999 produced between 1962 and 1966. It successfully competed against the Maserati 3500 GT and Jaguar E-type 2+2.

Powered by a twin-cam, 2.6-liter straight six and featuring a full leather interior and power windows in a classic Giugiaro-penned body, the 2600 was designed to be an effortless continent crosser. As the late Pat Braden wrote in the April 2002 issue of SCM, *"A well turned-out 2600 Sprint is an all-day 90-mph cruiser that is easily the equal to nearly any GT car built in the same period." The factory brochure boasted that, "one may change up into top (fifth) gear at 100 mph."*

Reading this auction listing elicited a pair of sharply contrasting reactions. As the former owner of three 2600 Sprints, I recalled the great power, comfort and classic looks of these high-speed tourers, and the many hours of great driving I had in my 2600 Sprints. But having bought one of those three cars sight unseen, I also recalled the horror when I saw the rusty fright pig that was delivered to my house. You can probably guess from the photos which of those two memories is more relevant to this car.

Any project car is a risky buy, but this one raises more red flags than a May Day parade in Beijing. The first is that the auction listing incorrectly called the car a 2600 Sprint "Speciale." No such designation exists, as that moniker was applied only to specially bodied Giulietta and Giulia coupes.

No date is given for the alleged engine rebuild, while the photos show a dirty motor that's missing its manifold and carburetors. If this doesn't make us suspicious, the seller's identification of the original carbs as "Strombergs," when the 2600 used Solexes, should. And "fitting dual Webers"? That would be quite a trick, as all 2600s came with triple dual-throat carburetors.

With no photographic evidence of all the missing trim pieces, great potential exists for an exhausting and wallet-depleting search for them. "Body sections taken mainly from other vintage Alfas" isn't particularly encouraging, and I wonder if those pieces might not be as rusty as this car apparently once was (or still is).

The photos do not clearly show the quality of the current bodywork, missing what should be obligatory undercarriage or trunk floor close-ups. As the car has supposedly been in the body shop for six years, it would be nice to know more about when and how this work was completed. Are there new body trim gaskets to go with the car? Was the glass taken out when the body was refinished?

To put the car pictured here right would take considerably more than "a professional coat of paint and some time." We all fantasize about landing an easy restoration, but this isn't it.

The best of my 2600 Sprints was a one-owner 35,000-mile California "black plate" example, purchased after the car had been painted by the seller and mostly re-assembled. But I still had to locate and then install all the chrome trim using new old stock or re-plated pieces, neither of which come cheap. (Nor are there any original attachment clips available.) I also sorted out the electrical system, rebuilt the steering box, replaced the clutch (a unit shared with the Ferrari 250 and priced accordingly), and completely overhauled the braking system. All of this was done to a car that I was able to drive at some speed and with some confidence before *I bought it!*

Given that the nicest 2600 Sprint in the world can be had for $15,000, it's quite unlikely that this eBay project, even bought at only five grand, could be brought up to that standard for an additional ten.

Perhaps the buyer of this car is a capable mechanic and body man who is also a holder of vast stocks of vintage Alfa parts. If so, he may have gotten a good deal. But for anyone who is not a do-it-yourselfer, and has to write checks to get things done, this was not the best way to get into a 2600 Sprint.

From the March 2004 issue of SCM. ◆

1966 2600 SZ Coupe

That the car was restored in Germany indicates a thorough mechanical overhaul, though it seems un-Teutonic to have "mislaid" the paperwork

by Donald Osborne

Chassis number: 858075/856075 (see below)

The Alfa Romeo 2600 coupe, which made its debut in 1962, marked a return to the high-speed GT cars Alfa was known for prior to the four-cylinder Giulietta series. The six-cylinder, 2,582-cc twin-cam was Alfa's first "over-square" engine. It produced a lusty 145 bhp and, to cope with the power and the 125 mph which resulted, Alfa Romeo specified servo-assisted four-wheel disc brakes as standard. It drove through a five-speed gearbox and the gear change was floor mounted.

The 2600 series was never a big seller (over 11,000 made, 1962-68) because it was expensive, at list prices starting at $4,700 and going up past $6,000. Most cars had saloon bodies but a very few had special bodywork. This car is one of the rare, lightweight, Zagato-bodied coupes which are the most desirable of all 2600 variants. Built with performance-oriented touring in mind, just 105 SZ models were made and they were capable of more than 135 mph/216 kmh.

This rare car is finished in white with deep red leather upholstery and is fitted with optional alloy wheels. In 1992 it underwent cosmetic and mechanical restoration in Germany said to have cost DM 120,000 (approximately $80,000 at the '92 exchange rate). The car's documents have been mislaid, but Bonhams will be happy to assist the buyer in registering this car in the U.K. if required.

The SCM analysis: This car sold for $34,336, including buyer's premium, at Bonhams' Geneva auction, held March 10, 2003.

The price, at the high range of the SCM Price Guide, still represents good value in a rare Zagato-bodied automobile.

This car is listed in the auction catalog as a 1962, which is impossible. Serial production of the 2600 Sprint Zagato (SZ) didn't begin until 1965 (a prototype was shown in 1963). In fact, this same car was listed as a 1966 model at the March 2000 Brooks Geneva auction, where it sold for $33,803. Also, the serial number listed by the auction company, "858075," is outside the range of chassis numbers for this model (856001-856105). Assuming that the number should be "856075," it should be considered a 1966 model.

Over 11,000 2600s of all types were sold over a six-year span, a respectable number for a top-of-the-line car. The most numerous (6,999) were the very attractive Giugiaro-designed Bertone coupes.

Like most Zagato-built cars, the 2600 was built in very low numbers, just 105 leaving the factory. The Alfa 2600 SZ is unusual for a Zagato-bodied car in that its coachwork was steel rather than aluminum (the hood is made of alloy).

Even with the steel body, it was still lighter than the standard Bertone 2600 coupe by almost 300 pounds. This helped to eliminate the major drawback of all the 2600s, which is very heavy low-speed steering (our editor has referred to 2600s as "the best trucks Alfa ever made"). It also featured a slightly shorter wheelbase than the standard coupe, further helping handling.

Potential problem areas with this model mostly revolve around the mechanicals. The triple two-barrel Solex carburetors must be carefully maintained with regular lubrication of the vacuum-operated mechanism that controls the secondary in order not to burn valves. (The Solexes are actually not, strictly speaking, two-barrel carbs, but a primary and a vacuum-controlled secondary on a shared plenum.) A rare and desirable option is triple two-barrel Webers in place of the Solexes.

Be wary of non-factory Weber conversions. Unless the original shared runner Solex manifold is replaced, or sleeved to match the intakes of the Webers, the cars can never be made to run correctly. Another issue is the 165 x 400 tires required, which are expensive and available from few sources.

The unique bodywork, trim and glass, the dashboard, center console and four individual bucket seats are particular to the SZ. Further, very little was shared between the big six-cylinder Alfas and the smaller Giuliettas and Giulias; this, combined with the lower production numbers and survival rates, can make sourcing parts both challenging and expensive.

The seemingly poor hood fit seen in the photo of the auctioned car is not a concern—few fit much better. Generally speaking, the fact that the car was restored in Germany would indicate the likelihood of a thorough mechanical overhaul, albeit ten years ago. The Germans usually like to drive, rather than simply show, their cars. However, we must note that it is quite un-Teutonic for the seller to have "mislaid" the paperwork.

You might reasonably assume that the combination of low production and Zagato coachwork would result in high market values, but that is not the case here. The SZ has no competition history, which is important to collectors. Further, not all agree on the attractiveness of its lines. In a certain sense, it might be considered a precursor to the Zagato-built ES-30 of 1989-91, known as "il Mostro," (the Monster)—fast, not many built and cheap.

This Alfa is a stylish, rare and fashionable highway cruiser, and a great choice for the many thousand-mile touring events held every year. I've owned three standard 2600 coupes and found them to be a delight on the freeway. While this SZ is unlikely to appreciate significantly in the future, for someone looking to own a low-production Zagato from a famous marque, it represents a very good buy.

(Photo, historical and descriptive information courtesy of the auction company.)

From the May 2003 issue of SCM.◆

1966 2600 Sprint Coupe

When you consider some of the cars that have been wrecked, burned or even buried, and then brought back to respectability, the challenge of the car pictured here is relatively mild

by Pat Braden

Chassis number: ARS25528

This 1966 Alfa Romeo 2600 Sprint coupe was formerly owned by Pat Braden, author of *Alfa Romeo Owner's Bible*. It has covered approximately 36,000 miles. A complete car, it needs a straightforward, but total, restoration. It "ran when parked," but that was years ago. The gauges are functioning (or at least they light up and the appropriate needles move when you turn the key), the fuel pump works, the car cranks well from the key—she really "wants to go." And she probably would, if the spark plug wires hadn't completely deteriorated from age.

The car is 95% complete, with all the difficult-to-get parts in place. Most of the rusty problem areas are readily apparent, as the car has been in this paint and in the California sun for some 17 years now. It is surprisingly straight. Due to floor and spare tire well rust, I recommend complete pan replacement and trunk floor replacement, not patching. The tire jack went through the passenger floor at one time due to improper jacking. There is bubbling under the paint.

Alfa 2600s have a classic 2.6-liter, DOHC, alloy straight six-cylinder engine with a five-speed manual transmission. The engine alone is valued at $2,000 to $2,500. Other features include triple Solex PHH carbs and disc brakes all around. The Giugiaro design, executed by Bertone, is timeless and echoed in cars like the Iso Rivolta and Gordon-Keeble.

This is the very car that at one time inspired the statement "If you simply must have a classic six-cylinder Alfa, this is probably the model to buy. Although the 2600 is the most bulletproof Alfa of all time, according to an Alfa engineer who knows such things, they never had the charm of smaller Alfas and were not successful in the U.S."

Please be aware that the photo makes the paint look better than it really is.

The SCM analysis: This car sold for $1,900 on eBay Motors, February 7, 2002. There was no buyer's premium, and the initial minimum bid was $1,500.

It was in regular use when I purchased it for $1,500 from an Alfa enthusiast in Ohio in 1985. The Sprint suffered a broken windshield as it was being transported to California. A fellow Alfista called to tell me that the transport company had been searching high and low in attempts to locate a new windshield for the car. I called the company and, without identifying myself, asked if they needed a windshield for a 2600. "Yeah," came the hopeful response, "do you know where we can find one?" I assured them I could, and found a used windshield locally, but it too was broken in transit. I then located what was probably the last new 2600 windshield in the world, at AFRA in Italy. Fortunately, the transportation company picked up all costs. Clearly, for even a semi-exotic, the windshield is often the most problematic part to replace.

As soon as I got the car, I had the windshield installed and gave it

The parts car had a wild, multi-colored paint job; **I presumed it had belonged at one time to a wealthy hippie.** The new owner followed up on the hunch and found that **it had been registered to a "J. Lennon at Capitol Records."**

a new red paint job. For several years I tinkered with the car, starting it regularly to keep things lubricated. I also bought a $750 "parts car" against the day I'd be able to afford a complete restoration. The parts car was complete, but it wasn't running and had a badly dented rear fender. It also had a wild, multi-colored paint job with "lace" patterns laid over green, red and yellow geometric shapes. Because I found this car in the San Francisco area, I presumed it had belonged at one time to a wealthy hippie.

In 1998, when I finally realized that I'd never get around to restoring the red car, I traded the pair of 2600s (even up) to a friend for a nice Alfetta Sport Sedan with an automatic transmission. The new owner followed up on the hunch that the parts car belonged to a wealthy hippie, and found that it had been registered to a "J. Lennon at Capitol Records." The parts car with the hippie paint job was ex-John Lennon. The value of the two 2600s suddenly reversed.

After about a year of ownership, my friend ran out of garage space, so I agreed to store the cars for him until he found a buyer. With the two 2600s sitting in my driveway, I repeatedly confronted the temptation to own them once more. I finally decided that they represented a phase of my Alfa experience that I should not revisit. My friend's advertisement for the pair focused on the "ex-John Lennon 2600" and attracted an Alfa enthusiast in Wisconsin, who bought them. Since the deal did not involve me, I never

The cost of renewing this car will far exceed its market value for the foreseeable future: Only enthusiasts need apply.

asked the purchase price. The Wisconsin owner was intent on restoring the Lennon car, so there was now a real danger of my red 2600 becoming the "parts car." Fortunately, instead of being parted out, it was put up for sale on eBay to raise funds for the restoration of the Lennon car. A noble motive, but $1,900 isn't going to get him very far.

When you consider some of the cars that have been wrecked, burned or even buried, and then brought back to respectability, the challenge of the car pictured here is relatively mild. On the other hand, the objects of most automotive archaeology are inherently valuable and justify the money required for a proper restoration. The cost of renewing this car will far exceed its market value for the foreseeable future: Only enthusiasts need apply.

There's no doubt regarding the attractions of this model. The 2600's elegant Bertone body adds to the lure of Alfa's alloy, twin-cam, inline six. The Giulietta arms-akimbo posture does not apply to this ultimately comfortable tourer: the seating position is high and well-cushioned. Though the transmission on this car has the same gear ratios as the Giulia box, the 2600's 4.7:1 final axle ratio (compared to the 4.5 of the Giulia) makes first gear a real stump-puller. You can easily get underway in second with the added torque and mechanical advantage of the 2600, and third through fifth gears are optimum for anything up to about 110 mph. A well turned-out 2600 Sprint is an all-day 90-mph

cruiser that is easily the equal, in comfort and safety at high speeds, to nearly any GT car built in the same period.

The $1,900 paid here is slightly less than the value of this 2600's component parts. Moreover, it represents a very modest appreciation over the $1,500 I spent for it some 17 years ago. From one perspective, the new owner is getting one of the real bargains in collectible cars. The fantasy of an inexpensive restoration looms large here, especially for those whose enthusiasm exceeds their means. The reality, however, is that anything less than a professional restoration will doom this car either to certain destruction or to still another restoration by some future, better-funded owner. In its current state, this car is a still-unfulfilled promise.

There's a larger issue, however, and that's the survival of an important Alfa model that deserves conservation. My ownership of the car only saved it from destruction. As time passes, should the value of this car increase, the investment of a professional restoration would become more reasonable. But the break-even point between the cost of a restoration and the car's market value is still probably at least a decade away. If you must have a 2600 Sprint, an admirable ambition from my perspective, set aside $15,000 and go buy the best one in the world. You won't be sorry.

From the April 2002 issue of SCM. ◆

Restoring a 2600 Sprint doesn't pay off when you can find a great car for $15,000.

Crossing the Block

1900

#431-1954 ALFA ROMEO 1900 CSS Coupe. S/N AR190001678. Wine/Cognac. Odo: 1,301 kilometers. 1975-cc, twin Webers, 5-sp. Mileage since Swiss resto. Spotless bodywork with good panel fit to long doors. Paint and brightwork excellent. Leather and

carpets like new. Cond: 1. **$128,831.** *The glossiness of the restoration boosted bidding to $12,000 above top estimate. Buyer thought it was worth it! A new current period record price for a 1900. They are comfortable for touring, but offer rather uninspired performance from the cast-iron block engine.* **Coys, Monaco, 5/04.**

#228-1954 ALFA ROMEO 1900 SERIES 2 SUPER SPRINT Coupe. Body by Touring. S/N 1900C01822. Maroon/tan, maroon pinstripe. LHD. Odo: 52,799 km. 1957 2-liter motor, five-speed gearbox fitted. In receipt of $70,000 U.S. resto pre-1998 import to U.K., acquired at 2000 Geneva auction

for $62,121. Cosmetically only very slightly worn paint, brightwork and trim. Cond: 2+. **SOLD AT $54,959.** *$11,290 below estimate wisely accepted for non-period-correct S1 SS. Having never apparently driven it, one cannot help wondering why vendor bought car in first place. Price was in current predictable range for 1900s.* **Bonhams, Monte Carlo, Monaco, 5/03.**

#229-1954 ALFA ROMEO 1900SS AMERICA Coupe. Body by Ghia. S/N 01838. Eng.# AR1308.00888. Red/beige leather. LHD. Bucket seats. Chrome wire

wheels. Ghia's 1954 Paris Show car which was acquired by president of Ford Motor Company. Restored 1995. Cond: 1-. **SOLD AT $31,014.** *A one-off which raised just over its top estimate. Slightly odd looking perhaps, but one-offs sometimes turn out that way.* **Brooks, Geneva, Switzerland, 3/00.**

#162-1954 ALFA ROMEO 1900 SUPER SPRINT Coupe. Body by Touring. S/N 1900C01822. Eng.# 102000110051. Maroon/tan leather. LHD. 5-speed. Bucket seats. Chrome wire wheels. Said to have been in receipt of $70,000 U.S. restoration by Al

Cortes (mechanics) and Mossier (bodywork). Maintained by Chris Robinson in U.K. since 1998. Cond: 1-. **SOLD AT $62,121.** *Upgraded Super Sprint spec model with 1975cc motor and 5-speed transmission in near mint condition fetched more than top estimate.* **Brooks, Geneva, Switzerland, 3/00.**

#19-1954 ALFA ROMEO 1900 SUPER SPRINT Coupe. S/N 1900C01822. Burgundy/tan leather. Odo: 52,881 miles. Excellent paint and interior, fine doors and panels, scratch on windshield, tiny dent on right

front fender. Car didn't sit quite level: weak spring? Cond: 1-. **SOLD AT $79,554.** *Sold*

for $62,121 by Bonhams Europe in March, 2000 and again in May, 2003 for $54,959. Seller did fine providing no further dramatic investment was needed in the interim. But why doesn't anyone simply want to hold, drive and enjoy this attractive car? **Artcurial, Paris, France, 2/04.**

#170-1955 ALFA ROMEO 1900 SUPER SPRINT Coupe. Body by Zagato. S/N AR1900C 02056. Dark red/gray leather, red piping. Bid-dollar restoration in '90 by Epifani restorations, used very little since. Tasteful and mildly exciting body style.

Striking interior. Only strikes coming from missing air cleaner and some bubbling paint under brake reservoir from spilled brake fluid. Cond: 1. **SOLD AT $217,000.** *1900 Zagatos have been making a comeback during the past twelve months. While this car (bought by a European SCM subscriber) was over the top in price, it was merely ahead of the market, not a crazy stupid amount.* **Bonhams & Brooks, West Palm Beach, FL, 1/01.**

#373-1955 ALFA ROMEO 1900C Coupe. Body by Ghia. S/N AR1900C02186. Dark gray, black/cream leather. LHD. 4-cylinder DOHC engine with 5-speed transmission. Sold new to the Spanish royal family and imported to the U.S. in 1990 from Italy. California registration. Chipped, flaking paint

and chrome; worn carpeting. Cond: 3. **NOT SOLD AT $55,000.** *A tiring restoration on a tiring body style. This is a restrained example of the gaping-grille theme Ghia explored in the '50s. There are much prettier 1900s, and any rarity of this design can be attributed to a lack of desirability. Plenty of money.* **Brooks, Carmel, CA, 8/00.**

#89-1955 ALFA ROMEO 1900 SS Spider. Body by Ghia Aigle. S/N 01959. Red/tan leather. LHD. Odo: 38,845 km. Bench seats. Chrome wires. 1955 Geneva Salon-displayed and spent all but last year in Switzerland, where it was exhibited in

Muriaux Museum. Last restored during 1980s with paint and trim still sharp. Cond: 2+. **SOLD AT $76,218.** *Bodied in Switzerland and likely to be like no other Alfa 1900 SS in your neighborhood, it made slightly more than auctioneers' forecast. Not the most handsome of cars, but at least with the SS engine has enough power to get out of its own way.* **Coys/Barrett-Jackson, Monte Carlo, Monaco, 5/00.**

#455-1955 ALFA ROMEO 1900C SPRINT SERIES 2 Coupe. Body by Ghia. S/N AR1900C02186. Gray/black, white leather. LHD. Odo: 89,670 km. Older paint finish deteriorated, many cracks and chips. Right side door hard to close. Chrome pitted. Leather seats still presentable, carpets are

worn though in spots. Tired overall appearance. Rare Ghia coachwork. Cond: 4+. **NOT SOLD AT $34,500.** *Reported to be unrestored, known ownership history and actual miles. Won Best Unrestored Car award at Concorso Italiano in 1999. Bid was in the reasonable range for condition and provenance. Sold Christie's 8/2002, $35,320. NS Brooks 8/2000, $55,000.* **Bonhams & Butterfields, Brookline, MA, 5/03.**

#23-1956 ALFA ROMEO 1900 SUPER SPRINT Race Coupe. Body by Touring. S/N N/A. Red/black. LHD. Odo: 69,492 km. Paint very good. Full cage, bucket seats, Luke full harnesses within. On/off internal/external battery cut-out. Engine freshly rebuilt. Borranis with Cinturatos and Dunlop-shod mag wheels included. Cond: 2. **SOLD AT $41,213.** *Mille Miglia eligible, clearly fully sorted*

for more track work and correctly valued by all concerned. These cars are surprisingly fast when properly done, but most are just worn-out coupes with shiny paint jobs. **H&H, Derbyshire, UK, 12/02.**

GIULIETTA

#163-1955 ALFA ROMEO GIULIETTA SPRINT Coupe. Body by Bertone. S/N AR 149300777. Red/gray. Odo: 25,816 km. Cosmetically restored outside and inside not that long ago, and still generally acceptable.

Engine was said to have been "excellent" and transmission "good." Cond: 2+. **SOLD AT $11,956.** *Still very shiny, offered without reserve and instantly retailable, it made top estimate. Sprints are more popular in Europe than the U.S., as vintage events here often involve long, hard miles, which a GT car is much more suited for.* **Bonhams & Brooks, Geneva, Switzerland, 5/01.**

#26-1957 ALFA ROMEO GIULIETTA VELOCE Spider. S/N 149502103. Eng. #1315-30751. White/black vinyl. Odo: 81,145 miles. 1290-cc, dual Webers, 4-sp. Excellent paint, great brightwork. Correct chokeless Weber DC03s and tunnel-case gearbox. Very good gaskets and glass. A full and excellent restoration on a car where corners are often

cut. Underhood tidy, clean but not fresh, not overdone. Clean and tight-fitting seats, good carpets. Excellent dash. Cond: 2. **SOLD AT $41,800.** *Factory built as a Veloce, not a*

single-carb Normale that was converted. Lots of pre-auction interest here. As usual, there was plenty that the experts picked apart, but in the end the market spoke and loudly. When commissions were added in, sale price succeeded the high estimate. Giulietta Veloces were the true factory hot rods of their era, and are gradually being recognized by the market as having a value above equivalent MGs and Triumphs.* **Gooding & Co., Pebble Beach, CA, 8/04.**

#74-1958 ALFA ROMEO GIULIETTA SPECIALE Spider. S/N AR 1495 03801. White/red vinyl/black. LHD. Odo: 88,510 miles. Floor-shift 4-speed manual. Seen at McCormick auction in March where it sold for $9,240. Borrani steel wheels. Correct early model tranny. Still has mechanical fuel

pump on head. Thick recent paint, overspray on headlight rubbers. Incorrect material and pattern to seats. An inconsistent resto. Cond: 3+. **NOT SOLD AT $10,700.** *It will take an Alfa aficionado to pay much more than the amount offered for the car. While not hugely expensive to restore, very nice Alfas can be found in the $14,000-16,000 range, and this car will take more than $5,000 to become very nice.* **Silver Auctions, Portland, OR, 4/00.**

#319-1958 ALFA ROMEO SPIDER NORMALE. S/N AR149503801. White/red vinyl. Odo: 88,503 miles. Borrani steel wheels. Correct early model tranny. Still has mechanical fuel pump on head. Thick recent paint, overspray on headlight rubbers. Incorrect material and

pattern to seats. Gauges need re-do. Messy engine. An inconsistent restoration. Cond: 3-. **SOLD AT $9,240.** *The most difficult thing will be NOT to restore this car. If it runs and drives well, it is a mildly attractive example of an early Alfa. However, start a major fix-up program, and you'll be into the car (and out of the market) in a heartbeat.* **McCormick, Palm Springs, CA, 2/00.**

#132 -**1958 ALFA ROMEO GIULIETTA Spider.** S/N AR149504616. Odo: 34,032. Light blue/black vinyl/black top. A pretty little car, overall finish less-than-perfect, but appears original and correct. Good

chrome, good panel fits, a decent but not show quality car. Engine detailed nicely and correctly. No rust. Cond: 3. **NOT SOLD AT $14,400.** *This was fair market for the car, and could have been sold without a backwards glance. Why and where would you expect to get more for it? RM, Newport Beach, CA, 11/99.*

#43-**1958 ALFA ROMEO 750 SPRINT VELOCE Coupe.** S/N 149306552. Silver/ blue-gray corduroy and vinyl. LHD. Early "eyebrow" car. Correct factory-built, numbers-matching Veloce with dual Webers.

Restored to a very high standard. Cond: 1-. **SOLD AT $36,300.** *Many Sprints had Veloce features added later; to find a car that is complete with all its original factory performance bits intact is very unusual. A very high price, but justified by this Alfa's superb condition. RM, Monterey, CA, 8/02.*

#315-**1959 ALFA ROMEO GIULIETTA SPRINT ZAGATO Replica Coupe.** S/N AR10126_00082. 4-cyl. Red. 5-speed. DOHC alloy engine. Numerous details are not correct and, considering the considerable expense of

building a car like this, inexplicable. Cond: 3-. **SOLD AT $19,440.** *This car sold for $49,500 at Monterey as a genuine Giulietta SZ but*

has since been identified as one of about 28 replica SZs extant. *Well bought if you never park it next to a real one.* **Barrett-Jackson, Scottsdale, AZ, 1/01.**

#1018-**1959 ALFA ROMEO SPIDER VELOCE 750 GIULIETTA.** Body by Pininfarina. S/N 1495F05317. Red/black vinyl, red piping. LHD. Odo: 74,975 miles. Good panel fit, excellent chrome, some door dings and loose fit on the cloth top but altogether a nice car. California blue plates.

Last year of the short wheelbase 750 series Giulietta. Cond: 3+. **SOLD AT $20,140.** *A tiny bit pricey, but close to worth the money. This was the only Alfa in an auction of over 800 cars, quite a change from a few years ago. The new owner bought a nice driver, and a good investment too. Barrett-Jackson, Scottsdale, AZ, 1/00.*

#11-**1960 ALFA ROMEO GIULIETTA SPRINT SPECIALE Coupe.** Body by Bertone. S/N AR1012000239. Red/tan leather. Clean, straight car with later Giulia 1600-cc engine and five-speed gearbox. Original 1300 engine goes with car. Excellent door fit. Rear

panel painted incorrectly, otherwise no cosmetic problems. Missing stainless sill trim. Cond: 2-. **NOT SOLD AT $25,000.** *Vendor, a subscriber, told SCM it was "going to sell" but it didn't. High bid was generous enough for a car with incorrect components. A few postblock regrets may be in order here. RM, Amelia Island, FL, 3/01.*

#5-**1961 ALFA ROMEO GIULIETTA SZ Coupe.** S/N 1012686. Red. Charitably described by catalog as "restored in South of France." Neatly cut aluminum rectangles riveted to the floor, hidden by rubber mats, with matching pieces on the doorsills. Engine compartment filthier than my no-star hotel room, missing air box. Modern Nardi steering wheel and cheap new paint. Cond: 3-. **NOT SOLD AT $39,000.** *I have rarely seen anything worse than this example. This is definitely a real car—no one could build a fake this bad.*

Would probably make sense at $20k, as you could get a new body from Galbiati and have a decent car for under $50k. **Poulain Le Fur, Monaco, 5/01.**

#156-**1961 ALFA ROMEO GIULIETTA SPRINT Coupe.** Body by Zagato. S/N AR 1012600067. Metallic silver/black. Odo: 11,527 km. Subject of total restoration by Zagato specialist Galbiati in 1994, when engine changed for another of correct type. Still immaculate and appearing to have been

only very slightly used. Cond: 1-. **SOLD AT $59,587.** *Lack of resto bills or paperwork on file would have worried some. However, delightfully minimalistic with patina of nicely settled-down refurb. Even though only 1.3L powered, an SZ like this is good for 125 mph, making it fastest of Giuliettas. Yes, please.* **Bonhams & Brooks, Geneva, Switzerland, 3/01.**

#154-**1961 ALFA ROMEO GIULIETTA SZ Coupe.** Body by Zagato. S/N 0012000571. Eng.# 0012000571. Dark blue, yellow stripe/ black. LHD. Floor-shift, bucket seats. Recent

engine rebuild and bare-metal respray. Cond: 2. **SOLD AT $46,000.** *Potentially very competitive in up to 1300-cc class of Historic Races/Rallies, this lightweight Sprint Zagato duly sold for over top estimate.* **Brooks, Geneva, Switzerland, 3/00.**

GIULIA

#445-**1962 ALFA ROMEO GIULIA 1600 Spider.** Body by Pininfarina.

S/N 10123AR374067. Red/black. Odo: 97,798 miles. Shipped from California in 1989. In receipt of Veloce twin side-draught Webers upgrade. Paint and trim just about okay. Trunk lid fit poor. Driver's side finisher ratty. Cond: 3+. **SOLD AT $13,248.** *Mid-estimate result for below-average car. Certainly the Webers help, but has the rear axle ratio been changed out to Veloce spec as well? Or will this car buzz along doing 4,000 rpm at 60 mph?* **Bonhams & Brooks, London, UK, 4/01.**

#685-1963 ALFA ROMEO GIULIA Spider. S/N 383152. Eng. #AR051454107. Blue/beige. RHD. Odo: 4,972 miles. Veloce-spec engine. Mileage likely to be post-restoration. Panels and fit good. Repaint, rechrome,

and retrim, including top fabric, all excellent. Cond: 1. **SOLD AT $31,223.** *Faultless cosmetics brought considerably more money than could be seen for this car in the retail arena.* **Bonhams, London, UK, 4/04.**

#134-1963 ALFA ROMEO GIULIA Spider. Body by Pininfarina. S/N 101 23 375817. 4-cyl. Tomato red/black leather. LHD. Odo: 29,223 miles. 5-speed manual. Factory steel wheels. Minor paint

nicks that have been touched up. Leather is starting to get stiff. Very good engine room cosmetics, plus motor runs out fine. A few pieces of brightwork could use some attention, but nothing that some Simichrome polish

can't put off. Cond: 3+. **SOLD AT $14,438.** *Bought well, sold even better.* **Mecum, Elkhart Lake, WI, 7/00.**

#273-1963 ALFA ROMEO GIULIA NORMALE Spider. S/N AR 374906. 4-cyl. 1600cc. Red/black vinyl. Black canvas top. LHD. Odo: 47,245 miles. Floor-shift 5-speed manual. Disc wheels. Normale fitted with later 105, dual-Weber eng. Wrinkle

in driver's side front bumper. 3-shoe drums, Euro car with side turn signals on fenders. Early Giulietta gauges (correct for interim car). Seat tops have electrical tape on them. Straight, shiny paint. A driver. Cond: 3. **NOT SOLD AT $15,000.** *There were just too many warning signals popping up with this car for it to bring the $20-$25k a no-excuses, no-stories car can command.* **RM, Meadow Brook, MI, 8/00.**

#410-1964 ALFA ROMEO GIULIA SPRINT Coupe. Blue/blue. RHD. Odo: 14,250 miles. Webasto sunroof fabric torn. Very distressed front fenders. Passenger side

window cracked. Truly awful. Cond: 4+. **SOLD AT $1,316.** *Posibly worth buying for 1570-cc motor, transmission and other parts—but not for car.* **Bonhams & Brooks, London, UK, 2/01.**

#38-1964 ALFA ROMEO GIULIA TZ Coupe. Body by Zagato. S/N 750030. Eng.#

44. Red/black vinyl. LHD. Badly crashed and caught fire in a 1967 Italian hill climb.

Subsequently carefully and fully restored. Registered for vintage racing in Europe. Looked sharp and ready for road or track. One of 101 TZs built. Cond: 2+. **NOT SOLD AT $98,963.** *Crash and fire history may have scared off some bidders. No-stories TZs are now approaching $175,000, but "badly crashed and caught fire" aren't exactly reassuring words for a potential buyer.* **Christie's, Paris, France, 2/02.**

#75-1964 ALFA ROMEO GIULIA SPRINT SPECIALE 1600 Coupe. Body by Bertone. S/N 381350. Silver/black. LHD. Totally restored by XK Engineering (U.K. Jag specialists) in 1999. Repaint, rechrome and retrim still excellent (apart from

one fender scratch). Cond: 1-. **SOLD AT $21,543.** *Correctly valued at $1,500 above guide price. One of the most beautiful production cars ever, hugely expensive to restore due to their many one-off body, glass and chrome bits. In the late '80s, these were $50,000 cars. Today, $20-$30k is all there is.* **H&H Classic Auctions, Buxton, UK, 10/03.**

#59-1964 ALFA ROMEO GIULIA Spider. S/N AR383092. Eng. #AR0011212241. Gray/red. RHD. Odo: 72,988 miles. 1.6-liter, 5-sp. Believed genuine two-owner car. Repainted in 1997 and

still good. No rust apparent. Front chrome scratched, driver's seat squab torn. Cond: 2-. **SOLD AT $25,662.** *Good value at this price, vendor/auctioneers had been looking for $2,000 more. Great looker, super motor, lovely driver—shame about the dull color.* **Christie's, London, UK, 3/04.**

#250-1965 ALFA ROMEO GIULIA TZ Coupe. S/N 047. Eng. #0052. Red/black. Odo: 91,111 kilometers. 1570-cc I4, 5-sp. 150+ mph top speed. 1 of only 101 of these mini GTOs built, this one amazingly never raced. Original chassis, body, engine, and ransmission. Color-changed from white to

tmore traditional red. Repaint still very good. Wheels scruffy. Original interior good. Cond: 2+. **NOT SOLD AT $261,622.** *This should have been more than enough. The extra $35,000 sought seemed excessive for a TZ without the right period competition provenance. Nonetheless, TZs three or four years ago were $175,000 cars at best; those days are gone for no-stories examples.* **Bonhams, Monaco, 5/04.**

#70-1965 ALFA ROMEO GIULIA SPRINT SPECIALE Coupe. S/N AR380419. Eng. #AR0012100970. White/gray fabric. Odo: 38,831 kilometers. 5-sp. Delivered new in France. Likely to be all genuine. Panels good, fresh repaint very glossy. Openings scruffy, sealing rubbers renewed,

door fit poor. Chrome excellent, no corrosion. Interior cord slightly marked, period Blaupunkt push-button radio intact. Cond: 2+. **SOLD AT $29,939.** *Both in terms of exterior design and mechanically, the Sprint Speciale was very innovative for its time. Considering the disappointing door fit, high estimate money paid was a tad strong. These cars come to market infrequently, though.* **Christie's, London, UK, 3/04.**

#5525-1965 ALFA ROMEO SSZ Coupe. S/N AR381238. Red/black. Odo: 15,634 miles. 1570-cc I4, 5-sp. This was the first of four Sprint Speciale Zat protoypes built by

Tom Zat on Giulia SS chassis. Capable of 140 mph. Zat campaigned the cars in SCCA and won three national championships. Only two of the cars remain. Well maintained but not

restored. Documented history. Cond: 2. **SOLD AT $48,400.** *Interesting car that brought a sizeable premium due to its history and rarity. Hope its next stop is at the Historics next year at Laguna Seca. (Personally, I find the SSZ odd, a caricature of the real Sprint Speciale that is a striking car. —ED.)* **Russo and Steele, Monterey, CA, 8/04.**

#5424-1965 ALFA ROMEO SSZ Coupe. S/N AR381238. Red/black. LHD. Odo: 15,615 miles. Rust bubbles on both doors and left rocker panel. Rear emblem missing. Cracks in paint near right headlight. Wiper scratches on windshield. Engine bay dirty and underside greasy with rusted-through floor pan. Passenger seat leather split and driver's

seat dry as well. Gauges and headliner dirty. Driver's window won't roll up and the hood pull is hanging loose under the dash. Cond: 4. **SOLD AT $17,500.** *One of a few botched-up speciales built in the Midwest some years ago. No hope of ever making it back into a real car. A sad ending for a Sprint Speciale, one of the most beautiful cars ever built in serial production.* **Russo and Steele, Scottsdale, AZ, 1/04.**

#4053-1965 ALFA ROMEO SPRINT SPECIALE SSZ PROTOTIPO Coupe. S/N 10121. Red/black vinyl. LHD. Odo: 5,607 miles. Original interior has sun damage to top of back seats, dye worn from carpets. Repainted in 1980, still good with only minor scratches. Unusual deep dish wheels with

Pirelli Cinturato radials. No bumpers, remaining brightwork fair to good. Cond: 4+. **SOLD AT $22,578.** *Car card states this is the first SSZ prototype, and one of three remaining. Looks from here to be a dechromed SS with really cool wheels. (Probably one of the Tom Zat cars that were only legendary in Mr. Zat's mind and dreams.—ED.)* **eBay Kruse, Auburn, IN, 8/02.**

#147-1965 ALFA ROMEO SSZ PROTOTYPE Coupe. S/N AR381238. Blood red/black front and red rear vinyl. Odo: 5,605 km. First of four prototypes (so claimed). Newer vintage steel road wheels.

Sunburnt rear seat back. Nice repaint. Cond: 2-. **NOT SOLD AT $18,100.** *Really a fakey-doo; a car with no past and no future. Looks like an SZ modified by a body shop for visually- and taste-challenged students. Makes the Norwood fake 288 GTO look really, really good.* **Mecum, Road America, 7/01.**

#57-1965 ALFA ROMEO GIULIA SPRINT GTA Competition Coupe. S/N AR613096. Eng.# AR00532/A19783. Red/black. LHD. DOHC alloy engine with dual ignition. Ex-Autodelta, with sliding box location for solid rear axle. Restored in Italy during 1988 to full Autodelta specifications,

with additional modifications to make the car more roadable. Cond: 3+. **SOLD AT $58,750.** *Most GTAs have lived a strenuous life, and a largely-original GTA is rare, especially one from Autodelta. Restoration was directed to originality with concessions for public road use. At high end of the SCM Price Guide, this versatile car was still a good investment.* **Christie's, Pebble Beach, CA, 8/00.**

#157-1965 ALFA ROMEO GIULIA TZ BERLINETTA Coupe. Body by Zagato. S/N 10511AR750090. Eng.# 10511-0100. Red/black. LHD. Odo: 5,562 km. Raced during 1965-68. Last restored 1988 and only occasional Alfa reunion outings since. Some

engine work 1999. Wider, more modern Campagnolo TZ2s fitted, with chipped spare wheel. Set of TZ1s included. Well presented. Cond: 1-. **SOLD AT $199,122.** *TZs are in much demand. This one had plenty of original features and eventually cost its new owner $57,000 over top estimate. TZs have recovered from their $125k days, but may never again see the $750k numbers of the '80s. This was a very good car.* **Brooks, Monte Carlo, Monaco, 5/00.**

#108-1965 ALFA ROMEO GIULIA SPRINT GTA Coupe. S/N AR613096. Red/black. LHD. Apparently Autodelta team raced 1966-1968 at Monza, Jarama, Zeltweg and Oulton Park. Vendor owned since 1988,

since when reasonably faithful restoration to period-correct GTA spec has been carried out. Cond: 2+. **NOT SOLD AT $38,160.** *Not really mint enough to warrant the reserve, so unsold. A really good GTA with period history can probably command more.* **Christie's, London, UK, 3/00.**

#392-1965 ALFA ROMEO GIULIA GTC Spider. Body by Touring. S/N N/A. Red/black cloth. LHD. Original Giulia engine replaced with later 1750 engine. Two owners from new with a total mileage of 125,000. Rebuilt in 1997-98 and shown at the

Lafayette and Hillborough concours. Cond: 3. **SOLD AT $11,500.** *The later engine is a more-powerful, unobtrusive upgrade. In spite of its recent restoration, the car has several faults, including a slightly worn interior and damaged metal flashing across the top of the windshield frame. Low price reflects car's condition.* **Brooks, Carmel, CA, 8/00.**

#527-1965 ALFA ROMEO GIULIA SPRINT GT Race Coupe. Body by Bertone. S/N 753437RHD105.04. Eng. #AR00502. Red, white front fenders/black. RHD. Odo: 85,496 miles. Rot-free South African, modified for racing Denmark 2001, further mods

for FIA long-distance events UK 2002. 1.6 race motor, stripped-out caged interior, latest high-back Sparco, Sabelt harness. Well detailed, glossy paint race marked. Cond: 2+. **NOT SOLD AT $27,540.** *Considering standard of prep and added value of spares package, race-ready Alfa should have sold for $32,000 required. However, you are getting awfully close to scruffy GTA money here, and that's a real car, rather than a tarted-up GTV.* **Bonhams, Susex, UK, 7/03.**

#68-1966 ALFA ROMEO GTA Race Coupe. S/N AR613699. White/black. LHD. Body modified by Conrero. Driven in period by Giunti/ Baghetti. A genuine GTA, but very distressed and hugely expensive to revive. Cond: 3-. **SOLD AT $30,624.** *Near the top*

estimate was forthcoming. Much more than this will be required to put it back on the grid. Yet with perfect GTAs having $70,000 asking prices in the U.S., there may be room to restore and come out okay. **Coys/Barrett-Jackson, Monaco, 5/02.**

#1543-1966 ALFA ROMEO GIULIA GTA Coupe. S/N 10502613535. Red/yellow/blue cloth/black vinyl. Very good paint, with some stone chips. Plexiglas windows; racing-modified interior with Simpson driver seat, 1750 GTV passenger seat, and 1300 Giulia rear seat. Campagnolo racing alloy

wheels. Clean engine, modern dual-circuit racing brakes. No listed period racing history. Carries a German-market ID tag with

a standard GTV prefix and a chassis number that doesn't fit with either the normal coupe or GTA sequence. Cond: 2-. **NOT SOLD AT $92,000.** *Vintage race history in Germany beginning in the 1980s. Bid was under the value of a more fully documented GTA, but the car was well prepared and could not be duplicated for the price bid. Could have been sold at the high bid.* **Bonhams & Butterfields, Carmel, CA, 8/04.**

#175-1966 ALFA ROMEO GIULIA SPRINT GT Coupe. S/N AR62030. Red/black vinyl. LHD. Odo: 53,760 miles. Plenty of paint wounds, especially heavily touched-up front fender tops. Talbot mirrors, aftermarket stereo speakers and antenna (with a broken mast). Musty interior smell. Older tires.

A nice 80-footer. Cond: 4. **NOT SOLD AT $6,800.** *Car looks like it really needs an end user to spend a lot of time and money on it. The basic chassis and body are decent.* **Silver, Fountain Hills, AZ, 1/02.**

2500

#720-1947 ALFA ROMEO 2500 Cabriolet. Body by Pinin Farina. S/N 915417. Ice blue/dark red leather. Red canvas top. RHD. Odo: 28,141 kms. Excellent top and door fit. Paint excellent too, but an oddball color. Interior as new. Ready to tour,

would need some freshening to show competitively. Great dash. Older restoration, paint beginning to check a bit on the nose. Superb dash. Cond: 1-. **SOLD AT $108,000.** *Not the fastest Alfa ever built, but Alfisti say they are ultra-reliable and comfortable for long-distance driving. This handsome example will probably seem cheap in years to come.* **Barrett-Jackson, Scottsdale, AZ, 1/01.**

2000

#636-1959 ALFA ROMEO 2000 Spider. S/N AR1020400407. Red/black. Odo: 60,249 miles. Very nice paint with some minor flaws. Very good chrome, but reworked grille shows light dings. Corrosion in windshield area.

Excellent interior with crisp appearing seats, good carpets. Clean dash, original gauges could use cleaning. Disc wheels. Cond: 3+. **SOLD AT $45,475.** *The seller hit this one straight out of the ballpark and on to the surrounding streets. The new owner obviously thought more of this car than I did. Exactly double the price I would have expected had this car been in #2 condition.* **RM Auctions, Boca Raton, FL, 2/04.**

#339-1959 ALFA ROMEO 2000 Spider. Body by Touring. S/N AR1020400407. Red/black vinyl. LHD. Odo: 60,089 miles. Nice body and paint, but cracking windshield gasket left in place. New interior. Some light staining on the cloisonné emblem on the nose,

seams in the upper package shelf area lifting, pits chromed-over on vent window frames. Parking brake inoperable. Cond: 2-. **SOLD AT $24,600.** *It could hold its own at local shows, but would need more detailing to make the concours circuit. Power-to-weight ratio poor compared to most other Alfas, so show circuit is the way to go with it. A huge price for a cast-iron Alfa.* **Silver, Ft. McDowell, AZ, 1/03.**

#758-1959 ALFA ROMEO 2000 Spider. Body by Touring. S/N AR1020400407. Red/black vinyl. LHD. Odo: 60,110 miles. Very nice restoration, well done through

out. Excellent paint. Pitted chrome has been replated on windshield header. Well detailed underhood. Owner says engine has been rebuilt. Cond: 2. **NOT SOLD AT $28,500.** *Owner told an interested bidder that it was a Pininfarina body and looked like a Ferrari. Substitute "Touring" and "Maserati" and he would be correct. Very nice car; Rawhide wasn't the venue to sell this pretty red roadster.* **Kruse, Scottsdale, AZ, 1/03.**

#29-1960 ALFA ROMEO 2000 Spider. Body by Touring. S/N AR1020401698. Eng. #AR 00204. Red/black. LHD. Odo: 21,376 km. Older restoration with good panel fit, respray is polish-marked.

Engine bay neglected apart from polished air-intake rams for Weber quartet. Comes with factory hardtop. Cond: 2. **SOLD AT $31,189.** *Thanks to competing bidders, near top estimate was paid for apparently rot-free example of a great looker. The Webers (replacing the factory Solexes) are a real plus if they are set up properly. Full market, but not a stupid price.* **Christie's, Apeldoorn, Holland, 8/03.**

#127-1960 ALFA ROMEO 2000 "PRAHO" PROTOTIPO Coupe. Body by Touring. S/N AR10205-00001. Eng.# AR00204-01345. Silver gray/beige and brown leather. LHD. Odo: 833 km. Touring's attempt to style a 2000 coupe. Totally original, excepting 1966-vintage paint, which is holding up well. Chrome fading on front and rear

bumpers, otherwise good. Leather sagging but acceptable. Wacky dashboard popular with viewers. Great interior. Cond: 3+. **SOLD AT $39,770.** *Too many design features to list, but it takes a real connoisseur to appreciate this car, whose slightly American styling (read that as an Edsel wearing glasses) is not what the average Alfa collector is looking for. Belongs in a museum.* **Bonhams, Nurburgring, Germany, 8/02.**

#428 -1961 ALFA ROMEO 2000 Spider. S/N 1020401018. Odo: 18,063. Red/black vinyl/tan top. Inexpensively redone interior.

Bondo cracks behind passenger door and on rear wheel arch. Taillight lenses faded and cracked, but generally a good looking, presentable old car. Cond: 3. **NOT SOLD AT $9,500.** *This one was strange. Spirited bidding just stopped at $9,500, which wasn't enough to persuade its owner to kiss it goodbye. He was probably right, but only by a few thousand dollars. Conversely, a hard sell at any time.* **RM, Newport Beach, CA, 11/99.**

#1269-1962 ALFA ROMEO 2000 Spider. Body by Touring. S/N AR1020402879. Red/red with black piping. LHD. Odo: 51,869 miles. Redone interior, but not correct. Two-tone seats with contrasting piping, dash painted body color instead of black crackle.

Excellent glass. Clean underhood but incorrect, bare brass radiator header. Good chrome, fine paint. Missing correct grille badge. Cond: 2+. **NOT SOLD AT $24,000.** *Very attractive presentation with much money spent. Incorrect detailing spoils the car, though, and raises doubts about the mechanical work. Last seen at 2001 RM Monterey, where it sold for $26,400.* **Russo and Steele, Scottsdale, AZ, 1/02.**

#522-1962 ALFA ROMEO 2000 Spider. Body by Touring. S/N AR102 04 2825. Eng.#AR00202402824. Red/black. LHD. Odo: 97,321 miles. Restored in 1989.

Many minor chips. Pitted chrome. Mechanical refurb in 1997. Cond: 2-. **SOLD AT $5,796.** *Tired looking, but said to work well enough. Cheaply landed. Price will no doubt cause*

much emotional distress to 2000 owners everywhere. **Bonhams & Brooks, Silverstone, UK, 8/01.**

2600

#110-1962 ALFA ROMEO 2600 Spider. Body by Touring. S/N AR1020401835. 8-cyl. Tomato red/black vinyl. LHD. Odo: 18,887 miles. 4-speed manual. Factory steel wheels. Converted in mid-'60s to a then-new Ford 289 Hi-Po. Repaint

sprayed right over door weatherstrips. Recent top. Vintage Blaupunkt radio, Raydyot mirrors, Hurst shifter. USAF surplus web seatbelts. Dual side exhausts. Cond: 3. **SOLD AT $14,175.** *Sold at established level for an unaltered example, despite the fact that it is now actually powerful and dependable. Since the new owner is Alaskan, perhaps being a hybrid is a definite plus, since there aren't too many Italian car shops in Fairbanks.* **Mecum, Elkhart Lake, WI, 7/00.**

#189-1963 ALFA ROMEO 2600 Spider. Body by Touring. S/N AR192083. Red/white vinyl. LHD. Odo: 60,150 miles. Like so many of marque and type, formerly California-owned. Paint and brightwork aging. White vinyl and engine bay untouched. Not run for two years. Cond: 2. **SOLD AT**

$18,354. *Offered without reserve, it made more than expected. If it runs out well, fair enough. But if it needs anything, the equation falls apart. These are not cars that command huge sums even when perfect.* **Christie's, London, UK, 11/00.**

#53-1963 ALFA ROMEO 2600 Spider. Body by Touring. S/N 13018. Red/black vinyl. LHD. Odo: 20,812 km. Mostly original, equipped with three Solex carbs and tool kit. So-so paint and chrome, tired interior. Black paint below the doors not a good sign. Lippman Collection. Cond: 3-. **SOLD AT $19,800.** *The 2600 is an open-air tourer and should not be mistaken for a performance car. They rusted badly, as well, so finding a complete, running one is becoming more difficult. A surprisingly high price for a 2600 in*

this condition. Perhaps values are on the rise. **Blackhawk, Hershey, PA, 10/02.**

#1552-1964 ALFA ROMEO 2600 Spider. S/N AR 191540. Red/tan/brown leather. Odo: 67,740 miles. Good panel fit. Very good paint, with some sanding marks on trunklid and polish swirls. Most chrome good, but thinning on left headlight trim and pitting on windshield pillars. Good interior with some wear on top

of instrument binnacle, incorrect two-tone seat inserts. Weber carbs fitted. Cond: 3+. **NOT SOLD AT $30,000.** *California black plate car. Sometimes troublesome Solex carburetors replaced with Webers, on correct original manifold. Car presents itself very well, and incorrect interior would be an easy fix. 2600 Alfas are fast, comfortable touring cars whose values have been rising. They have not, however, gotten higher than the price bid. This one should have been sold without regret.* **Bonhams & Butterfields, Carmel, CA, 8/04.**

#406-1964 ALFA ROMEO 2600 Spider. Body by Touring. S/N AR192546. Silver/putty leather. Odo: 70,374 km. Painted but not restored. Current owner

purchased from a police officer in Milan, Italy. Needs a little of everything but would be a great car to clean up and drive—no restoration, please. Three Solex carbs. Magnets stick in most places. Cond: 3-. **SOLD AT $8,798.** *An honest and mostly original example, could run forever with a little care and feeding. The dealer purchaser will spend some time on a clean-up and hang it out for sale for $5,000 or*

so more—and it will still be a very good buy. **The Auction, Las Vegas, NV, 4/01.**

#4-1965 ALFA ROMEO 2600 Spider. Body by Touring. S/N AR191882. 6-cyl. Red/gray leather/black. LHD. Odo: 20,412 miles. 5-speed. Reverse not working, hole in exhaust system. Correct dog-dish hubcaps. Old paint has lost its luster. Tired chrome. Straight.

Some rust in passenger rocker. Worn interior matches rest of car. A driver. Cond: 3-. **SOLD AT $10,575.** *While the days of $50,000 2600 spiders are long gone, $10k for a decent driver still seems cheap. However, the reverse could be a $2,500 fix ("let's replace the clutch assembly while we're in here") and suddenly you're very near market.* **Christie's, Los Angeles, CA, 6/00.**

#189-1966 ALFA ROMEO 2600 SZ Coupe. Body by Zagato. S/N 858075. White/red leather. LHD. 9,359 2600-series cars

made between 1962-68, just 105 SZ models were made. Subject of a $196,000 (DM 120,000) German restoration in 1992. Cond: 1. **SOLD AT $33,803.** *Rare Zagato-bodied 2600 lightweight still looked freshly done and cleared lower estimate.* **Brooks, Geneva, Switzerland, 3/00.**

#175-1966 ALFA ROMEO 2600 SZ Coupe. Body by Zagato. S/N 856075. White/red. LHD. Odo: 97,035 km. Optional alloys. Expensive German refurb 1992, still cosmetically sharp, only very minor wear. Documents

missing. (Catalog had S/N, model year incorrect.) Sold by Bonhams Geneva in 2000 for $33,803. Cond: 1-. **SOLD AT $34,090.** *1 of only 105 coachbuilt lightweights. No-reserve rarity nearly made lower estimate. Probably the cheapest way to get into a true Zagato. And they perform well enough, too.* **Bonhams, Geneva, Switzerland, 3/03.**◆

Section III
The Modern Era

In this section, we take a look at the cars from the modern era, beginning with the 105-series GTV and Duettos and reaching all the way to the last Alfa to be sold in the U.S., the 164. We also touch on some Alfa exotica, ranging from the underappreciated four-cam Montreal to the ultimate racing Alfas, the Formula 1 cars.

More than any other section, this is a pot-pourri of the Snake and Cross. From 1968 on, due primarily to ever more stringent smog and safety regulations, the cars we got in the U.S. became less and less interesting. However, unlike other marques like Austin-Healey and MG, Alfa refused to simply give up and go away. The shortcomings of the U.S. models have become a boon to aftermarket shops, as they have developed the parts and expertise necessary to make our short-changed American Alfas perform like the real thing.

Alfa Romeo left the U.S. market over a decade ago, and the newest Milano is now just a used and often very badly maintained car. Yet under the quirky "butt-in-the-air" styling, the rear-drive, transaxle-equipped Milano still has copious amounts of Alfa DNA coursing through its veins. The front-drive 164, our final American Alfa, has been more problematic, as its electricals and mechanicals have not stood the test of time. But the 164 remains a strikingly attractive four-door sedan, the first Alfa that a grown-up wearing an Armani suit could drive and not feel silly.

I'd like to give a quick nod towards the Montreal. I've owned several, and with its short-stroke V8 and slick-shifting ZF five-speed, this model represent Alfa's interpretation of a purebred, high-performance exotic. No, they'll never get any respect in the marketplace, but that simply means you have the chance to own a classic super-car for the price of a modern econobox, which is not a bad deal at all.—*Keith Martin*◆

1967 Duetto Spider

From a period of manufacture that represents the best of times, Roundtail Spiders are among the most desirable everyday Alfas to own

by Keith Martin

eBay Motors, item #2413790064

Last month, we wrote "How to Get Bottom Dollar for Your Alfa," and described a pathetically written eBay auction—item #2410837134—that resulted in the sale of a nasty Duetto for $2,651. As chance would have it, as that issue went to press, we came across another Duetto on eBay. Beautifully presented, the car, even though in a generally not-sought-after color of ivory (crème), brought a top-of-market $15,950.

Below is the description from the eBay listing, our analysis follows.

Alfa Romeo produced the so-called roundtail spider from 1966 to 1969. The Spider was called that due to the sloped shape of the decklid, which differentiated it from later Spiders.

Roundtail Spiders have a most beautiful design, which makes them among the most desirable everyday Alfa Romeos to own. They were from a period of Alfa manufacture that represents the best of times, just prior to major emissions and safety changes, yet benefiting from many of the modern advances of the mid-to-late 1960s.

Powered by a twin-cam four cylinder of 1570-cc, the Duetto offered good performance and an attractive "Spider" body. The body featured bumpers that were set into the front and rear wings as well as a front grille set below the front bumper.

The Duetto came with twin carburetors and four-wheel disc brakes. Production of the Duetto finished in 1967 after only 12 months and only 6,325 were ever produced, making them a rare collector's car.

The example offered here is a very straight and unmolested survivor. It had lived in Southern California most of its life and the last owner enjoyed her for the last 18 years.

The exterior has recently been refinished to its original luster, painted in its original ivory and is free of dents or scratches, showing only minuscule imperfections (i.e., chips). The black interior has also been recently updated. It still retains the correct engine and transmission in their stock configuration.

The form of the entire front end is completed by the still-intact headlight covers.

From the direct front and rear, one can see the integrated design of the bumpers for the car. These bumpers were much more style than substance, serving to protect the car little from actual damage.

A lot of money has been spent to enhance its already stellar performance. It is not a show car, but a very beautiful and powerful driver.

Happy bidding and good luck!

The SCM *analysis: After 58 bids, this Duetto sold on May 8, 2003, for, as mentioned above, $15,950.*

First, let's start by trying to learn a little something about the car from the photos. Unfortunately, neither the chassis number nor the engine number were listed in the description, perhaps the only thing I could fault the seller for. However, there is a photo of the chassis tag, and it reveals that this car was originally built for the German market. The orange, Euro-spec turn signal lenses, rather than U.S.-legal red, support this.

However, since the speedometer reads in miles rather than kilometers, this instrument was clearly changed out at some point. The seats appear to be redone in leather, an acceptable upgrade from vinyl. The standard rubber floormats have been upgraded to carpet, and the vinyl pattern to the top appears a bit too smooth. Finally, the Alfa Romeo script on the trunk appears to have been bent and then painted black, which is strange, as this script is widely available in the aftermarket. The engine bay itself appears correct but isn't detailed, which is unfortunate given the way the rest of the car is presented. The unusual clips used to fasten the air-cleaner crossover tube are missing. Finally, the engine cam covers appear to be painted with a black-crackle finish, which is incorrect but common.

But at a computer monitor's 72 dpi, everything else on the car looks scrumptious. It appears to have all of its dainty stainless-steel bumpers intact, and the headlight covers that came in the trunk of the 1967s (they were illegal by DOT standards) have been properly installed, with the headlights "frenched" into the fenders.

The little raised area behind the grille is still in evidence, a detail that is often lost when Duettos get their inevitable Bondo nose jobs following the equally inevitable collision.

The wheels and tires appear to be the correct 15 inches rather than the 14 inches that followed in 1969 (there was no 1968 model year for Alfa in the U.S. due to smog and safety issues), and the dash top doesn't seem to have any cracks.

$16,000 is all the money in the world for a Duetto, and for this amount, one might expect a car with a detailed engine bay. But good Duettos are hard to find, and ones that aren't painted red even more difficult.

Clearly, the bidders interested in this car were attracted by the professional and thorough presentation of the car in its online venue and were prepared to pay up to own it.

Assuming the car is as good as it looks, I would call this deal a good one for seller and buyer both.

(Descriptive information provided by classbenz@aol.com.)
From the July 2003 issue of SCM. ◆

1969 1750 Spider

You'd certainly be better off just buying a done car than stripping the paint off of this can of Italian worms

by Keith Martin

Below is the seller's description of eBay Motors, item #2410837134, sold on April 12, 2003.

This Alfa has a 1750 injection engine, 63,000 miles, five-speed. Stored inside 25 years. Does not run. Totally complete. Needs someone to breathe life into her.

Has extra top. Inside of engine looks perfect! Excellent candidate for restoration.

Alloy wheels. Bumpers are great. The body is almost rust-free and seems perfectly straight. The fender has the paint lifting off—it looks like something was left on it and it held moisture and bubbled the paint. Surface rust except what you see in the pics.

The SCM *analysis:* This car sold for $2,651 after a three-day auction. The seller had a feedback rating of 7, the buyer of 110. There were 24 bids in all. The serial number of the car was not provided.

This is a near-perfect example of how to get bottom dollar for your car. Most importantly, having a three-day auction instead of a seven- or ten-day one means there is no time for the "buzz" about your car to build, as the link to your auction is mailed and re-mailed within the body of enthusiasts.

Given what I can see from the pictures, this was a rust-infested car. I would make it wear a SARS mask before putting it on a car-hauler, lest its mere passing cause every paint job within 20 miles to start bubbling as it went by.

The description was relatively straightforward, although I would like to know what kind of X-ray vision the seller had to be able to say, "The inside of the engine looks perfect." I wonder if Mr. See Through noticed that the engine bay was white, indicating that this was once a white car that has been color changed.

I did appreciate the pictures that pointed out how truly horrible the car was, with paint bubbling on every surface, the surround missing off the steering column (why?) and the home-boy attempt at repair of the trunk lid.

Given what I can see from the pictures, this was a rust-infested car. I would make it wear a SARS mask before putting it on a car-hauler, lest its mere passing cause every paint job within 20 miles to start bubbling as it went by.

If I had been selling this car, I would have opted for a seven-day auction. I would have tried to turn the engine over by taking out the

sparkplugs, pouring some Marvel Mystery Oil down the plug holes, letting it sit for a couple days and then trying to rock it back and forth while it was in fifth gear. Further, I would have had a photo of the interior of the trunk and a couple of shots from underneath the car.

Alfa Romeo roundtails are fairly straightforward, robust cars. Purists prefer the 1967 1600-cc carbureted models, known as Duettos. The 1750 models, while having a slightly more powerful engine, were saddled with problematic SPICA fuel injection and trouble-prone dual brake boosters.

Values of roundtails have never been what they should be, given the mechanical sophistication of the car. Consider that MGBs of the same era had primitive, 1800-cc overhead-valve engines, while the Alfa sported an alloy engine, gearbox and differential, with chain-driven dual overhead cams.

Yet we are now seeing concours Bs cross the $20,000 threshold, while roundtails struggle to get to $15,000.

This low market value means that the car pictured here, if not broken up for parts, may get a haphazard amateur restoration, with Bondo slathered on rocker panels and sheetmetal welded into the floors. Let's hope not.

But a first-rate restoration of this car would easily cost more than $15,000, and you'd certainly be better off just buying a done one than stripping the paint off of this can of Italian worms.

As this car was presented on eBay Motors, a prudent buyer would only assume the worst, and that what he was seeing on the screen was just the tip of the corrosion monster that was trying desperately to devour this car. If that's the case, then the seller was shrewd in revealing as little as possible and hoping for a bidder whose dreams colored the reality.

But if the car were actually better than described, and the seller had put a little more energy into letting buyers know exactly what they were bidding on, he might have even gotten another $1,000 out of this beater.

From the June 2003 issue of SCM. ◆

1969 1750 Spider

A Weber-carbureted Duetto is the lightest, most sporting and most easily maintained of the Alfa Spiders imported into the U.S. since 1967

by Pat Braden

Chassis number: AR1410753
Engine number: AR0051258160

A modern classic by Pininfarina, the simple yet elegant Spider bodywork premiered in the U.S. on the 1967 1.6-liter Duetto would prove enduringly popular, lasting into the 1990s. The Spider's mechanics were essentially those of the Giulia sedan, comprising independent front suspension, a coil-suspended live rear axle and four-wheel servo-assisted disc brakes, while the engine was the Giulia Sprint GTV's 1.6-liter, double-overhead camshaft four. The U.S.-market Duetto was made for just one year before being superseded in 1969 by the 1.8-liter 1750 Spider Veloce, which carried the same symmetrical bodywork as the Duetto (due to EPA and DOT regulations, there was no 1968 or 1970 model year for Alfa in the U.S.). In 1971, the 1750's "round tail" was modified with the "sawed-off" Kamm-type tail, which would characterize the successor 2000 model.

A most attractive and sought-after post-war Alfa, this early left-hand drive "roundtail" 1750 Spider Veloce was recently imported into the U.K. from South Africa. The car is reported to be in good condition mechanically, with very good bodywork and paintwork, and a good original interior and top. The car also has a new exhaust system and tires.

The SCM *analysis: This car sold for $10,865, including buyer's premium, at the Bonhams & Brooks Beaulieu sale on September 9, 2001. This price is within* SCM*'s estimate of $9,000 to $12,500, and represents a solid investment.*

The symmetric Duetto, with its tapered front and rear, available in the U.S. in model years 1967 and 1969 (called a Spider Veloce), is something of a cult piece. The 1967 models are more highly prized because they carry dual Weber carburetors instead of the SPICA mechanical fuel injection, which was introduced on the 1969 U.S.-specification 1750 Spiders (series 105.62). Another roundtail attraction is its lack of the "comfort and convenience" accessories—air conditioning, power windows and side mirrors—that came to weigh down later versions of the Spider. A Weber-carbureted Duetto is the lightest, most sporting and most easily maintained of the Alfa Spiders imported into the U.S. since 1967.

Although elegant, the Duetto's almost-bumperless nose and tail sections proved overly susceptible to damage, and the later squared-off "Kamm" tail gave Alfa's engineers a more substantial body structure from which to suspend functional bumpers.

As the auction catalog copy suggests, the Alfa Spiders derived from the original Duetto achieved one of the longest production runs of any marque, spanning 28 years. European taste for the model soured long before the American attraction, and the model ended its run as a U.S.-only "Commemorative Spider." The reason for the Spider's longevity has much less to do with enduring design than Alfa's marketing incompetence, however. From the mid-'60s to the middle of the '90s, Alfa blundered from model to model, using a trial-and-error approach that eventually sapped the company of its resources and kept it from updating its venerable Spider. Also, Alfa's various approaches to U.S.-mandated smog and safety regulations

always seemed to be of the Band-Aid, "what's the least we can do?" variety rather than an overall, thoughtful approach.

When the Alfetta models were introduced in 1975, only a Sprint and Berlina appeared, and enthusiasts wondered where the new Spider was. In 1972 Pininfarina had proposed a replacement for the Duetto and intended it to appear with the Alfetta Berlina and Sprint, but there were simply no funds for its development. The Pininfarina Alfetta Spider prototype is now housed in Alfa's museum at Arese.

So American enthusiasts, who since the middle 1950s had been accustomed to driving Alfa Spiders that featured state-of-the-art engines and suspensions, were saddled with the increasingly heavy, unattractive, outdated two-liter cars of the '80s and '90s.

Expensive surprises are few with a well-kept roundtail. Finding unbent front and rear decklids can be difficult, and used stainless steel bumpers and reflective rear "lollipops" in good condition are costly.

But the mechanicals are robust, with parts available from a variety of sources. Best of all, with long-legged gearing and a well-designed five-speed gearbox, these cars are comfortable cruising at 75 mph all day long, something that can not often be said for $10,000 1960s sports cars.

Roundtail Spiders can be upgraded to later two-liter engines relatively easily, and while the performance is definitely increased, something quite wonderful is lost in the change: the sound and feel of the 1600-cc and 1779-cc engine with its free-revving characteristics. Somehow the two-liter engines exchanged increased horsepower for a feeling of mechanical ponderousness.

There is something virginal about the early Duettos: the sense of a true sports car unspoiled by the rough hands of marketers or advertisers. The Duetto is about as close to a pure sports car as you can get, especially if cars like the Morgan or MGB are a bit too spartan. The new owner can reasonably anticipate many miles of pleasant motoring, with little fear of mechanical complications. And because of its seminal design, which looks better with each passing year, a good Duetto or Spider Veloce is likely to be a fine long-term investment.

From the March 2002 issue of SCM. ◆

1992 Spider Veloce

The nimble little sportster of "The Graduate" fame is now a mature, if slightly portly, cruiser with a tidy little tuck to its nose and tail

by Donald Osborne

Chassis number: ZARBB32N7N7004239

As described by the seller: One registered owner, West Coast car, totally as new condition in every way. Virtually like the day it left Italy. Only 22,500 careful miles, no accidents, never smoked in. Attractive yellow exterior draped inside with luxury features including original black suede leather seats and door panels. Uniquely factory equipped for a European 2.0-liter roadster with power steering, air conditioning, power windows, locks and mirrors, AM/FM stereo with cassette, factory Campagnolo alloy wheels, correct Pirelli P-Zero tires, plus speed control. LoJack keyless entry alarm with interior movement sensor, color Alfa logo mats for shows, plus an extra daily set of mats and a fitted car cover. Original high-quality cloth top and window, and like the entire car, beautifully preserved. A very rare opportunity to capture a daily drivable reliable classic Italian sports car.

The SCM analysis: This car sold for $27,540, including buyer's premium, at the Barrett-Jackson Scottsdale auction held January 22-25, 2004. The price, at nearly triple the high SCM Price Guide value of $10,000, represents an extraordinary result.

The 1991-94 model Spiders were the last series of a 23-year production run for the 2-liter open Alfa. From the time the "square tail" model was introduced in 1971, the evergreen Spider went through many changes due to safety and emissions regulations. Most did not enhance the sporting nature or the looks of the car. Power decreased, ride height was raised, and large rubber bumpers and spoilers spoiled, if you will, the looks.

But not all changes were bad. The SPICA fuel injection system was jettisoned in 1979 in favor of a Bosch system. This finally solved most starting and drivability issues. The chassis was re-engineered in 1982, adding stiffness and vastly reducing cowl shake, although even with the car here you could easily mix a milkshake by just setting a glass on the dash and driving down the road.

The final updates came in 1991. The rear of the car lost the rubber-lipped spoiler for a smoother, more integrated tail, and newly fashionable body-colored bumpers appeared. A driver's side airbag was also added. For the upmarket "Veloce" model (the name at this point denoted only a higher level of trim, with its 120-hp, four-cylinder engine identical to the base car), these changes joined leather and suede seats, air conditioning, power windows, power steering and stereo cassette radio. The nimble little sportster of "The Graduate" fame was now a mature, if slightly portly, cruiser with a tidy little nip and tuck to its nose and tail. In other words, it had gone from being Kathleen to emulating Mrs. Robinson.

Since most older Alfa Spiders have had at least one impecunious owner ("if it ain't broke, don't fix it, and if it is, how cheaply can I have it done?"), buying a '90s car offers at least some reassurance against age-related afflictions. Yet even these cars are now over a decade old, meaning the factory warranty is long expired and a documented service history is just as desirable as on a vintage example.

Spiders from the 1990s are more resistant to rust than earlier models, though their steel is still not up to galvanized Porsche standards. This said, it is necessary to make sure that the drain holes in the doors have not been blocked or they will collect water and corrode from the inside. A prospective buyer should also watch out for badly repaired front-end damage on the nose, a common problem in areas where "touch parking" is practiced.

Interior trim was also improved from earlier models, though is still prone to looseness, rattles and breakage. Parts are easily obtained, however. While the suede and leather seats are attractive and comfortable, they do not wear well.

The interior of the car pictured here was one of the reasons it stood out. The seats were unmarked and the carpets were as-new, making the observed 22,587 miles believable. Even the printed Alfa logo on the AM/FM cassette radio was unfaded. The original Campagnolo wheels were free of curb rash and were wearing new tires. The panel fit was excellent, and the original yellow paint was in very good condition—its only blemishes were a few minor stone chips touched-up on the front bumper.

So for a nearly new car, was the price that far out of line? Well, to compare, a 1991 Alfa Spider with under 19,000 miles recently sold on eBay Motors for $14,000 (ending early with the "buy it now" option). This was a Florida car in white with a tan interior, with all service records that, from the pictures, appeared to be as nice as the Barrett-Jackson car.

Furthermore, as Alfa Spiders are rarely used as year-round transportation in parts of the country that experience winter, there are no shortage of low mileage cars from the early '90s for sale. While many may not be as well preserved as our example, they offer good value if you're not concerned about a door ding or two.

As a collectible, the pre-1970 roundtails will always be the "real deal," though the final Spiders are the best of the post-1974 cars and therefore should hold their values better. But it will be a long time before a '92 Alfa is anything other than a used car. Buying one in as-new condition is a viable alternative to a Mazda Miata or four-cylinder BMW Z3, but for $27,000 you can order a new Miata and have change left over.

This sale appears to be a combination of a superb car and a little of that legendary "Barrett-Jackson magic" at work. While we often say the price guide goes out the window for a #1 condition car, in this case the buyer's wallet went with it.

(Photo, historical and descriptive information courtesy of the auction company.)

From the May 2004 issue of SCM. ◆

1970 GTAm

This is a car that stirs the boy racer in all of us, and represents what every GTV owner wishes his car were

by Pat Braden

Chassis number: 1531231

The GTAm models are derived from Alfa's 1750 Veloce coupe. The Am suffix is a shortened version of "America," and refers to the U.S. model, which required fuel injection for emission reasons. With full development, the GTAm engine brought twice the brake horsepower available from a standard carbureted car. The bodywork featured fiberglass doors, hood and dashboard and riveted fiberglass fenders. It featured the typical Autodelta sliding-block rear suspension to lower the car's roll center, thereby improving handling. The cars ran on 13-inch Campagnolo wheels and had ventilated disc brakes. A new dual-plug cylinder head was used, and the engines were available with either 1779-cc or 1985-cc displacements.

Autodelta, Alfa Romeo's competition arm, prepared the GTAm for the European Touring Car Championships. In 1970, the works won six of nine races, and the Dutch driver Toine Hezemans secured the European Driver's Championship. In 1971, the class was divided and a new minimum weight introduced, but Hezemans was able to retain the Championship.

Figures suggest that there were 40 GTAms built, although the confirmed number is closer to half that. Fifteen cars were supplied directly to Autodelta for their own use—the recorded works cars. A handful of cars were sold to privateers who commissioned Autodelta to upgrade them to GTAm specification. Three were exported to America and Angola, one to the Jolly Club in Italy, and this car, 1531231, to Luigi Cecchini of Lucca, on May 26, 1970, as confirmed by Alfa Romeo Autodelta. The remainder of the 40 or so produced is accounted for by privateers who bought parts from Autodelta and carried out conversions themselves.

This car debuted in the hands of Cecchini in the Copa della Collina in June 1970. It suffered a minor incident, and there appears to be no racing history after this event. The Alfa then went to Spain and was eventually bought by the present owner in Sicily in 1986. It was subsequently restored over a period of four years to its original condition and features full Autodelta specs, being fitted with correct 2-liter fuel injection and twin-spark head. On completion of the restoration, the car was used in various historic competition events, including the Alfa day at Monza in 1990. It has been featured in a number of Italian publications in April 1992, and December 1996. The car was driven by Teodoro Zeccoli, an original works driver who wrote to the owner thanking him, and confirming the car was as it was when it originally raced and is "unbelievably fast."

Use since restoration has been limited to 60 miles and the car is reported to be in excellent condition. The car is eligible for the Tour Auto, Youngtimer series and a number of track events. It is offered for sale with a file containing a letter from Alfa Romeo, copy for the specification for the model, various photographs and the magazine articles the car was featured in.

The SCM analysis: SCM *gave this car a #3+ rating when it sold for $50,055, including buyer's premium, at Christie's London sale on* December 4, 2001. That is a surprisingly low condition rating for a freshly restored car, and may in part explain the reason the car sold for such a low price.

The Alfa GTAm is a car that stirs the boy racer in all of us. Based on a standard production chassis, it represents what every GTV owner wishes his car were. The GTAm was a serious effort by Autodelta at a time that Alfa was also developing the Type 33 cars and trying to stay afloat financially. The TZ and TZ2 models had been cancelled in favor of the Type 33, and it is quite likely that the GTAm could have been developed further, given added resources. Even so, it was a very successful racer, both in Europe and the U.S. Many GTAms offered alloy panels instead of plastic, and the shapes of the flares varied between cars.

GTAm engines developed 220 hp at 7,200 rpm, compared to 118 hp of the stock 1750 engine. There is no mention made by the auction catalog whether this GTAm is fitted with either a Bosch or SPICA sliding-plate throttle-body injection system, or a competition-use-only narrow-angle competition head.

There are more questions here. The chassis number 1531231 is listed in Tony Adriaensens's book, Alleggerita, *as a GTAm, but without any other information. This makes the chassis number ripe for a variety of creative interpretations. The fact that the only documentation that comes with this car is a letter from Alfa Romeo, a copy of the general specifications of the GTAm model, and recent magazine articles, is enough to give one pause.*

By the way, Adriaensens also prefers "America" as an interpretation of the Am in GTAm; the other reading is "Alleggerita maggiorata" (lightweight modified), but he thinks that is inappropriate, as the GTAm was much more than a modification of the GTA. There never was an "official" factory name other than GTAm.

The sale price is at least $25,000 below SCM's *Price Guide, but this does not necessarily mean that it was well bought. Since its restoration appears to be old and deteriorating, even though declared to be fresh, this GTAm needs a thorough going-over before being raced, or a complete restoration if it is to be shown. In either case, more money will be required before the car satisfies its new owner's fantasies.*

Given the condition of this car, and the lack of documentation of its provenance, the price paid should be viewed as market correct.

(Photo, historical and descriptive information courtesy of the auction company.)

From the May 2002 issue of SCM.◆

1973 Junior Zagato

Unlike virtually all other Alfa Zagatos, this is not a race car, but a dependable, nimble, daily driver

by Pat Braden

Chassis number: 3060352

One of the things which marked Alfa Romeo from lesser makers from the 1950s through to the 1970s was that it was able to make small runs of special, lightweight, coupe versions of its mainstream cars. The most prized of these were the cars bodied by Zagato, an expression of the historic relationship between the two companies.

The Alfa Romeo 105 series of Spiders and sedans provided lively performance. Equipped with both 1.3- and 1.6- liter powerplants, the larger DOHC engine produced 109 hp, with 103 lb/ft torque low in the rev range. Combined with a five-speed gearbox and Alfa Romeo's sweet chassis with four-wheel disc brakes, it was an outstanding performer in its class.

Zagato's two-seat coupe body weighed 182 lb less than the stock Giulia GT. Top speed increased to 118 mph, but that does not tell the whole story. The car was much more nimble and responsive, and the brakes had less work to do, so it was astonishingly rapid over winding roads, or in the mountains. Zagato made just 402 examples of the lightweight coupe with the 1.6 engine, and the Swiss-registered car pictured here is a fine representative of the type.

The SCM *analysis: This car sold for $9,962 at the Brooks Europe Auction in Geneva on March 6, 2000.*

When Alfa introduced the 1570-cc Giulia engine in 1962, it disappointed many customers who valued the lower Italian circulation tax of the 1290-cc Giulietta engine. Because of the lukewarm reception of the new Giulia Sprint GT, and in part to retain its 1300-cc clients, Alfa re-introduced the Giulietta Sprint with a 1290-cc version of the Giulia engine at the 1964 Geneva show. This car was the progenitor of Alfa's Junior line. From 1964 on, Alfa offered a range of displacements for its passenger cars, always including the 1300-cc tax bracket. The Junior designation was first applied to the 1966 GT coupe. When the 1750 series was introduced in 1967, the Junior range was enlarged to include both 1300 and 1600 engines. In 1969, Alfa showed a Junior Zagato with the 1290-cc engine at the Turin show.

Typical of Alfa, the production version did not appear until much later, and well after the initial excitement had abated. The Junior Z finally went on sale at the end of 1970. Two years later, the 1570-cc version of the Junior Zagato was shown at the Turin show. A slightly revised Junior Zagato, with heavier bumpers and changed interior appointments, debuted at the 1972 Turin show. The confluence of the Junior and Zagato lines in this car focuses not on engine displacement, however, but on its bodywork. Zagato-bodied Alfas have been benchmark cars in design and performance since the RL SS of 1926. Zagato bodied the 1950-51 championship Alfettas, and about 35 coupes on the 1900 floorpan in 1956-57. But when they began producing Giulietta Sprint Zagatos, Alfa refused to sell them bare chassis. The Zagatos were forced to buy finished Giulietta Sprints off the showroom floor, and then remove the bodywork, an almost prohibitively expensive procedure. Alfa remained dedicated to Bertone for its special-bodied coupes, and only agreed to cooperate with Zagato when they finally identified the need for a lightweight, aerodynamic coupe which was more competitive than the Sprint Speciale. The results were the SZ and SZ Coda Tronca Giulietta Zagatos, among the most collectible Alfas extant.

Alfa Zagatos are typically dressed all in aluminum alloy. However, the Junior version carries steel in its most strategic areas. As a result, at 2,094 lb it is significantly heavier than the 1,455 lb of the Giulia Tubolare Zagato or the 1,675 lb of the alloy-paneled GTA Junior. Unlike virtually all other Alfa Zagatos, this is not a race car, but a dependable, nimble, daily driver. The Junior Zagato is very similar to the Sprint Speciale in that it is a unique long-distance grand touring car that assures high average speeds in spite of its diminutive displacement. The interior of the Junior is spacious, the seats and driving position are comfortable and there's ample glass for excellent outward visibility.

It's impossible to miss the striking similarity between the Junior Zagato and Honda's first CRX. Ultimately, this has to be taken as an honor for the Zagato design, which is crisp and still distinctive, even in the 21st century.

SCM's Price Guide gives a range of $17,500 to $20,000 for the 1570-cc Junior Zagato. Taking the worst possible interpretation of its "fine" condition, the parts needed to fix this car mechanically are plentiful and relatively inexpensive. The buyer has a roadable project at half-price. Its low production volume assures that the Junior Zagato will remain a valued collectible, while its steel body means that it will resist everyday wear and tear better than an all-alloy lightweight. Historically, the most rewarding collectibles are also the most useable examples of their era. The Junior Zagato is a practical, as well as a good, investment. That this car sold for less than half the Price Guide high figure is an indication that either there were evils lurking with this car that could not be discerned from the catalog, or that some lucky buyer got a terrific buy.

(Photo, historical and descriptive information courtesy of the auction company.)

From the June 2000 issue of SCM. ◆

1974 GTV

By any measure, $30,000 is a huge price, as these cars usually trade in the $10,000-$15,000 range

by Donald Osborne

Chassis number: AR3026032

*A*s described by the seller on eBay Motors: This is a one of a kind 1974 Alfa Romeo GTV 2000. It is in absolutely mint condition, with 12,776 documented miles. It was purchased new by my wife from Alfa of Tacoma in 1976 and reportedly was one of the last GTVs to be imported to the States. It has been kept garaged and covered since new.

After the car was repainted in 1985 we decided to put it away and it has only been driven for occasional pleasure and upkeep since then. This car is mechanically perfect. Its only cosmetic flaw is that some of the stitching on the driver's seat is worn. Other than that you'd be hard pressed to find any other fault with this beauty.

The car comes with factory air conditioning and limited-slip differential. It has also had a number of options installed on it over the years. The major items include: Cromodora wheels with Pirelli P6 tires, Alpine cassette stereo and speakers, factory GTA headers and complete exhaust system, factory European cams, Koni shocks, Shankle sway bars, lowered springs, blueprinted injection pump and injectors, European taillights and side markers, Carello headlamps, chrome outside mirror, sump guard, power antenna, battery master switch, updated fuel pump and a new high-torque starter from an Alfetta. In addition the car will come with most of the removed OEM parts.

The SCM *analysis:* This car sold on eBay Motors for $30,101, on November 13, 2004.

Designed by the young Giorgetto Giugiaro for Bertone, the GTV was an instant classic from its introduction as the Giulia Sprint GT in 1963. With simple and elegant lines and perfect proportions, over the ensuing 14 years of production its body changed only subtly, in details such as the grille, headlights, taillights and instrument panel design. The biggest revision came in 1969, with the elimination of the early "stepped" hood. It was then that the Giulia coupe became known as the GTV.

Underhood was another story entirely. Engine displacement grew over the years, changing the GTV's character. The original high-revving, carbureted 1570-cc DOHC four (1600) was supplanted by a 1799-cc four (1750) with a SPICA mechanical fuel injection system in the GTV of 1969, which caused owners no end of trouble as they struggled to get the primitive unit set up correctly. The 1962-cc (2000) GTV of 1973-74 had a smoother, torquier, but lower-revving motor that, despite its greater power, left many Alfisti longing for the classic "on-edge" feeling of the 1600.

Regardless of the engine, all these coupes are superbly balanced cars, with slick gearboxes and nimble, predictable handling. There's really no more tossable sports car in its class. Mechanically, GTVs are robust and reliable, with weak second-gear synchros and a tendency to blow head gaskets as their main potential problems.

Build quality is good and the GTV has the feel of a much more expensive piece of machinery. That said, bodies are as prone to rust as all Italian cars of the era. Particular spots to check out are the double-skinned rocker panels, trunk floor (especially the battery box) and the floor under the pedal box. The drain holes in the bottom of the doors should also be checked to make sure they are not clogged, as this can lead to rust in the bottom of the door skins.

Interior trim can be an issue on GTVs, with weak seam stitching on the seats and rear seat tops, which can split from sun exposure through the rear window. Replacement upholstery kits are readily available to solve these problems. A more serious concern is cracking in the vinyl dashboard top. Although glue-on pads are sold, the only proper way to deal with this is to replace the entire vinyl dashboard unit. Redoing the seats and dashboard in a GTV could cost upwards of $3,000 in parts alone, with labor extra.

The GTV 2000 pictured here was indeed the last of the line. Though the GTV actually continued in production through 1977, it was no longer sold in the U.S.—the new Alfetta Sprint replaced it for the 1975 model year. The popularity of the Alfetta at introduction can be gauged by the fact that it took a year of sitting on the dealer's lot for the car pictured here to sell when new. Today, however, the tables have turned, as even traditionally affordable late-model GTVs are becoming increasingly attractive collectibles, while "good" Alfettas are still a challenge to peddle at no reserve on eBay.

This car is stated to be a low-mileage, one-owner car, with the factory limited-slip differential and air conditioning, both desirable options. Less attractive, at least to my sensibility, is that this car has been rather extensively though tastefully modified. The Cromodora five-star wheels are nice, but GTA headers and exhaust, Euro cams, Koni shocks and Shankle sway bars lead me to think that the "occasional pleasure" the seller has had in this GTV has been on the track. The battery master switch installation is the icing on the competition cake.

The car was repainted when it was eleven years old, which is not surprising, given the usual life of the original lacquer finish. The windshield was not removed during this work, though the original U.S.-spec side-marker lights and taillights were replaced with European ones at this time. Detailed photos show panel fit to be variable, with the left side door off at the rear edge and the right side of the trunk lid raised. The interior is in very good condition, with the all-important dash top appearing to be excellent, although the carpets cannot be seen underneath the red floor mats.

All in all, whether this GTV was a weekend track toy or not, it appears to be in exceptional shape. But by any measure, $30,000 is a huge price for a '74 GTV, as most trade within the SCM Price Guide range of $10,000-$15,000. I thought the performance mods would have suppressed the price, but the bidders (seven who offered more than $20,000) felt otherwise. Perhaps the extremely low mileage and single ownership history counted more in their minds.

As interest in these cars continues to rise and the number of one-owner, no-stories cars continues to drop, I would certainly expect more cars to break that $20k barrier. But still, the new owner here may have to wait a while for the market to catch up to what he paid. The seller, on the other hand, hit a grand slam.

From the February 2005 issue of SCM.◆

Affordable Classic: 1980-86 GTV-6

No Alfa since the 6C 2500 is more comfortable, or more suited to long distance travel

by Pat Braden

The Alfa Romeo GTV-6 was produced at a time when Alfa Romeo was hemorrhaging money. Yet the engineers at Alfa managed to create one of the most sophisticated sports cars of its era. An all-alloy SOHC V6 engine driving a rear five-speed transaxle with deDion suspension is world-class engineering. This was also the last two-door sports coupe Alfa imported into the U.S. before its retreat from the market in 1995.

Alfa wanted its new car to be bug-free, so GTV-6s built in 1980 were used exclusively by the factory for testing. The model was finally considered ready for public sale in 1981, but fortune was not with the new Alfa. Porsche's 944 was introduced at the same time, and robbed Alfa of many sales in its inaugural year. Then, a clerical error caused virtually the entire 1982 U.S. allotment to be silver with a blue interior. Mechanical problems included weak head gaskets and a hydraulic cam belt detensioner, which, if it failed, could require a major engine overhaul.

By 1985, the car's mechanical difficulties were behind it, and the GTV-6 underwent some desirable styling changes. These included a redesigned interior with new seats and a more attractive trim scheme for the exterior. The following year, however, Fiat bought Alfa and withdrew the coupe from the market in anticipation of the Milano sedan.

The car's short market life, along with its technical problems, turned away many potential buyers. However, faithful Alfisti find a great deal to enjoy about the car. Its 2.5-liter, all-alloy V6 engine gives ample power over a very broad range of engine speeds. No Alfa since the 6C 2500 is more comfortable, or more suited to long-distance travel. The car offers reclining seat backs, power windows and a reasonable air conditioning system. (Demonstrating a perhaps well-founded lack of confidence in the Italian power window motors, a manual crank was included in the glovebox.) Many models carried a manual sunroof, and several special editions were offered in an effort to inspire sales.

Years produced: 1980-86
Number produced: 19,400 (6,500 for the US)
Original list price: $16,983 (1981)
SCM Price Guide: $3,000-7,500
Tune-up/major service: $250
Distributor cap: $15
Chassis #: Bulkhead
Engine #: Passenger side of engine
Club: AROC, 10 Raskin Road, Morristown, NJ 07960
Web site: aroc-usa.org
Alternatives: Nissan 280Z, Toyota Supra, Porsche 944

GTV-6s are just now passing the nadir of their value, which will rise for low-mileage cars in excellent condition, as they become more rare. Special edition models, such as the Balocco or the Maratona (called the "Marijuana" by some Berkeley-area wags) bring only a small premium, since most of their uniqueness was either glued or screwed to the body.

Shoppers should try to find a 1985 or '86 model. The health of the driveshaft is the first thing to check. A careful visual inspection will reveal the condition of its three rubber donuts (one inside the front bell housing). A vibration at idle, or at about 3,500 rpm, indicates that the driveshaft is not in balance. If the cam belt shows traces of oil, its detensioner is in immediate need of repair; more reliable non-hydraulic tensioners are available. By now, every GTV-6 has been fitted with an improved head gasket, but if the oil on the dipstick looks milky, get ready for a quick $750 interaction with the local ATM. Later improvements to the engine in the Milano and 164 sedans can be easily retrofitted to the GTV-6, and a GTV-6 equipped with a 3-liter engine from a Milano Verde is a joy to drive.

Look for rust in the usual places, including the rockers and the wheel arches. Be sure all the switches work, as replacing them, or the motors they control, can be expensive. Since best-in-the-world GTV-6s are under $10,000, it doesn't make sense to buy one that has major needs—unless, like so many Alfisti, you are a do-it-yourselfer. Virtually every part necessary to restore a GTV-6 is available either new aftermarket or in good used condition.

Any Alfa that has style and performance will eventually become collectible. The GTV-6 is an inexpensive way to enjoy a future collectible with superb engineering, at a very reasonable price.

From the November 2000 issue of SCM.◆

1984 GTV-6

With a later 3.0-liter V6 from the high-performance 'Verde' Milano, this GTV-6 should be a fast, fun and affordable sports car

by Donald Osborne

Chassis number: ZARAA6693E1005744

As described by the seller on eBay Motors: A classic Alfa, mechanically sound, with a 5-speed manual transmission and a 3.0-liter V6 from a 1988 Milano (with approximately 90,000 miles). The car runs very strong with no oil leaks. It has been garage kept and adult-driven.

My father bought it brand new in 1984 and I took it over in 1999 and put the new motor in it, along with many other new parts. These include an ANSA exhaust, K&N filter, rebuilt shift linkage, and new drive train seals.

The car has a sunroof, new Sony stereo, power windows, tilt wheel, and A/C. It is 99-percent rust-free, with only some small spots on the right corner panel. Comes with car cover. I bought a new car so it's just sitting around, and has been driven less than 100 miles in the last six months, but I have started it periodically to keep everything fresh.

The SCM *analysis:* This car sold on eBay Motors (item 2488305017) for $4,800, September 6, 2004.

The GTV-6 was the successor to the Alfetta GT, which itself replaced the 2000 GTV coupe in 1975. On paper, the Alfetta was a major step up in sophistication from the GTV, with such race-bred features as a rear transaxle and inboard rear disc brakes. Another new feature was the instrument panel layout, which put the tachometer alone in front of the driver, with the speedometer and remaining gauges in a cluster in the center of the dashboard. Yet neither the cockpit design nor the car itself was well appreciated.

The Alfetta used the same twin-cam, 2-liter four-cylinder engine of the outgoing GTV, fitted with the same problematic SPICA fuel injection system. It was widely believed that its chassis was capable of handling much more power—sorely needed to give the sluggish Alfetta some life. That power came in 1981, when Alfa dropped in a Bosch-injected 2.5-liter V6 and created the GTV6.

The V6 was acknowledged as a terrific powerplant—flexible, smooth and strong. It transformed the character of the car, and made the GTV6 a true GT car. But the V6 was not without its weaknesses, as it had a two-piece head gasket which was prone to blowing if the car was driven hard before its alloy block was fully warmed up. The good news for collectors is that a factory recall replaced the faulty gaskets with redesigned, one-piece gaskets, fixing most of these failures long ago.

The V6 engine did not cure all the Alfetta's problems. After years of being known for one of the slickest, most direct gearboxes in the business, Alfa Romeo had introduced the terms "vague" and "rubbery" to the Alfisti's vocabulary with the Alfetta's underwhelming shift linkage to the rear transaxle. To make matters worse, the rubber donut driveshaft joints would first create unpleasant driveline vibrations as they deteriorated, and then bring the car to a halt as they self-destructed. These issues were carried over to the GTV-6 without improvement.

The GTV-6 did get some styling changes, most notably a hood bulge to clear the bigger engine, black plastic body trim on the C-pillar and sills, larger rear light clusters, and new alloy wheels. The interior was also upgraded with leather, a revised dashboard with a traditional instrument layout, air conditioning, tilt wheel, and power windows.

In considering a GTV-6, the usual Alfa caveats about rust apply.

These cars rust, not only in the usual spots (rocker panels and front and rear valances), but also in the windshield frame and around the rear hatch glass, both areas that are difficult and expensive to repair. It is also important to check the channels of the GTV-6's sunroof to ensure that its drain holes have not been blocked. The car pictured here appears to be in very good condition and is stated to have minimal rust, which would be surprising given that it has lived all its life in New Jersey.

This GTV-6 has had a number of mechanical modifications, the most important of which is the replacement of the original engine with a later 3-liter V6. This engine was introduced in 1987 in the high-performance "Verde" model of the Milano sedan, and is more powerful, with a peak 183 hp and 181 lb-ft of torque vs. 154 and 155 for the smaller 2.5. This swap is not unusual and should add to the driving experience, provided it was performed by a competent mechanic.

That the car has been in a single family is a good thing, as we can assume a continuous record of work performed (and deferred), leaving the new owner minimal guesswork as to what needs to be done. With no mention of major engine work, it must be assumed that after 90,000 miles a valve job looms in this motor's future, but at just $1,500, no one should be going hungry in order to pay the bill.

At $4,800, the price paid here was near the lower end of the SCM Price Guide range of $4,500-$7,500. For a fast, fun, and affordable sports car, this could be a great buy. However, I would have wanted to do a complete mechanical inspection before bidding on this car, simply because it has not been driven any great distance in the past six months. No old car likes to sit, and older Italian cars don't like it more than most. Periodic starting doesn't keep anything "fresh" if the car is not brought up to full operating temperature and put under some load, and just starting the engine can do far more harm than good.

Even if its one-family ownership has caused this car to avoid the usual deferred maintenance that accompanies most Alfas trading in this price range, its recent period of inactivity could mean that the buyer will have to undertake a total re-commissioning, including oil change, hoses, filters, brakes, driveshaft donuts, timing belts, tensioners and a replacement of the head gasket. Add a few more "minor" repairs to the project, like dealing with the encroaching rust, recovering the sheepskin-clad front seats, or replacing the exhaust, and it's easy to see why the market for these cars is so thin. Let's hope the new owner enjoys driving this one and nothing breaks.

From the December 2004 issue of SCM.◆

1969 1750 Berlina

What factors would cause someone to pay twice the going rate for an unloved car? You will find them familiar: rarity and condition

by Pat Braden

Chassis number: AR1555614

As described by the seller on eBay Motors: This is a USA car converted to carburetors (Webers) as a European model. Engine redone 3,000 miles ago. New transmission, new $3,000 paint with new rubber throughout. Original interior in near-mint condition. No cracks on dash. Extensive work mechanically and otherwise. Drives and looks like new. $500 remote control stereo system. Excellent, almost-new Pirelli tires. Doesn't need anything. Your gain, my loss. Between last owner and me, over $22,000 in this Alfa. I've never seen a better one. Turn key, fast and classic. I have the original fuel injection gear, European manual from 1969 and many receipts. Serious buyers only, please. This car is the real thing. Starts every time and I'm open to inspections.

The SCM *analysis: This car, item number 1843160613, sold on eBay Motors for a mind-boggling $6,995 on July 16, 2002.*

From time to time, a sale comes along that blows a hole in the Price Guide *large enough to drive a Lincoln Navigator through. Rarely, however, is the vehicle in question a four-door sedan, and in this case, arguably the least interesting model of Alfa saloon ever imported to the United States.*

What factors would conspire to cause someone to pay twice the going rate for an unloved car? Strangely enough, you will find them familiar: rarity and condition.

It is a seemingly oxymoronic truism in the collector car world that the most common cars often have the lowest survival rates. Who would want to preserve, for instance, a Chevette or a Mustang II? But after the drudgery of daily use has decimated the ranks of these plebian commuters, the survivors develop an attractiveness all their own. Witness the 1979 Ford Pinto, as-new with only 328 miles showing, that sold at the 2001 eBay/Kruse Spring Auburn auction for $6,466, nearly twice what the car cost new. So, even though more than 100,000 1750 Berlinas were built, there are few left today, and far fewer in excellent condition.

When introduced to the U.S. in 1969, the Alfa Berlina was the stylistically uninspired follower of the quirky but cute Giulia Super.

While the predecessor Giulia sedans got everything right, the 1750 seemed to get almost everything wrong, beginning with a fuel-delivery system that the factory refused to make user serviceable, and a dramatic propensity to rust. A dual-circuit brake system was one of the federal mandates for this model, and the 1750 fitted two failure-prone and expensive (at $300 each) Binaldi brake boosters in the engine bay. A 60-mm increase in wheelbase made the car roomier but less nimble than the Giulia sedan. Interior changes included less supportive seats and a secondary instrument cluster placed on the center console, out of the driver's line of sight.

As time passed, Berlinas, like Alfas in general, aged poorly and expensively. While the values of Berlinas plummeted on the resale market, the costs of a valve or clutch job remained the same as the more cherished sporting models. Who would bother to put a $3,000 paint job on a $1,500 car?

And that brings us to the car in question.

For an Alfa enthusiast who, for whatever reason, is looking for a perfect Berlina, this was a brilliant buy. The previous two owners, perhaps after smoking something stronger than Camels, succeeded in reportedly "investing" more than $22,000 in this car.

They addressed the SPICA issue by converting the car to European-spec Weber induction, and one would hope that it was done properly, with the correct European intake manifold, conversion of the throttle linkage and installation of the cold-air canister.

Assuming that the $22,000 spent went for proper overhauls and refurbishments of the suspension and mechanicals, for less than $7,000 the new owner has a better-than-new car, a perfect example of one of the last of the front-mounted transmission, 105-series four-door sedans.

Is this a good investment? Perhaps. At the 1988 Alfa National Convention held in Tulsa, OK, a burgundy Berlina, similar to this car, and restored to showroom perfect, attracted the most attention of any car in the concours and was awarded the "People's & Judge's Choice." Why? Because, while restored Giulietta Spiders and even SZs are a relatively common sight at Alfa gatherings, rarely does a restored Berlina make an appearance.

So long as the car is kept in its current pristine condition, the owner is likely to be able to get his money back upon sale. But there lies the conundrum. If he drives and enjoys his new 30-year-old car, he is subjecting it to the risk of rock chips, parking lot dings, worn upholstery and all the other indignities that accompany daily use. This car is only a few imperfections away from being a $3,000 Berlina.

Our advice? Since the car will never be worth significantly more than it is today, holding it for investment purposes is futile. Far better to take it out and enjoy it, and should it depreciate to half its current value through use-induced road rash, view that as simply the price paid for driving a time-warp car.

From the September 2002 issue of SCM.◆

1988 Milano Verde

If you can get over the looks and deal with less than ideal ergonomics, the driving experience is terrific

Donald Osborne

Chassis #: ZARAA6693E1005744

As described by the seller on eBay Motors: I am too old for all my toys so I am selling. This is a nice car, all original and totally rust-free. It has always been stored inside. It has the 3.0-L motor with low miles—only 62,000 showing. This Milano runs and drives like a new car. It's a very dependable car so the winning bidder can fly in and drive it home.

The SCM *analysis: This car sold on eBay Motors for $7,600, on March 4, 2005.*

The replacement for the Alfetta-derived Sport Sedan, the Milano was introduced in 1986 as a 1987 model. As the last rear-wheel-drive car Alfa made, it's considered by many to be the last "true" Alfa. A further development of the Alfetta platform, it retained the rear trans-axle and inboard rear brakes of the earlier cars but carried the superb alloy V6 first seen in the U.S. in the GTV-6 coupe.

At introduction, three Milano trim levels were available: the base Silver, mid-range Gold, and luxury Platinum. The cars were well equipped, with standard air conditioning (on the Gold and Platinum), power windows, central locking, heated mirrors and a tilt steering wheel. The Silver had a tweed interior, the Gold velour interiors, and there was attractive suede-and-leather seating in the Platinum.

Initially powered by a 2.5-liter V6 making 155 hp, for 1988 a hotter three-liter version offering 183 hp debuted in the sporty "Verde." Included were anti-lock brakes, a limited-slip differential, stiffer springs and Recaro sport seats, as well as a body kit that added plastic fender flares and side skirts. For those who wanted even more power, noted performance tuner Callaway offered a twin-turbo setup for the Milano that bumped the Verde's horsepower rating up to 242.

The Verde name came from the green cloverleaf featured on Alfa Romeo racing cars. For those who haven't heard the story before, an insomniac Alfa mechanic was said to have painted the cloverleaf on a white triangle on one of the team cars the night before the 1923 Targa Florio. The car went on to dominate and win the race, so with typical Italian superstition, all subsequent Alfa race cars have carried the insignia.

Intended to lift Alfa sales levels to new heights, the Milano ultimately disappointed. The design was perhaps too different for U.S. tastes. After the relatively clean and attractive design of the Alfetta GT and Sport Sedan, the Milano represented a return to what could kindly be called "quirky" styling. Depending on who you talk to, the sharply bent sheet metal in the back of the car either makes it look as though it had been rear-ended, or immediately brings Jennifer Lopez's primary asset to mind.

The interior was not spared the weirdness either, with a u-shaped hoop pull-up parking brake handle and a radio which was impossible to operate if the shift lever was in first, third, or fifth gear. Another "interesting" touch was front power window switches mounted on the roof console, while those for the rear windows resided on the center console, under the driver's elbow.

Worse than the styling, however, was the poor service and support given by the importer ARDONA (a joint venture between Alfa and Chrysler) and the notorious Alfa dealer network. Yet, despite the mid-dling sales performance of the Milano, Alfa didn't give up on selling sedans in the U.S. after discontinuing it in 1989. The sleek Pininfarina-

designed 164 replaced the Milano in late 1990.

Regardless of its short lifespan, the Verde was a capable sports sedan. Contemporary tests recorded a 0-60 mph time of 7.8 seconds and a top speed in excess of 135 mph. This, and the car could return up to 35 mpg on the highway.

The driving experience is terrific, with a well-balanced chassis that handles like an Alfa should—neutral and "chuckable." The V6 has good torque and high-end power all the way to a 6,500 rpm redline, making it flexible enough for all driving conditions.

Mechanically, the Alfa V6 is a durable engine, with the main weakness being its original two-piece head gasket. By now, most of these should have been replaced with an improved, one-piece design that was offered in a factory recall.

The vagueness in the shifting which afflicted the Alfetta was somewhat improved with a revised linkage in the Milano, but the gearbox still encourages deliberate, rather than quick, shifts. The problems relating to the rubber driveshaft "donuts" also carried over into the Milano. It's absolutely vital to make sure these are monitored and replaced in a timely fashion to avoid vibration, as they can ultimately lead to driveline failure. This is particularly an issue on the Verde, due to the more enthusiastic driving style that the car encourages.

By the time the Milano was produced, rust proofing had finally found its way to Italy—sort of. As a result, these cars suffer fewer corrosion problems than their predecessors; however, every Milano I've ever seen has a strange Achilles heel in the leading edge of the rear wheel openings, an area terribly susceptible to rust. This is exacerbated in the Verde, as the damage is usually hidden underneath the plastic fender flare and isn't caught until the trim piece falls off. Almost all Milanos, including those from warm, dry climates, will have had some repair work done in this area by now.

This Milano, a Michigan car, is said to be "rust free." That's a pretty bold boast for any Midwestern Alfa, but the mileage is low and if it has been garaged and maintained, perhaps I can believe it. The car appears to be in stock condition, with the exception of a big, 2 1/2-inch exhaust pipe that would look more appropriate on a slammed Integra. It seems like a strange accessory on a car being sold by an older owner, especially an Alfa. The only obvious sin I could see was some wear on the rather fragile driver's seat fabric, which isn't such a big deal, except that replacement fabric is no longer available.

The SCM *Price Guide shows a range of $3,500-$6,000 for Milanos, but the $7,600 paid here is still not a lot of money for a fast, comfortable four-seater that will offer its new owner a lot of driving fun if everything checks out. The Verde was a rare model (less than 900 made), so it's not like you'll be bumping into too many others out there in the real world. If you can get over the dated, slightly bizarre looks, mediocre build quality and marginal power accessories, it's a great choice for a rather special everyday driver.*

From the August 2005 issue of SCM.◆

Need for Speed Test Drive: The '94 4-Cam 164

At 3,500 rpm, the punch of the Alfa horsepower and the snarl of the four-cam engine kick in. 120 mph is nothing—and then you shift into fifth

by Keith Martin

After 25 years of owning Alfas, my car-buying habits had become predictable. In the '60s, all the used Alfas cost about $500; a Giulietta Spider Veloce, $600. I bought a couple of them. In the '70s, the price of '60s Alfas climbed to around $900. A good Giulia Super was $800; a Giulia Spider Veloce, $1,000. I think I ended up with around six or seven Alfas through that decade.

Inflation arrived in the '80s. I paid nearly $1,500 for a used '70s spider, and some friends spent over $5,000 for four year-old GTV-6s. In the '90s, beater Milanos fell below $3,000, and there were always a few spiders around for under $2,500—some of them even ran. The various Alfa models changed from year to year, but the song remained the same: Wait. Let someone else buy them new so you can use up the last good miles on the car.

Then Craig Morningstar, long-time public relations consultant for Alfa Romeo called one winter day, asking if I would like to fly to Phoenix to test-drive the new 1994 4-cam 164. Leave the cold February drizzle of Portland behind for sunny Arizona? It's called a no-brainer.

As soon as I hit Sky Harbor Airport, I happily ditched my umbrella and raincoat before heading to a press conference at the Biltmore Hotel. The room was full of "official automotive journalists." There was the ever-dapper Ken Gross, polite, knowledgeable, and interested in learning as much as possible about the new model. Then there were the Young Turks, staffers of large organizations like *Car & Driver, Road & Track, Automobile Magazine* and *Autoweek,* and the older generation, who had seen it all before.

The next morning at breakfast, I struck up a conversation with Jennifer Bott, assistant editor of *Ward's Automotive International*, and we decided to drive together.

Bott was driving, I navigated, and within three blocks I had us hopelessly lost. Her sense of direction saved us, and a few miles later we joined the seemingly endless stream of '94 Alfas heading against rush-hour traffic toward the desert.

Bott mentioned that it was difficult to carry on a conversation with me, as I kept rubbing the leather seats, saying "What a cool car." "Power seats." "An automatically-dimming rear-view mirror." "115 degrees, and the air conditioning blows cold."

Alfas have always had terrific drive trains. Even the poor maligned '75-'81 Spica Spiders, with a little emission-dodging help, could be made to move right along.

But the Snake & Cross cars have never been long on creature comforts. Yes, I know all about how efficient the space-utilization on a Giulia Super is, and how if you tilt the front seat back far enough in a Milano, even someone over 5'5" can fit comfortably.

But the 164 is a *real* car. You could wear a business suit in one, and it wouldn't drip oil on your pants leg. Even in the rain, your 164 would get you there dry and on time. Try that in a '70s Spider. (Don't even mention a Giulietta/Giulia Spider—for their time, they were terrific. But their anemic heaters and guaranteed-to-build-small-lakes-in-the-footwells weather protection just doesn't cut it for daily use.)

Bott was driving fast. So fast that she blew by the Young Turks in the 164Q. Bott didn't know much about Alfas, but she knew she liked this car.

Finally, the Turks caught us. Forty miles outside Phoenix, as U.S. 60 slimmed down to two-lanes, off they went, swerving and swaying all over the road, testing the "off-center response" of the steering, and maybe even trying to activate the airbag. A few miles later, we traded

into a five-speed LS 164, and I took my first turn driving.

This is power. The torque in the new four-cam 164 pushes you back in your seat beginning at 2,000 rpm. At 3,500 the punch of the Alfa horsepower and the snarl of the four-cam engine kick in. It's fast. 120 mph is nothing—and then you shift into fifth.

The Young Turks were trying to trick the automatic LS into thinking the desert was "ice" when we blew by and disappeared up into the hills. At El Capitan Pass, 123 miles into our run, elevation 4933ft, we switched to the 230 bhp 164Q.

I tried to explain the original Mille Miglia to Bott. Imagine a 1,000 mile road race, on public roads not closed to regular traffic. A race that started at night, just to keep things interesting. A race where, when sneaking up on a competitor, you drive with your lights off so they don't see you until you're ready to pass them.

Bott tried to look interested, but I think she suspected my explanation was just an excuse to demonstrate to her how Alfa's race-bred suspension was designed to go around the mountain curves (with 5,000 foot dropoffs) at three times the posted mph.

The 164Q has a cockpit adjustable suspension. I pressed the "Sport" button, and the difference was noticeable. Above 70 mph the car hunkers down, gives more road feedback, and tells you it's ready to be driven. Driven hard. Driven to your limits—which are probably far below ITS limits.

I think we backed off to 100 mph for one short stretch, when we had to slow down for traffic.

The rest of the time was spent pushing the car at speeds that would make an Italian proud.

"Aren't you worried about tickets?" Bott asked.

"I don't think Arizona sends ticket reports to Oregon," I replied.

The Alfa had been run near redline, for over two hundred miles, in 120 degree temperature, without missing a beat. It was quiet, and comfortable. Never once did Bott or I cause any of the 164s we drove to lose their composure.

If I were to have just one new Alfa in my life, it would be the 164 four-cam. It's quiet, comfortable, and will outrun and out-handle any Alfa I've ever owned. I can offer in trade a '67 Giulia Super and a '58 Spider Veloce. Plus a bunch of very valuable 750 parts like heater knobs and slightly dented hub-caps.

I love this car.

From the August 1993 issue of SCM. ◆

1976 Alfetta Sedan

When I first saw the car, it took my breath away. "Who would do a $65,000 restoration on an Alfetta sedan?" I wondered

by Donald Osborne

Chassis number: AR116330003126

This rare and sought-after four-door Alfa Romeo sedan features new exterior paint and new and correct interior. Its classic Alfa 2,000-cc inline four-cylinder has been treated to a recent rebuild, and it is fitted with dual Weber carbs. All the stainless trim has been restored, while all the chrome bits have been similarly redone. This is a fun, fast, and affordable four-door sports car. The new buyer will suffer no disappointments, as this one runs and drives as it looks.

The SCM *analysis: This car sold for $11,070 at the Barrett-Jackson Scottsdale auction, held January 26-30, 2005.*

Introduced in 1975 alongside the Alfetta GT coupe, the Alfetta sedan can trace its roots back to the Giulia TI sedan of 1962. The 1,600-cc TI begat the 1750 Berlina in 1969, which had a longer wheelbase, roomier and better-furnished interior, and a bigger trunk. In 1971, Alfa's two-liter engine was dropped into the package and the 2000 Berlina was born. With a revised interior further continuing the march up-market, and the smoother, torquier engine, it provided even more refinement. The 2000 Berlina didn't appear in the U.S. until 1972, and was superceded by the Alfetta three years later.

Named after the all-conquering post-war Alfa Romeo Grand Prix car, the Alfetta was a markedly different car than its predecessors. It was shorter, lower, lighter and wider than the Berlina, and offered styling by Bertone that was more shapely than the "square-rigged" Alfa sedans of the past. Finally, Alfisti no longer had to make excuses for owning a sedan.

The Alfetta represented a new engineering direction for Alfa as well, and boasted the sophistication of rack-and-pinion steering, a rear-mounted, five-speed transaxle, longitudinal torsion bar front suspension, and a DeDion rear axle with inboard disc brakes. The Spica-injected, two-liter DOHC four of the 2000 series was retained, good for 118 hp in the Alfetta.

Some of these changes to Alfa's proven technology were a good thing, while some weren't. While Alfa sedans had always been a pleasure to drive, the Alfetta took it to a new level, with near 50-50 weight balance thanks to the transaxle. The cars were a pleasure to steer with the throttle, yet still incredibly forgiving. I risked many tickets driving mine much too quickly on any road with S-bends, climbing corners or decreasing-radius curves. The Alfetta was truly a sports sedan.

On the other hand, the remote shift linkage was unfortunately vague, rubbery and balky. This was made even more galling as the ultra-direct Alfa gearbox was already a thing of legend, and Lancia had done a transaxle linkage so much better in the Aurelia way back in 1950. The shift forks could also bend or lose their clips if the lever was forced too quickly.

The other notorious weakness of the Alfetta is its rubber driveshaft donuts, three couplings that take the place of traditional U-joints. As they age, they develop cracks, which in turn cause driveline vibrations that lead to total failure. Count on replacing them on any car you buy. To make things a bit trickier, the design changed three times during the car's production run, so you must be sure to fit the proper type on your car.

The Alfetta's inboard rear brakes were also problematic, with pads that are difficult to change and a parking brake that greatly increases rear pad wear.

Alfetta interiors are a mixture of fragile materials. The velour sags and wears out, the foam padding dries out before turning lumpy and powdery, the hard plastics are prone to cracking and warping, and the wood veneer is given to peeling and fading. Sedans generally saw

more use than coupes as well, so their interiors tend to be more tired. Kits and materials are available for a total re-do of the interior, but are more expensive than those for the more valuable two-door cars.

Rust is a major issue with all Alfas of the 1970s as well. Alfa Romeo used low-quality Soviet steel thanks to a trade deal the Italian government (Alfa's owner at the time) made with the USSR. Although a lot of the rust tends to be cosmetic (around the trim mounting points and window trim, including the windshield) it almost certainly will have also attacked the main structure by now. The pedal box, driver's floor and seat belt mounting points are especially vulnerable.

When I first saw the car pictured here driving into registration at the auction, it took my breath away. "Who would do a $65,000 restoration on an Alfetta sedan?" I wondered. As I got closer, however, I realized I was mistaken. This wasn't a restoration at all, but rather a fairly thorough "refurbishment."

The paint was fairly thick, with a good amount of orange peel present—not unlike the original finish. The seats and door panels had been recovered with a proper velour kit, but with some sagging in spots. The front seat headrests were missing, and their mounting holes were covered with a patch of seat fabric. The horn buttons on the steering wheel spokes looked slightly melted somehow, and there was black electrical tape wrapped around part of the rim of the wheel. Underneath an aftermarket dashboard cover rug, the usual and expected cracks in the original dash top could be seen. There was no radio, and the car was not equipped with a/c.

The engine compartment was clean, with what looked to be a professional installation of twin Weber carbs in place of the hated Spica mechanical fuel injection system. The cam cover had not been changed however, and the broken brackets for the original air plenum hose were still there.

To top it all off, the car seemed to sit a bit too high, as if it had new springs with incorrect dimensions.

Having said all that, this was still the nicest Alfetta I've seen in at least 20 years. Was the price a Barrett-Jackson phenomena? Certainly, and even more so given what notorious cheapskates owners of Alfettas are. But how much is a good Alfetta worth if you're looking for one? They're not thick on the ground, so perhaps this new and unrepeatable record price will coax some more nice examples to surface. And let's face it—even if the new owner paid twice retail, he's only $5,500 upside-down, less than the cost of a valve job on a lot of the exotics we cover in SCM. Further, he has a four-door sedan capable of hustling down backroads with a family aboard, in keeping with the Alfa slogan for their 1900s, "the family car that wins races."

From the May 2005 issue of SCM. ◆

1979 Alfetta Sport Sedan

The no-reserve status suggests that the seller really had no idea what this four-door would bring

by Pat Braden

Chassis number: AR116582002690

While the post-war Alfa 1900 Berlina was advertised as "the family car that wins races," the slogan for the late '70s automatic-equipped Alfetta Sport Sedan could have been "a truly sale-proof car."

The Alfetta was Alfa's attempt to regain its technical edge with a sophisticated drive-train and suspension. Its previous models were powered by an engine dating to 1954 and a suspension dating to 1962. In 1975, the cash-strapped company offered the same twin-cam alloy engine, but with fresh Sprint and Sport Sedan (Berlina) styling, a five-speed manual transaxle and DeDion rear suspension. Hampered by a power-robbing Rube Goldbergian approach to emissions, Alfettas proved as sluggish as their sales, and quickly reaffirmed Alfa's reputation for blown head gaskets and terminal rust. New features included heavy steering, a rubbery shift linkage and an insatiable appetite for driveshaft donuts. The American distributor, attempting to explain away Alfa's plummeting sales, pleaded for a sedan with an automatic transmission, surely an essential enhancement for the American market.

In 1978, a batch of 2,000 Berlinas with air conditioning and a ZF three-speed automatic transaxle was assembled for our market. Not surprisingly, buyers attracted to air-conditioned cars with automatic transmissions did not shop Alfas, and Alfa enthusiasts were offended by the unsporting nature of the car. More than half of these "Alfamatics" were shipped back to Italy as unsaleable. Italians immediately fell in love with the luxury of an air-conditioned, automatic Alfa. The repatriated cars, now badged "America," sold well enough that the model was put back into production for the Italian home market.

The SCM *analysis: I recommended an "Alfamatic" to the former owner of the car pictured here. He wanted the convenience of an Alfa four-door, and I observed that the Alfetta's reputation for destroying donuts did not apply to the ZF-equipped cars since they avoided the driveline shocks of the clutch-equipped cars. During his possession of the car, the owner improved its already good condition to better-than-new. Its heavy stock bumpers were replaced with stainless units from an earlier Berlina, and fog lights and mild cams were added. The car passed a smog test after a careful tune-up and fresh catalyst.*

Several months ago, however, the worst possible failure happened to this car: Its rare ZF gearbox gave up. Fortunately, a used unit was located at Alfa Parts Exchange. The last time I saw the car, it was sitting tail-high on jackstands waiting for the replacement transaxle to be installed. Fearing this might not be the last of his problems with the car, the owner decided to sell. He could not find a buyer who would offer as much as $1,000. He finally let it go for less than that.

An alert SCM *reader then forwarded me the following listing from eBay Motors for this same car, being offered for sale at no reserve by its new owner:*

"This is a 1979 Alfa Romeo Sport Sedan with a clear title. The engine is solid and runs strong. It is in great running condition. The exterior is black and the interior is tan and brown. The car has the original Alfa Romeo wheels with expensive Goodyear AquaTred tires in near-new condition. The engine is in great condition. The automatic 3-speed transmission is also in great condition. The car has a few extra parts including two cams, four armrests, smog gear, etc. The paint is nice and the interior is fabulous. Fog lights are in complete working condition and come with the yellow covers. The seats are in great condition. All the gauges work, as far as I know. Decals are in good condition."

The no-reserve status suggests that the seller really had no idea what this Alfa would bring. The high bid of $3,606 on May 19, 2001 is astonishing for (arguably) the least loved of all Alfa Romeos, and is no doubt prompted by the car's remarkable condition. The real question: Who would so cherish an Alfa sedan that appeals to so few and struggles to make $1,500 on the open market? One possible answer: an Alfa enthusiast who is not deterred by the Alfetta reputation, and for whatever reason needs an automatic rather than a manual-shift car.

Alfettas are a problematic model. The SPICA system is difficult to get through smog tests, and those that have not already rusted into oblivion are at the nadir of their value. It's likely that this car, thanks to the care invested in it, will be one of the very few to survive. It's in the new owner's interest to hang onto the car and assure that it does: in 20 years, it will surely be rare (after all, this model is rare even today, with few being sold initially, and most of those already gone to that great Italian crusher in the sky) and may even have some small degree of collectibility. Most likely, the new owner should just drive and enjoy the car, and realize that if he decides to sell, he'll confront the same prejudices that prompted a previous owner to nearly give it away.

(Note: In spite of its "great running condition," this car had not changed hands ten days after the sale. The seller was still "tuning" the engine in an attempt to pass California's mandatory smog check.)

From the July 2001 issue of SCM.◆

1971 Montreal Coupe

Accelerating the car through its five gears, all problems are soon forgotten while listening to the intoxicating growl of the engine and song of the exhaust

by Doug Zaitz

Chassis number: AR1426425
Engine number: AR00564 01566

Inspired by an Alfa-based Bertone styling exercise (penned by Marcello Gandini) that had been exhibited at the 1967 Montreal Expo, the two-seater Montreal coupe debuted at the Geneva Salon in 1970. Unlike the Expo prototype that used Alfa's 1.6-liter twin-cam four-cylinder engine, the production Montreal used a "civilized" 2593-cc version of the T33 sports racer's four-cam V8.

Air vents behind the doors suggested a mid-engined layout like the T33's, but as installed in the Montreal the dry-sumped engine was front-mounted and drove the rear wheels via a five-speed ZF gearbox. Detuned for road use, this superb, race-pedigreed power unit produced 200 hp at 6,500 rpm courtesy of electronic ignition and Spica mechanical fuel injection.

The Montreal's running gear was sourced from the contemporary Giulia 1750 GTV, comprising independent front suspension and a live rear axle, plus disc brakes all around. Aided by its slippery, fastback body styling, the Montreal was good for a top speed of 137 mph and, in spite of a hefty price tag, proved very popular—3,925 examples found customers between 1970 and 1977.

Left-hand drive like the majority of Montreals, this example has formed part of an important private collection for the past ten years and is presented in excellent condition. The car is finished in red with black interior, and is fitted with an Airco air conditioning system. This rarely seen and highly desirable Italian Grand is offered with details of service history and previous owners.

The SCM analysis: This car sold for $13,993, including buyer's premium, at the Bonhams Goodwood Revival, held September 6, 2002.

Montreal ownership is stressful, yet rewarding. When I bought my Montreal some 12 years ago, I found myself in that pre-Internet era surrounded by snake-oil-prescribing Montreal doctors and greedy parts sellers.

The advent of e-mail and the Internet, increasing the availability of reliable information, has made Montreal ownership much less angst-producing. Cures for the car's weaknesses and idiosyncrasies are becoming more well known. Items such as the engine water pump jackshaft bushing replacement, the weak forged alloy transmission shift forks and easily cracked steering box mounting flanges are a few of the more serious issues that can now be dealt with relatively easily.

Bruce Taylor, an enthusiastic Monti owner from Geneva, Switzerland, has created a comprehensive Montreal resource, the Montreal Homepage (www.alfamontreal.info). Bruce also started the Montreal Digest, an e-mail list, which can be joined by visiting groups.yahoo.com/group/alfamontreal/join.

The Montreal has an unusual mechanical specification and is visually exciting. It is an excellent grand touring coupe, with sufficient interior space for two adults and limited luggage. The steering, while quite heavy at low speeds, is light and accurate when motoring along. The soft suspension makes for a comfortable ride however, the body does experience the typical Alfa cornering roll (Portlander

Dave Rugh or Harvey Bailey Engineering of England have sport suspensions for the Montreal).

If purchasing a Montreal, be sure that it has its original "turbina" style wheels as they are a unique size for this application. Oversize wheels and tires are ill advised, as they will overstress the steering box and affect the handling adversely as well. Only buy complete cars; the trim bits are expensive and hard to find. Run fast from cars with visible rust and/or evidence of home-boy accident repairs. You're buying a car outside of the collector mainstream in the first place; don't make it worse by picking up a bad one.

The driving posture is typical of Italian cars: arms outstretched to reach the wheel with knees bent outward and feet offset from center. The clutch is heavy, and the ZF gearbox notchy. As with all Alfas, a proper warm-up of the engine and drivetrain is essential for long life. Be sure that your mechanic has an excellent understanding of Spica fuel injection; you don't want to finance his Montreal education.

This particular Montreal's sale price was right in line with the SCM Price Guide. For a similar car in the States, a similar sales price could be expected with motivated buyers present. Excellent Montreals will typically sell with little advertising, most often by word of mouth through the local or national club. There are plenty of rats and fright pigs out there, lurking for unsuspecting, uninformed buyers.

I whole-heartedly support SCM's value assessment of the Montreal: it will languish near the bottom of the collector car market. Future substantial increases in market value are quite unlikely, as many collectors who remember the Montreal at its introduction have moved on to higher-tiered collectibles. Younger collectors may not be cognizant of Alfa Romeo and the Montreal, and may avoid it.

This leaves a small pool of prospective owners, found mainly through the Alfa club. The clutch of 100 or so U.S. Montrealisti form a small, tight-knit community.

However all the problems are soon forgotten as I accelerate my car through its five gears while listening to the intoxicating growl of the engine and song of the exhaust. When the car is running right, the mechanical woes are left behind and the pleasures of being behind the wheel of an affordable exotic come to the fore.

(Photo, historical and descriptive information courtesy of the auction company.)

From the December 2002 issue of SCM.◆

1980 179C Formula One

This car is the poster child for the vintage racing truism that 'the cheapest thing you will ever do is buy the car'

by Thor Thorson

Chassis number: 179/C-006

Alfa Romeo had dipped a toe into the waters of Formula One in 1971 when it supplied a V8 engine for Andrea de Adamich's works March. Then in 1976, Alfa supplied engines to Brabham. From there it was just a short step towards creating its own F1 team for 1979.

This car began as a 179B but was converted to C specification for 1981 with the hydro-pneumatic suspension that sophisticated teams used to circumvent the ban on sliding skirts. Chassis 006 first appeared in the 1980 British Grand Prix in the hands of Bruno Giacomelli, who used it for the rest of the season.

The highlight of the year was the United States Grand Prix at Watkins Glen, where Giacomelli put it on pole nearly a second in front of the field. He led from pole until just after half-distance, when he was eliminated by an electrical fault. At the final race of the season in Las Vegas, Giacomelli secured a podium spot by placing third. Mario Andretti was so impressed that he left Lotus to join Alfa Romeo.

Chassis 006 has now been restored to race-ready condition without regard to cost. The vendor reports that 520 hp has been delivered on a dynamometer, and the car has not been raced since restoration. It is sold with many receipts and bills, FIA documentation, and a vast quantity of spares valued in excess of $60,000.

This is a thoroughbred Grand Prix Alfa Romeo that set pole, dominated a Grand Prix, and rewarded its driver with a podium finish.

The SCM *analysis: This car sold for $153,750, including buyer's commission, at the Bonhams Europe Nürburgring auction, held August 9, 2003.*

This race car is the poster child for the vintage racing truism that "the cheapest thing you will ever do is buy the car." There are only two sorts of buyers for such a car. The first is a starry-eyed novice with quixotic dreams and a lot of hard experience in his near future, not only behind the wheel but also with checkbook out and pen ready. Hopefully, the car was purchased by the other sort: an experience-hardened Alfa cognoscenti with another Alfa F1 car who needs the spares. But the real question here is why the car was sold in the first place. We'll get to that, but first, a little background.

In contrast to their superb sports and production car programs, Alfa Romeo's F1 program was classically Italian in the "Cyclops" cartoon tradition, i.e. lots of people, huge egos and ambitions, chaotic organization, and neither enough money nor development. The Alfa engine was a beautiful concept and probably made the most horsepower in the series at the time, not to mention the most sensuous exhaust note (with the possible exception of the Matra), but it was heavy and wildly unreliable. Alfa used to show up at races with three engines per car and would change them every night. They'd have changed them at lunch too, had there been enough time. Even then they seldom finished. That was 20 years ago, when they were new. See where I'm going with this?

Aside from the engine, the cars are well constructed. The titanium suspension is a wonder of fabrication that was designed for the "sliding skirts" level of aerodynamic downforce, so it is plenty strong for normal use in this configuration. The transaxle is a Hewland FG six-

speed, so it works like it's supposed to, doesn't break much, and is easy to get parts for. Beware of reverse, though—it's only there to meet regulations and won't survive any use.

As a ground effects F1 machine with 520 hp, this is not a car for an amateur pilot. The challenge of driving such cars—with or without skirts—is described by my business partner like this: "For a given corner, you can drive through at 80 mph on mechanical grip or you can make it through at 100 mph on aerodynamic grip, but at 90 mph, you're in the gravel trap." You not only have to have the ability, but the cojones *to step across the chasm to reliance on aerodynamic grip—and then stay there. This is easier imagined than practiced, and not for the faint of heart. But once mastered, it is fun.*

Mechanicals aside, these are glorious cars. To quote the old line from "Gumball Rally," "It's such a handsome design!" The Alfa 179 is unique, beautiful, and stands out, even in as exotic a crowd as a vintage Formula One grid. The headers are titanium sculptures worthy of a museum. And at the risk of being repetitive, the sound! Everybody at the track will be waiting to hear you come past.

So on to the Sherlock Holmes question: What can we deduce from the circumstances surrounding this auction sale? Let's see. You can buy a garden-variety, mid-1970s, DFV-powered Surtees or March that will run in the upper middle of the pack for $120,000–$140,000. You can buy a top-line ground effects car (also DFV-powered) for $200,000–$250,000. A collector grade 12-cylinder car (Ferrari, BRM, Matra) goes for $300,000-$700,000. Why then is someone offering a ground-effects Italian V12, freshly restored, never raced, along with $60,000 worth of spares for a published low estimate of $125,000?

My educated guess is because it will cost at least half that per year to actually race it. Phil Denny (a specialist who actually supports several of these cars in vintage racing) explained that if you turn the engine to 12,500 rpm, (which is where you make the magic horsepower and the great noises), it's good for 200 miles of use before it needs a rebuild costing about $20,000 in labor, plus parts. We're talking about $25,000 per weekend if you want to really run it and be competitive.

Whoever actually put up their hand to buy the car was either very brave or very knowledgeable. If they were just very brave, the knowledge part will arrive soon enough.

(Photo, historical and descriptive information courtesy of the auction company.)

From the December 2003 issue of SCM.◆

1995 RZ Zagato

The ultimate failure of the series was that it never delivered on its visual promise—it looks like it should be the fastest car in the world

by Pat Braden

Chassis number: ZAR16200003002172

Alfa Romeo has produced a lot of cars that have remained memorable, whether commercially successful or otherwise. The RZ, as a high-performance convertible, is one of those cars.

The RZ was designed and built by Zagato. The coachwork was a thermoplastic resin, reinforced with fiberglass composite material and bonded to a steel chassis with special adhesives to produce a body with extraordinary torsional rigidity. The result was dramatic and the Italian press described the car as "Il Mostro," or "the Monster." It was immediately loved or hated.

The mechanical concept of the RZ prototype was the fruit of work by Alfa Romeo, together with an important contribution from Alfa Racing. The RZ is the synthesis of traditional technology pushed to its highest level. It is not, and does not pretend to be, a high-tech car. Engineers specified a 3-liter V6, double overhead camshaft, light alloy engine, with maximum care being taken with the timing, the camshafts, the compression ratios and the geometry of the manifolds. The engine produced 210 bhp and gave the RZ a top speed of 151 mph.

The transaxle scheme, with front engine, rear gearbox and DeDion axle, guarantees exceptional stability, thanks to optimal distribution of the load across the two axles. The RZ's restricted ground clearance prompted the adoption of a hydraulic lifting suspension system, operated by means of a button on the dashboard. The driver can raise the car by 50 mm in order to get over speed bumps and the like.

Production of the RZ commenced at the beginning of 1992 with a total of 278 units produced. The car pictured here is number 81. It comes complete with the appropriate Zagato certification and is finished in classic Giallo (Fly Yellow) with a black hide interior. This example came to the U.K. in 2000 and has seen very little use since being registered, the odometer showing a total of some 37,000 km. It is rare that this exclusive coach-built piece of exotica is available in the U.K. and this excellent ready-to-roar example offers exhilarating top-down summer motoring with unprecedented levels of head-turning style.

The SCM *analysis: This Alfa RZ sold for $23,124, including buyer's premium, at the Coys of Kensington Rockingham sale on May 27, 2001. Below* SCM*'s Price Guide, one could not have bought a more striking car for the price.*

Zagato has been in search of an identity for some time. After the war, its Giulietta SZ and Giulia TZ coupes regained the carrozeria's pre-war reputation for bodies of exceptional beauty and functionality. More recently, however, the company has delegated most of its fabrication to Galbiati and is striving to become a pure design firm. If Zagato's vision of the automotive future is accurate, we may have real cause for concern.

The convertible RZ is a conversion of the SZ coupe, the real owner of the "Mostro" title. These two limited-production Zagatos continued Alfa's abrupt, "crashed-into-a-brick-wall" styling theme established with the Milano and reflected in the current Spider and Sprint. The auction catalog's copy, when run through the SCM *truth translator, properly evaluates the model: It was a commercial failure, controver-sial, not high-tech and inherently impractical over speed bumps (i.e., for everyday driving). The ultimate failure of the series, however, was that it never delivered on its visual promise—it looks like it should be the fastest car in the world. You can think of it as a funny-looking Milano, or a spike-haired groupie who can't sing or play guitar.*

Development of the SZ began in the summer of 1987 and it made its debut in 1989. The basis of the car is the Milano Verde, with which it shares its driveline. Unfortunately, Alfa's SOHC V6 engine (as in the RZ) was first introduced in 1979 in the Alfa 6 (some ten years after its initial design) and the SZ chassis derives from the Alfetta sedan, which was introduced in 1975. As a result, the components of the SZ were well aged at the time of its introduction. The RZ, a chop-top, appeared in the winter of 1992, probably as an attempt to sell off the remaining SZs.

The SZ's finest moment of valuation came before it was introduced. Recall that 1989 was near the peak of the speculative era for collector cars. Alfa announced it was limiting production of the SZ to 1,000 and contracts for future delivery of the cars traded hands for as much as $100,000. However, when the car market crashed, this "instant collectible" became just a rebodied Milano and values plummeted to current levels.

In the SZ's defense, SCMer David Cohen at one time kept an SZ in Europe, and told us, "It's one of the most satisfying high-speed touring cars I've ever driven." And, of course, Mr. Cohen has driven more than a few.

So, who would buy this car? Those who want to stand out from the crowd and use their cars to bolster their image. It is the aesthetic successor to the Daimler SP250—you simply can't ignore this car. Its presence is so overwhelming that performance and beauty, or lack thereof, seem hardly relevant.

To become a true classic, however, a car must offer superior performance, beauty and utility. The price paid suggests that the SZ and RZ fail all three tests, and their market will probably trend downward for the foreseeable future. Well bought at the price if you have to have one, but not a sure-fire long-term investment.

(Photo, historical and descriptive information courtesy of the auction company.)

From the October 2001 issue of SCM. ◆

The Modern Era Cross the Block

OPEN CARS

#S433-1967 ALFA ROMEO DUETTO Spider. S/N AB662917. Red/black leather. LHD. Odo: 22,015 km. No reserve sale. Guatemala 2002 vehicle sticker in windshield. Glove box door vinyl covered. Good paint, fresh carpets, excellent dashboard, pitting to

door handles, scratches on bumpers. Pirelli P6000 radials. Cond: 3. **SOLD AT $16,500.** *Lots and lots of pre sale interest here; perhaps being the only Alfa in the sale has its upside. This represents a high sale price for a Duetto in this condition. Sale price is full retail or better, but these cars have been going up.* **Kruse, Hershey, PA, 10/03.**

#471-1967 ALFA ROMEO DUETTO Spider. S/N AR665528. White/red leather. LHD. Odo: 23,156 miles. Saggy fit on new leather seats, but clean interior fitted with full carpets instead of original half-mat, half-

carpet configuration. Good dash, brightwork fair to good. Rear bumpers still have "lollipop" reflectors. Weak gaps. AM/FM cassette. Cond: 3+. **NOT SOLD AT $10,000.** *Not an unfair bid for a car that appeared ready for use, but not for show.* **ebay/Kruse, Santa Clara, CA, 8/01.**

#431-1969 ALFA ROMEO DUETTO Spider. S/N AR1481379. Red, yellow/black cloth. Odo: 85,682 miles. Straight panels. Some paint chips and touch-up in the door edges. Plexi windshield. Competition-prepared seats and gauges. Rallye wheels, roll bar, headlight covers, competition paint. Raced in vintage rallies in New Zealand and Europe. Cond: 3. **NOT SOLD AT $8,500.** *Seller bought this car at auction a year ago. He was holding out for $15,000 to $18,000 here.*

Actual market value is somewhere between this and the price bid. **Kruse International, Seaside, CA, 8/04.**

#662-1969 ALFA ROMEO 1750 VELOCE Spider. S/N AR1410753. Red/black leather. LHD. Odo: 99,150 km. Excellent paint and upholstery, cracked headlamp cover and taillamp lens, good door fit, presents very well. South African import,

so no fear of the dreaded tinworm. Cond: 2+. **SOLD AT $10,865.** *Nice buy on a nice round-tail. These cars seem to bring about the same on both sides of the Atlantic. As a plus, this car had a factory-carbureted setup rather than the US Spica.* **Bonhams & Brooks, Beaulieu, UK, 9/01.**

#1883-1969 ALFA ROMEO 1750 VELOCE Spider. Body by Pininfarina. S/N AR1470386. Green metallic/tan. RHD. Early round-tail Spider, one of only 633 produced in RHD. Spent entire life in Transvaal,

where restored. Good retail presentation. Cond: 2. **SOLD AT $11,5753.** *Desired money was forthcoming, with some profit potential in spring.* **Bonhams & Brooks, Olympia, UK, 12/00.**

#5099-1971 ALFA ROMEO SPIDER. S/N 1486793. Red/black. LHD. Odo: 30,670 miles. Panel fit even and paint good but with the usual door edge chips.

Both tail light lenses cracked and luggage rack holes plugged with chrome bolts. Engine bay clean with a washer canister hole taped over. Driver's floor pan looks rough. Newer undercoating. No radio and misfit trim on the center console. Cond: 2-. **NOT SOLD AT $12,000.** *The doors slam solid and the top appears to fit tight. The car has some issues but nothing serious. This is a car I would feel confident to buy and drive home. Well, maybe not to Illinois in January, but perhaps Tucson or even L.A. Seemed like a fair offer to me but the owner was looking for around $15,000. Anywhere else in the world, this is an $8,000 car.* **Russo and Steele, Scottsdale, AZ, 1/04.**

#58-1971 ALFA ROMEO 1750 SPIDER. Body by Pininfarina. S/N AE1486793. Red/black vinyl. LHD. Odo: 30,503 miles. Excellent paint, with good chrome. Some pitting in door handles. New seat covers, correct floor mats and dash cover cap. Some cracking in console edge, non-factory radio blanking plate. Period aftermarket

trunk rack. Cond: 3+. **SOLD AT $17,280.** *A very pretty car, still wearing the original hubcaps and trim rings and sporting SPICA injection. Purchased at a dealer auction by a savvy SCMer who detailed it within an inch of its life, and got a world-record price.* **Barrett-Jackson, Scottsdale, AZ, 1/03.**

#445-1973 ALFA ROMEO SPIDER VELOCE. S/N 3040518. Red/black vinyl. Odo: 74,685 miles. 5-sp. Older repaint with little or no maintenance since the respray. Tired interior trim bits. Top was ready for replacement. No signs of rust-out from the exterior, but some problems in the most critical hidden areas, especially the rear quarter panels. Cond: 4. **SOLD AT $3,210.** *A lot of money for the seller, considering the consignor spent the money to buy the entry slot and transport the car, but decided not to*

have it detailed before running over the block. The "wash me" written on the decklid didn't help either. **RM Auctions, Novi, MI, 4/04.**

#623-**1974 ALFA ROMEO 2000 Spider.** S/N AR3045148. Yellow/black vinyl. Odo: 16,904 miles. 5-sp, Spica FI. Very good paint and panels, right door fit off, excellent interior, Marelli electronic ignition added during

mechanical restoration. Cond: 2. **SOLD AT $9,200.** *In very nice driver condition. Color not to everyone's taste, but car reported to run very well and reliably. A decent deal for an open Alfa. Last year for the chrome bumper cars, and they seem to be slowly climbing in value.* **Bonhams & Butterfields, Brookline, MA, 5/04.**

#1-**1974 ALFA ROMEO 2000 GTV Convertible.** S/N AR2411086. Eng. #AR005124284. Blue/black vinyl. RHD. Odo: 36,141 km. Presentable conversion from coupe, but older repaint looking very tired. Badly mismatched paint on trunk.

Chrome equally tired. Nice interior, though. Road worthy. Cond: 3+. **SOLD AT $8,100.** *Classic Italian motoring, sans roof. Sold at a fair price considering its coupe heritage and need for further investment.* **Shannons, Melbourne, Australia, 3/03.**

#427-**1975 ALFA ROMEO 2000 VELOCE Spider.** Body by Pininfarina. S/N 2472070. Primrose/black. RHD. Odo: 65,555 miles. Mileage appeared to be correct. Paint very flat—almost matte on back panels—with severe bubbling on rear wings. Door handles pitted. Cond: 3. **SOLD AT**

$4,802. *$1,000 less than the lower estimate was wisely accepted for this shabby car in need of a full cosmetic makeover. One shudders at what might be discovered beneath those bubbles.* **Bonhams & Brooks, London, UK, 4/01.**

#2526-**1975 ALFA ROMEO SPIDER.** S/N AR3048046. Black/black leather. LHD. Odo: 82,496 miles. It's early in the year, but this could be the worst car at auction for 2004. Cracked paint over poor bodywork. Bubbles, lifting and badly fixed paint. Some badges are missing (witness protection program?). Bumper trim largely gone,

balance Armor All-ed. Rust showing below trunk lid. Nice but not new cloth top and decent steering wheel. Cond: 5-. **SOLD AT $918.** *Not sold for $1,800 at Silver's Fountain Hills, AZ, sale. (See April '04 SCM, page 60.) Now found a new home for a touch more than half that. Interestingly, it has 75 more miles on the clock—did someone drive this thing from one auction to the next, or was it just towed? Worth the high bid for parts, but only for the truly needy.* **Kruse, Scottsdale, AZ, 1/04.**

#740-**1975 ALFA ROMEO SPIDER VELOCE.** S/N AR3048046. Black/black leather. LHD. Odo: 82,421 miles. Dented in the snout, and covered with semi-gloss and matte spray-can paint. Krylon restoration continued over the rest of the cracked

original paint. Driver's door glass drops about 4 inches when the door is opened. Radial tires are down to the wear bars. Very grimy under the hood, interior isn't all that dissimi-

lar. Approximately 5-year-old soft-top is the nicest thing about the whole car. Either running rich or very lightly burning oil, maybe both. Cond: 5. **NOT SOLD AT $1,800.** *Parts car special, money pit, or the next beater for that kid down the street. Either way, no one here was interested in a crappy Alfa today as it spent less than a minute on the auction block.* **Silver, Fountain Hills, AZ, 1/04.**

#171-**1976 ALFA ROMEO VELOCE Spider.** S/N AR3050086. Red/black vinyl. LHD. Odo: 21,389 miles. Paint is so new that several front and rear emblems weren't reattached (perhaps they wanted the paint to aerate evenly?). New interior and top, original

trim acceptable (what was reattached, that is). Engine compartment appears to be original. Cond: 3. **SOLD AT $5,408.** *With the paint so haphazardly and recently applied, one has to wonder what the mechanical side of the car is like. Fully priced—usually the best place to buy older Alfas is from Alfa Club members.* **Silver, Fountain Hills, AZ, 1/02.**

#335 - **1976 ALFA ROMEO SPIDER Convertible.** Body by Pininfarina. S/N AR3048506. Odo: 40,413 miles. LHD. Resale red/black vinyl. Top: white vinyl. Turbine alloy wheels (repainted), headlight washers, wrong shift knob. Quickie resale

spray job over a few good body divots on the nose. Missing rear bumper trim and Spider nameplate off rear face. Overall, a tired old tart. Cond: 4. **SOLD AT $3,502.** *No reserve for a lot of good reasons. '76s are burdened with the dreaded Spica injection, which, unlike wine, doesn't improve with age. This car should be driven until it drops and then abandoned.* **Silver, Fountain Hills, AZ, 1/00.**

#120 - **1977 ALFA ROMEO SPIDER.** Body by Pininfarina. S/N AR115410001100. Odo: 35,891 miles. LHD. Red/black vinyl. Top: black vinyl. WARNING: One can of red spray paint was sitting on the passenger's seat (yes, it was still sticky). Fuzzy black seat covers, driver's headrest was sitting in the back. Dash cracked, top seams

were sealed with RTV. At least it moved under its own power. Cond: 4. **SOLD AT $2,369.** *This car was doing everything possible to reinforce bad Italian car stereotypes.* **Silver, Fountain Hills, AZ, 1/00.**

#394-1978 ALFA ROMEO SPIDER. S/N 002594. 4-cyl. Beige/brown. Tan top. LHD. Odo: 69,586 miles. 5-speed manual. Bucket seats. Cromodora wheels. Bumper rubber torn, door handles pitted. Chrome pitted on headlight bezels,

mirror, side markers. A beater that's seen better days. Cond: 3-. **SOLD AT $3,150.** *The right money for a car that is now getting very long in the tooth. However, some Italian car mechanic is going to be delighted when his new client drives up in this car—like getting a Christmas bonus in January!* **McCormick, Palm Springs, CA, 11/00.**

#49-1979 ALFA ROMEO VELOCE Spider. S/N AR115410005482. Black/saddle leather. LHD. Odo: 441 miles. AM/FM, wood steering wheel. Original miles. Last seen at "The Auction" 2002, where it was a $14,250 no-sale. As seen then, though now thankfully

with a detail job. Quality issues relating to original build still exist. Lippman Collection. Cond: 2+. **SOLD AT $18,150.** *Essentially a new car, but a new car with build issues and an unknown storage history. My guess is that many thousands of dollars will need to be spent in the next 2,000 miles. With Spica injection, this will never be a highly desired model.* **Blackhawk, Hershey, PA, 10/02.**

#106-1980 ALFA ROMEO 2000 VELOCE Spider. Body by Pininfarina. S/N AR 115 38 2469607. White/black. LHD. Odo: 68,000 km. Mainly one Swiss lady owner. Sills renewed 2002, thick repaint fair, Perspex headlamp covers intact, fenders poor.

Windshield blade-marked, new top fabric, flat storage area instead of occasional rear seats. Campagnolos in need of repaint. Cond: 2. **NOT SOLD AT $8,635.** *Not quite sharp enough to raise the $11,000 required. Based on a 1954 suspension and drivetrain design, these poor old dogs aren't aging very well. Not a terrific color, either. Bid should have been enough, though.* **Christie's, London, UK, 4/03.**

#452-1982 ALFA ROMEO SPIDER VELOCE. S/N ZARBA5414C1015174. Ivory/brown leather. Odo: 52,438 miles. FI. Solid straight panels with good gaps. Paint touch-up to both rear fenders, door-edge dings. Chocolate brown

leather interior appears new. Good glass. Rubber bumpers are deteriorating. Cond: 2. **NOT SOLD AT $8,500.** *Big reserve on this little car, and this was the right environment too. I wonder what the seller expects for it. It's a cool Italian convertible in attractive colors. But $10,000?* **Kruse International, Seaside, CA, 8/04.**

#138-1982 ALFA ROMEO SPIDER VELOCE. S/N ZARBA5414C1015174. Cream/tan leather. Odo: 54,250 miles. Cost $15k when new. Power windows standard.

Aftermarket stereo added; a/c. Body straight with no signs of rust. Paint decent with no glaring issues. Glass not chipped. Ugly rubber bumper. Cond: 2-. **NOT SOLD AT $6,800.** *'82 was the first full year for Bosch FI. Both the* SCM Price Guide *and* NADA *put this car in the $4k range. The high bid should have done the job and then some. A nice car but not exceptional. Certainly not worth the $10k the auctioneer said the owner needed.* **Palm Springs Exotic Car Auctions, Palm Springs, CA, 11/04.**

#307-1984 ALFA ROMEO 2000 Spider. S/N WPOAB091XHS1203. Red/black leather. Dark blue top. Wear and tear kept to a minimum. Some natural chemical break

down of a few components noticed in the soft trim. Top replaced in 1994, still looked fresh. Hard starting even when warmed up. Cond: 3. **SOLD AT $4,850.** *These cars are valued on condition alone, with nice cars like this around $5K-$6K, and beaters at $3K or less. They're never going to increase in value, so should just be driven, enjoyed and then thrown away.* **Kruse, Atlantic City, NJ, 2/01.**

#000-1984 ALFA ROMEO SPIDER VELOCE. S/N ZARBA5417E1019609. Aqua/black. Odo: 56,288 miles. 5-sp. Paint okay; nose stone-chipped. Panel fit good. Leather seats cracked. Some wear to cloth top. Appropriate level of

wear for a 20-year-old car with below-average miles. Cond: 2. **NOT SOLD AT $5,100.** *This seems like perfectly good money to me, given the car's low miles but indisputably well-used condition. Perhaps Italian-centric venues could bring more. Owner apparently thought it was worth the time to try.* **Silver Auctions, Portland, OR, 10/04.**

#2-1985 ALFA ROMEO SPIDER VELOCE. Body by Pininfarina. S/N ZARBA5419F1023288. Black/black. LHD. Odo: 89,205 miles. Aftermarket stereo.

Various levels of chrome quality. A couple of interior knobs are missing, glovebox fit askew, rearview mirror fogging up. Engine room detailing not befitting of this consigning dealer's usual quality level. Cond: 3+. **SOLD AT $6,195.** *Post-block sale. Fair price for one of the nicer Alfas we've seen recently, although no councours contender. With pathetic build quality and cars that melt after 75k miles, the Italians can't make fun of Detroit. To GM, we say, get out of the Fiat deal. **Silver, Ft. McDowell, AZ, 1/03.***

#119-1986 ALFA ROMEO GRADUATE SPIDER. S/N 2ARBA5415G10442. White/black, cloth top and vinyl interior. Odo: 145,683 miles. Factory 5-spokes. Newer top and paint.

Black seat covers. Hard to start, hot or cold. Typical high-mileage shift linkage shudder. Mrs. Robinson is now a tired old tart. Cond: 4. **SOLD AT $3,952.** *As used Miatas decline in price, they drive the value of Alfa Spiders down even further. After all, which would you rather have—a 10-year-old Japanese car, or a 15-year-old Italian one? **Silver Auctions, Fountain Hills, AZ, 1/01.***

#390-1986 ALFA ROMEO GRADUATE Spider. S/N ZARBA5413610438. Red/black Black top. Odo: 69,716 miles. Primer overspray in door jambs. Paint on door handle rubber. Headlight bezel chrome pitted. With minor detail, could be a #3. Cond: 4+. **SOLD**

AT $4,725. *The Graduate was the base level Alfa Spider of these years, with vinyl seats, no a/c and disc wheels. As they grow longer in the tooth, they become more uneconomical*

*to own, especially compared to a Miata. Fair price. **McCormick, Palm Springs, CA, 2/01.***

#314-1987 ALFA ROMEO GRADUATE Spider. S/N ZARBA5647H10459. Red/tan. LHD. Odo: 63,143 miles. Local owner has had this car for many years. Seats freshly

redone. Original red paint looks good. A well-cared-for example. Cond: 2-. **SOLD AT $4,515.** *Alfa's entry-level Spider of the '80s, named after the Dustin Hoffman movie in which he drove a Duetto. If mechanicals are decent, a very fair buy, and lots of fun in the Palm Springs sunshine.*

#125-1987 ALFA ROMEO Spider. Body by Pininfarina. S/N ZARBA541XG1037329. Black/tan. LHD. Odo: 134,502 miles. Faded side window trim. Small ding in left quarter panel. Windshield scratched. Front seat inserts

replaced nicely. Reserve set at $4,600. Cond: 3+. **NOT SOLD AT $3,900.** *Overall a nice driver, but has too many miles to be worth much more. These poor old Spiders don't age gracefully, and the cost of an Alfa Botox treatment to make them frisky again will be more than they are worth. **McCormick, Palm Springs, CA, 11/02.***

#550-1987 ALFA ROMEO QUADRIFOGLIO Spider. S/N ZARBA5564H10522. Silver/gray leather. LHD. Odo: 42,700 miles. Hard and soft tops. Golfball-sized dent to left rear, light scratches

on original paint. Correct-style mags. Interior stitching holding up well, but seat leather appears hard in surfaces where the sun has hit it. Sold new in Missouri, in Illinois in 1994, on to Arizona in 1995. Cond: 3-. **NOT SOLD**

AT $8,000. *The owner should have jumped at this bid. Only truly exceptional examples can bring much more than $8,000, and this one was decidedly run of the mill. **eBay/Kruse, Scottsdale, AZ, 1/02.***

#286-1988 ALFA ROMEO GRADUATE Spider. Body by Pininfarina. S/N ZARBA5648J1062311. Beige/brown. LHD. Odo: 119,170 miles. Missing right rear hubcap. Rear carpet worn and sun damaged. Seats torn. Cracked windshield. Original paint still looks pretty good. Miscellaneous chips in

front and on mirrors. Cond: 3-. **NOT SOLD AT $1,900.** *Sold for $1,943 here last year in virtually the same condition, with 179 fewer miles. If the seller expects any more, he's going to have to do some detail work. These are disposable cars, bought on emotion alone. **McCormick, Palm Springs, CA, 11/02.***

#309-1988 ALFA ROMEO GRADUATE Spider. S/N ZARBA5648J10623. Beige/tan. LHD. Odo: 118,991 miles. Seats torn. All books and records. Original paint with some chips and dings. Broken windshield. A tired old Alfa offered with no reserve. Cond: 4+.

SOLD AT $1,943. *Seller was very gutsy to not place a reserve on this one. On the other hand, with any reserve, he probably wouldn't have sold the car. As a parts car, a terrific buy. As anything else, hopeless. **McCormick, Palm Spring, CA, 11/01.***

#NR17-1988 ALFA ROMEO SPIDER. S/N ZARBA556J1061385. Silver/gray leather. LHD. Odo: 8,664 miles. Some possible paintwork to front, but quite nice with believable miles. Slight wear to driver's seat, clean underhood and in the trunk. All brightwork good except for headlight trim rings. Pirelli tires appear original. Cond: 2-. **SOLD AT $14,734.** *Lots and lots of interest here. I must have listened as a dozen punters and potential owners tried to figure out what the auction price would be. Other than the*

genius who was thinking that $2,500 was too much, I heard estimates up to $12k. Well sold. **RM Auctions, Boca Raton, FL, 2/03.**

#388-1989 ALFA ROMEO 2000 Spider. S/N ZARBA5642K10630. White/tan leather. LHD. Odo: 65,709 miles. Some pitting on the chrome headlight trim. Panel fit good, as is paint. Fair to good interior. Closer inspection reveals a dropped area in the driver's floor pan and filler in both headlight areas. Possible significant front-end damage. Cond: 4. **SOLD AT $6,000.** *This car just had a dubious feel*

about it. There are plenty of other '89 Alfas to choose from that will bring less apprehension with them. Let's hope there are no bad surprises lurking here. **Mecum, Chicago, IL, 11/01.**

#350-1989 ALFA ROMEO GRADUATE SPIDER. S/N ZARBA5640K1063261. Black/tan leather. LHD. Odo: 47,434 miles. Very nice body prep and repaint. Rough cast, multi-spoke Alfa aluminum wheels.

Brightwork getting somewhat faded and tired looking. AM/FM/cassette stereo, trunk rack, accessory antenna. Seems to run nicely. Good original interior. Cond: 3. **SOLD AT $5,880.** *Consigned by an SCM subscriber, who wasn't overly surprised at the outcome. The right price for what is just a car. Does offer someone a lot of fun for not much money if the valves are properly adjusted, etc.* **Silver, Fountain Hills, AZ, 1/04.**

#908-1989 ALFA ROMEO CLOVERLEAF Spider. S/N 02486665. Eng. #ZAR1153. Silver metallic/gray and

red. Odo: 63,000 km. Mileage approximate. One Andorran owner until 1996. Seemingly still very original. Paint, alloys, and interior all good. Cond: 2. **SOLD AT $8,561.** *High retail money paid, but deserved in this case.* **Cheffins, Duxford, UK, 6/04.**

#302-1991 ALFA ROMEO SPIDER VELOCE. S/N ZARBB42N6M6008716. Red/tan. LHD. Odo: 63,045 miles. Owner by car to answer questions. Rear Alfa porcelain emblem cracked. Wheels dirty. Looks like original paint. Automatic, which is a shame.

Other than minor details, can't fault. Reserve set at $11,000. Cond: 2-. **NOT SOLD AT $8,000.** *These last-generation Spiders are really quite handsome, and the automatic is a good option for someone who won't or can't use a manual shift. But finding the buyer for an automatic Alfa at an auction can be tough. Car is worth another $1,500.* **McCormick, Palm Springs, CA, 11/02.**

#1000-1992 ALFA ROMEO SPIDER VELOCE. S/N ZARBB32N7N7004239. Yellow/black suede/leather. LHD. Odo: 22,587 miles. 2.0-liter, 5-speed. Excellent panel fit, very good paint with minor touch-ups on center front bumper; excellent original Campagnolo wheels, correct Pirelli P-Zero tires. Leather and suede seats unmarked, carpets as new. Cond: 1.

SOLD AT $27,540. *One owner, showroom-fresh example of last series Spider, down to its Alfa-branded cassette radio. A superb example, twice the* SCM *Price Guide price,*

as close to buying a new Alfa Spider as you can get today. Two people really wanted this cute yellow car on this day and weren't going to be bothered by a price guide. More power to them in terms of satisfying a fantasy; let's hope they don't try to sell the car next week and get their money back. **Barrett-Jackson, Scottsdale, AZ, 1/04.**

CLOSED CARS

#483-1969 ALFA ROMEO GTV Coupe. S/N AR1361294. Apple green/black leather. LHD. Odo: 110,223 miles. Engine punched out from 1750 cc to 2 liters. Body appears to have been stripped, prepped and painted, then had the original trim, chrome and glass reinstalled. New leather. Ding in lower center of right door. Appears partially restored. Cond: 3. **NOT SOLD AT $7,500.** *A frequent flyer between the two sales, it was also run on Monday to a high bid of $7,400. Despite*

our Editor's personal cars, green is rarely first choice of Alfa collectors. Not an unfair bid for a car that really needs major attention to be super nice. **Silver, Ft. McDowell, AZ, 1/03.**

#52-1970 ALFA ROMEO GTAm 2000 Race Coupe. Body by Autodelta. S/N 1531231. Red/black. Odo: 83,616 km. Autodelta uprated to GTAm provenance—though only one event charted in period. Okay-ish paint for old competition car. Perspex door windows very

frosted. Minimalist matte black interior in need of freshening up. Cond: 3. **NOT SOLD AT $57,200.** *Seemingly all original and correct. I loved it—but no bidder did sufficiently to part with the $64,350 required. Perhaps because the costs of a mechanical refurbishment might equal the reserve.* **Christie's, London, UK, 3/01.**

#47-1973 ALFA ROMEO GTV Coupe. S/N AR3022308. Fly Yellow/black vinyl.

Odo: 72,533 miles. Recently redone to meet SCCA rally specifications, most notably with the addition of a full roll cage. Several accessory gauges, Nardi steering wheel. Rather nice recent repaint. Won't hold a constant idle. Dealer consignment. Cond: 3+. **NOT SOLD AT $14,250.** *The modifications left little confidence in anyone seriously considering the car. I'm sure all the SCCA rally fanatics in the room could have been counted on the left fin of a trout. If there were that many.* **Mecum, Road America, 7/01.**

#709-1974 ALFA ROMEO 1600 GT JUNIOR Coupe. Body by Bertone. S/N AR115050001365. Alfa red/blck cloth. RHD. Odo: 49,000 miles. 5-speed manual. Factory

mags. Repainted and bumperless, though with original cloth interior. Cond: 3+. **SOLD AT $3,588.** *Panels all appeared to be rot-free and, if truly okay mechanically as claimed, this was one very cheap Alfa.*

#169-1991 ALFA ROMEO SZ Coupe. Body by Zagato. S/N 477. Light blue/tan leather. LHD. Odo: 15,000 km. Bucket seats. Aftermarket steel wheels. Unique example of SZ with coachbuilder's double

bubble roof treatment and supercharged 320 bhp engine. Cond: 1-. **SOLD AT $34,848.** *A one-off, sexy, very powerful SZ. At least it had not been painted in the obligatory Alfa red and seemed good value for the money paid.* **Brooks, Geneva, Switzerland, 3/00.**

#109-1972 ALFA ROMEO ALFASUD TI 2-door Fastback Sedan. S/N AS500003. Eng.# AS00001. Red/black. Odo: 15,839

miles. Factory-prepared rally car. Older restoration fresh out of storage, but tuned up and ready to race. Non-race bucket seat in bare, roll-caged interior. Race slicks. Cond: 2-. **SOLD AT $11,000.** *Consignor dropped reserve, but car crossed the block later in the evening with another lot number. That time, it failed to sell. Oh, well. Joins the other Alfasud offered in the "maybe it did, maybe it didn't" netherworld of auction results.* **Mecum, Road America, 7/01.**

FOUR-DOORS

#755-1967 ALFA ROMEO GIULIA SUPER Sedan. S/N AK344292. Green/tan vinyl. LHD. Odo: 7,117 miles. Dirt-cheap repaint. Tail lamp lenses crazed. Rear bumper dented and pushed in. Windshield wiper arm alignment off. Dent in right rear door. New seats, remainder of interior is original and

ratty. Five-speed, twin Webers. Grungy under the hood, difficult to start at times. Cond: 4. **NOT SOLD AT $5,600.** *A little hard for me to grasp, but our price guide pretty much has this right in the correct money for a sedan with needs. (ED. note: Giulia Supers are cult cars, and can be four-door rocket ships if properly prepared. This car, however, was not inspiring and the bid was plenty.)* **Silver, Fountain Hills, AZ, 1/04.**

#185-1974 ALFA ROMEO BERLINA 2000 Sedan. S/N AR3002755. Red/black vinyl. LHD. Odo: 78,831 miles. Rust-out in several odd locations on rear doors and rear quarter panels. Fresher replacement engine

with dual side-draft Webers. Weatherstripping and glass seals are chewed up or heavily

torn. Trim scuffed and pitted. Fuzzy seat covers. Cond: 5+. **NOT SOLD AT $3,300.** *Reran during the Monday push-pull-or-drag segment, bid to $2,200. A parts car waiting to happen, and the wait won't be too long. Bid for the value of the drivetrain.* **Silver, Fountain Hills, AZ, 1/02.**

ALFETTAS

#306-1976 ALFA ROMEO ALFETTA sedan. S/N AR116330003126. Dark green/black velour. Odo: 48,201 miles. 2.0-liter, 5-sp. Conversion to dual Webers. Very good shut lines. Very good paint with some orange peel and touched-up stone chips. Nice trim and rubber. Recovered seats and door panels have some fit issues; fabric patch covers holes for

missing front-seat headrests. Electrical tape on re-sprayed steering wheel; cracked dash top; mounting holes in center console. Very clean underhood. No stereo, a/c or sunroof. Seller wrote, "appraised at $18,000". Cond: 3-. **SOLD AT $11,070.** *Cleanest Alfetta anyone has seen in 20 years. Refurbished, not restored, but why? Price is at least double what it would have brought at any other venue. Further, the auction-queen fluff and buff was a little unsettling; I'd prefer to find a car that had a more honest, less pimp-my-Alfetta presentation.* **Barrett-Jackson, Scottsdale, AZ, 1/05.**

EXOTICA

#114-1971 ALFA ROMEO MONTREAL Coupe. Body by Bertone. S/N AR 1426425. Eng.# AR0056401566. Red/black. LHD. Odo: 97,740 km. Reasonable older repaint and original interior. Plating on door handles and door-mounted mirror bases pitted. Lest

we forget, the auction catalog misinforms us that the Montreal was powered by the civilized version of the four-cam V8 used in Alfa's T33 sport racer. Cond: 2. **SOLD AT $13,993.** *Sold in 1986 by Brooks Europe for $29,760. Mid-estimate result for a rather average example of Alfa's answer to the Mustang.* **Bonhams, Chichester, UK, 9/02.**

#139-1972 ALFA ROMEO MONTREAL Coupe. Body by Bertone. S/N AR1426222. Orange/black and gray cloth. LHD. Odo: 63,812 miles. Blaupunkt AM/FM cassette, Britax seatbelts. Very nice paint with a possible touch-up area in the right front. Excellent

brightwork. Very nice but incorrect interior, complete and holding up well. Owner proud of operational headlight covers. Cond: 2-. **NOT SOLD AT $16,000.** *Despite some issues with panel fit, this car has something rarely found in a Montreal: an ability to hold a magnet in every panel checked. However, given their limited following, the bid could have been taken without regrets.* **RM, Amelia Island, FL, 3/02.**

#924-1971 ALFA ROMEO T33/3 PROTOTYPE race roadster. S/N AR75080-019. Eng. #105800069. Red with white nose/black. RHD. Ex-Autodelta; 2nd in the 1971 Targa Florio. More recently restored for retro-eventing. 2002 Le Mans Classic raced. Spike Winter rebuilt engine. Only minor cosmetic event wear. Cond: 2+.

NOT SOLD AT $416,300. *One of these days, one of these 1970s Alfa long-distance racers WILL sell under hammer at public auction and true market value will be established. Not #019, not this time.* **Cheffins, Duxford, UK, 6/04.**

#458-1971 ALFA ROMEO TYPE 33/ TT3 COMPETITION Roadster. S/N 012/1. Red/black. RHD. Autodelta team raced in

1971, then 1973-74 Greek National Sportscar Champ winner. Restored in 1990s; rebuilt again recently. Panels, paint, alloys, and suspension unmarked. Cockpit good. Cond: 2+. **NOT SOLD AT $315,135.** *Eventually—perhaps—one of these Alfa 33s will sell in a public auction for the big bucks sought by their optimistic entrants. There were no takers here for this one.* **Coys, Monaco, 5/04.**

#118-1974 Alfa Romeo T33 T12 Prototype Racer. S/N AR11512008. Eng. #08. Red/black. RHD. 3-liter flat twelve, 500-hp. Older repaint slightly dull, period-authentic livery, well detailed to competition rather

than concours standard. Extensive documentation of history and current servicing come with. Cond: 2-. **NOT SOLD AT $584,800.** *Some really strong period Euro race history failed to extract necessary funds from new owner. Only 12 normally aspirated cars built (2 supercharged). Generally have been worth less than the V8 models. Very fair offer here.* **Christie's, London, UK, 12/03.**

#56-1980 ALFA ROMEO 179C GRAND PRIX racer. S/N 179/C-006. Red and white. Good body panels. Great looking car. Engine bay tidy but not perfect, engine started during viewing and sounded great.

Lots of interest. Comes with lots of spares. Cond: 2-. **SOLD AT $153,750.** *Originally a 179B and converted to "C" specification with hydro-pneumatic suspension in 1981. Seems cheap, but very expensive to maintain.* **Bonhams, Nurburgring, Germany, 8/03.**

#76-1981 ALFA ROMEO 179/C FORMULA 1 GRAND PRIX Race Car. S/N 179/C-006. Marlboro Red and White/ black. Last 179/C built, as driven into third-place at US GP in LA by Bruno Giacomelli and, more recently, Historic GP raced. Zero hours on 520-bhp V12, 5-speed gearbox and chassis since rebuild. Willans harness, minor race wear to Marlboro livery. Cond: 2-. **NOT SOLD AT $153,900.** *Great*

non-Ford DFV ride for Historic GPs failed to hook new owner with necessary $200,000 to buy it. Unless provenance is truly exceptional and/or motor is simple to run, single-seaters from this period are mighty difficult to move. **Christie's, London, UK, 6/03.**

#182-1982 ALFA ROMEO T182 F1 Single-seater Racer. S/N 001. 12-cyl. Marlboro pinky-red, white/black. Andrea de Cesaris drove this non-turbo F1 to capture pole position at Long Beach in its only GP, in U.S., where "De Crasheris" led for 14 laps

and held second for 18 laps before crashing. Last rebuilt in 1991 and only occasional demo-exercised since. Cond: 2+. **SOLD AT $105,000.** *Just under lower estimate money was accepted. F1 Alfas are just about the cheapest way to run with the big boys and get invited to all the neat meets. Price was a bargain by about $10,000.* **Brooks, Monte Carlo, Monaco, 5/00.**

#307-1985 ALFA ROMEO 185T GRAND PRIX Single Seater. S/N 003.

Benetton Green with red nose/black. Driven in F1 by Riccardo Patrese. Marked competition paint. Grubby harness. Matte black suspension. Dull V6 engine (in place of original V8) and transmission. Cond: 2-. **SOLD AT $50,687.** *Minimum required was forthcoming. Even with a different engine, this seemed like a good value for a working 1985 F1 car.* **Bonhams, Fontvielle, Monaco, 5/02.**◆

Section IV
Resource Directory

Duetto in front of the church used in the filming of The Graduate.

Price Guide

	Years Built	No. Made	Price Range Low	Price Range High	Grade	Rating	1 Yr. % Change
RL Normale/Turismo	22-25	1,702	$40,000	$50,000	C	★★	n/c
RL Sport/S. Sport	25-26	929	$60,000	$75,000	C	★★★★	n/c
RL Targa Florio	23-24	4	$275,000	$350,000	A	★★★★	4%
6C 1500 Normale	27-29	1,058	$60,000	$80,000	D	★★	22%
6C 1500 Sport	28	inc.	$95,000	$125,000	C	★★★	5%
6C 1500 SS Supercharged	28	inc.	$210,000	$260,000	B	★★★	6%
6C 1750 Turismo	29-33	2,259	$70,000	$90,000	C	★★	23%
6C 1750 Gran Touring	30-32	inc.	$85,000	$120,000	C	★★	24%
6C 1750 GS SC 2+2	30-33	inc.	$155,000	$195,000	B	★★★	4%
6C 1750 GS SC Zagato	30-33	inc.	$450,000	$600,000	A	★★★★	5%
6C 1750 GS Touring	30-33	inc.	$360,000	$425,000	A	★★★★	5%

(Deduct up to $100,000 for non-matching engines on previous two models.)

	Years Built	No. Made	Price Range Low	Price Range High	Grade	Rating	1 Yr. % Change
8C 2300 long chassis	31-34	130	$900,000	$1,500,000	A	★★★	20%
"Le Mans" Team Cars	31-34	12	$1,750,000	$2,500,000	A	★★★★	44%
8C 2300 short chassis "MM"	31-34	20*	$3,000,000	$4,200,000	A	★★★★	71%
8C 2300 "Monza"	31-34	26	$3,000,000	$4,200,000	A	★★★★	24%
Tipo B Monoposto (P3)	32-34	15	$1,700,000	$2,900,000	A	★★★★	35%
Tipo C Monoposto (8C-35)	35-36	6	$2,500,000	$3,500,000	A	★★★★	20%
6C 2300 saloon Coachwork	34-39	1,606	$32,500	$37,500	D	★★	n/c
6C 2300 Sp. Coachwork	34-39	inc.	$85,000	$105,000	B	★★★	n/c
6C 2300 Mille Miglia	38-39	inc.	$275,000	$350,000	A	★★★★	14%
8C 2900 short chassis	36-38	17	$6,000,000	$10,000,000	A	★★★★	64%
8C 2900 long chassis	36-38	27	$4,000,000	$6,000,000	A	★★★★	48%

(2,594 6C 2500 chassis of all types were built. Numbers below are included in that figure.)

	Years Built	No. Made	Price Range Low	Price Range High	Grade	Rating	1 Yr. % Change
6C 2500 SS (Coachbuilt)	39-43	50 - 100	$125,000	$175,000	B	★★★	13%
6C 2500 SS Corsa	39-40	10*	$225,000	$400,000	B	★★★	mkt
6C 2500 cabriolet (Coachbuilt)	39-53	50*	$150,000	$300,000	B	★★★	mkt
6C 2500 SS (Coachbuilt)	46-53	383	$175,000	$350,000	B	★★★	mkt
6C 2500 Frec. D'Oro	46-50	680	$40,000	$50,000	C	★★	n/c
6C 2500 Villa D'Este	49-53	250*	$175,000	$250,000	B	★★★	n/c
1900 5 Window coupe	51-54	949	$45,000	$60,000	B	★★★	n/c
1900M 4WD	51-53	1,949	$10,000	$15,000	D	★	n/c
1900 3 Window coupe	55-58	854	$55,000	$85,000	B	★★★	40%
1900 cabriolet	52	91	$50,000	$60,000	B	★★	n/c
1900 Zagato (SSZ)	55-57	28*	$200,000	$265,000	A	★★★★	48%
2000 Spider	58-62	3,443	$15,000	$22,500	C	★★	n/c
2600 Spider	62-65	2,255	$21,000	$30,000	C	★★★	19%
2600 Sprint	62-66	6,999	$10,000	$13,000	D	★	31%
2600 Sprint Zagato	65-67	105	$35,000	$55,000	B	★★★	20%
750 Sprint Normale	54-59	7,000*	$13,000	$18,000	C	★★★	24%
750 Spider Normale	55-59	7,000*	$15,000	$22,000	C	★★★	42%
750 Spider Veloce	56-59	2,300*	$25,000	$35,000	B	★★★★	14%

(Add 50% for 56-57 Veloces due to eligibility for prestigious vintage events.)

	Years Built	No. Made	Price Range Low	Price Range High	Grade	Rating	1 Yr. % Change
750 Sprint Veloce	56-59	1,100*	$25,000	$35,000	B	★★★★	20%
750 Sprint (Lightweight)	56-57	100*	$45,000	$55,000	A	★★★★	n/c
750 SS (Low-nose)	57-58	100*	$32,500	$40,000	B	★★★★	n/c
101 1300 Spider Normale	59-62	7,800*	$14,000	$22,000	C	★★★	33%
101 1300 Spider Veloce	59-62	500*	$18,000	$24,000	B	★★★★	9%
101 1300 Sprint Normale	59-62	17,000*	$10,000	$16,000	C	★★★	n/c
101 1300 Sprint Veloce	59-62	1,900*	$15,000	$25,000	B	★★★★	n/c
101 1300 Sprint Speciale	58-62	1,366	$22,500	$28,000	B	★★★★	12%
SZ-1	60-61	169	$70,000	$100,000	B	★★★	13%
SZ-2	61-62	44	$75,000	$110,000	A	★★★★	9%
TZ-1	63-64	101	$200,000	$280,000	A	★★★★	25%

	Years Built	No. Made	Price Range Low	Price Range High	Grade	Rating	1 Yr. % Change
TZ-2	64-65	12	$1,000,000	$1,250,000	A	★★★	n/c

(Note: TZs and SZs are easy to fake; prices are for authentic cars with paperwork.)

	Years Built	No. Made	Price Range Low	Price Range High	Grade	Rating	1 Yr. % Change
101 1600 Spider Normale	62-65	9,250	$14,000	$20,000	C	★★★	n/c
101 1600 Spider Veloce	64-66	1,091	$20,000	$28,000	B	★★★★	12%
101 1600 Sprint Normale	62-64	7,107	$12,000	$18,000	C	★★★	7%
101 1600 Spider Spec.	63-66	1,400	$22,500	$28,000	B	★★★★	17%
Giulia Sprint GT	63-66	21,542	$9,000	$12,000	C	★★★	8%
Giulia Sprint GT Veloce	66-68	14,240	$12,000	$15,000	B	★★★	20%
Giulia GTC	64-66	1,000	$15,000	$20,000	B	★★	23%
Giulia TI Super	63-64	501	$18,000	$24,000	B	★★★	20%
Giulia Super	65-72	124,590	$8,000	$12,000	B	★★★	11%
4R Zagato	66-68	92	$30,000	$40,000	B	★★★	8%
1600 GTA Stradale	65-67	560	$50,000	$60,000	B	★★★	n/c
1600 GTA Corsa	65-67	inc.	$60,000	$80,000	A	★★★	4%
1300 GTA Jr. Stradale	68-71	447	$40,000	$45,000	B	★★★	31%
1300 GTA Jr. Corsa	68-71	inc.	$45,000	$55,000	A	★★★	25%
1750 GTAm	68-72	40	$75,000	$95,000	A	★★★	n/c

(Note: GTA prices are especially affected by originality, completeness and history.)

	Years Built	No. Made	Price Range Low	Price Range High	Grade	Rating	1 Yr. % Change
TT 33/2 Stradale	67-69	18	$650,000	$850,000	A	★★★★	13%
TT 33/2 (2-liter)	67-69	30	$375,000	$500,000	A	★★★★	9%
TT 33/3 (3-liter)	69-72	20	$350,000	$500,000	A	★★★★	31%
TT 33 12 cylinder	75	12	$325,000	$425,000	B	★★★	7%
TT 33 SC 12 (Supercharged)	77	2	$250,000	$275,000	B	★★★	n/c
Duetto	66-67	15,047	$12,000	$16,000	B	★★★	8%
1750 Spider (Roundtail)	68-69	inc.	$10,000	$14,000	B	★★	12%
GTV 1750	69	44,265	$8,500	$13,000	B	★★★	19%
1300 Junior Zagato	68-72	1,108	$18,000	$22,500	B	★★★	n/c
1600 Junior Zagato	72-75	402	$25,000	$28,000	B	★★★	20%
Montreal	72-75	3,925	$13,000	$18,000	C	★	3%

(Deduct $2,500 if not properly state and federal certified.)

	Years Built	No. Made	Price Range Low	Price Range High	Grade	Rating	1 Yr. % Change
Berlina 1750/2000	69-74		$2,000	$3,500	D	★★	n/c
GTV 1750/2000	70-74	37,459	$9,500	$15,000	C	★★★	11%
Spider 1750/2000	70-74	n/a	$5,500	$8,500	C	★★★	8%
Spider 2000	75-81	n/a	$5,000	$7,500	D	★★	n/c
Alfetta Sedan	75-79	n/a	$2,000	$3,000	F	★	n/c

(Automatic trans, deduct $500.)

	Years Built	No. Made	Price Range Low	Price Range High	Grade	Rating	1 Yr. % Change
Alfetta GT (US)	75-79	13,715	$2,500	$4,000	F	★	n/c
Spider 2000	82-84	n/a	$4,000	$5,500	D	★	n/c
GTV-6	81-83	n/a	$3,000	$5,000	D	★★	n/c
GTV-6 Balocco	82	350	$4,500	$5,500	C	★★	n/c
GTV-6	84-86	n/a	$4,500	$7,000	C	★★	-4%
GTV-6 Maratona	84	n/a	$5,000	$7,000	C	★★	-4%
GTV-6 Twin Turbo	85	n/a	$10,500	$13,000	B	★★★	-6%
Spider 2000	85-86	n/a	$3,500	$6,000	D	★	n/c
Milano	87-89	n/a	$2,500	$4,000	D	★	n/c

(Automatic transmission, deduct $1,000.)

	Years Built	No. Made	Price Range Low	Price Range High	Grade	Rating	1 Yr. % Change
Milano Verde	87-89	n/a	$3,500	$6,000	C	★★	-5%
Spider 2000	87-90	n/a	$4,500	$7,000	D	★	n/c
Zagato ES-30	90-92	1,020	$22,500	$28,000	C	★★	-11%
164/164L	91-95	n/a	$3,500	$6,500	F	★	n/c
164S	91-95	n/a	$6,000	$9,000	C	★★	-3%

('94-'95 only, 4-cam 164L, LS add $3,000. '95 only, 164Q, add $7,000.)

	Years Built	No. Made	Price Range Low	Price Range High	Grade	Rating	1 Yr. % Change
Spider 2000	91-92	n/a	$5,000	$10,000	D	★★	-14%
Spider 2000 (com. ed.)	93	n/a	$8,500	$12,000	D	★★	-2%

(Automatic transmission, deduct $1,500.)

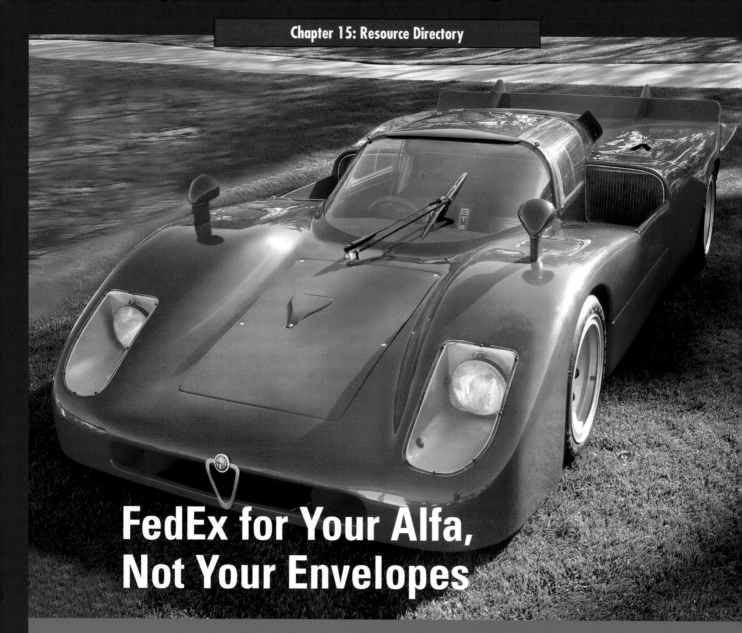

FedEx for Your Alfa, Not Your Envelopes

BIBA RESTORATIONS

1438 Arrow Hwy. Ste. H
Irwindale, CA 91706
acs@alfacybersite.com
www.alfacybersite.com/BRRest.html

Give me your tired,

your poor Alfa gathering dust,

yearning to be driven…

105

Take a Different Road

Introducing the Simple Lease®

At Premier Financial Services, we believe that getting out of

a lease should be as easy as getting into one. Our

Simple Lease® Program affords you the flexibility

of financing with the tax benefits of leasing, allowing

you the ability to change vehicles as often as you wish.

Mitch Katz, CEO

Experience the Premier Advantage • Call us today toll free at **877-973-7700**

Premier Financial Services
Vintage and Exotic Motorcar Leasing

www.premierfinancialservices.com
47 Sherman Hill Road, Woodbury, CT 06798

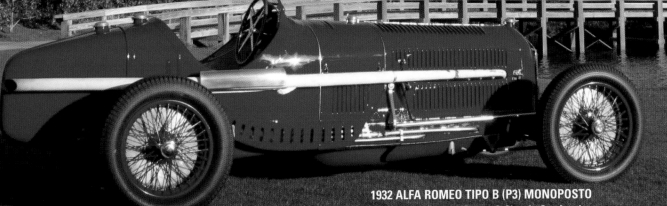

**Performance Consulting
Group, Inc.**

Helping you improve the performance of your sales team

Sales Management & Sales Team Development

Jim Griffin
griffinj1@cox.net
949-481-9160

Doug Gloff, MBA
dgloff@san.rr.com
858-487-0115

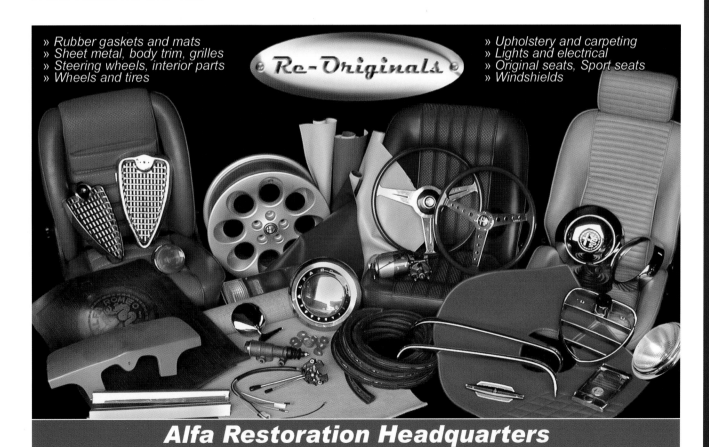

"Sports Car Market magazine is the *Cigar Aficionado* for collectible cars. It tells you everything you need to know about collecting, while at the same time being witty, entertaining and irreverent."

— Robert Lutz, President of GM North America, SCM subscriber since 1995

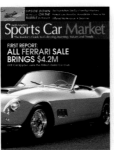

BUSINESS REPLY MAIL

FIRST-CLASS MAIL   PERMIT NO 890   PORTLAND OR

POSTAGE WILL BE PAID BY ADDRESSEE

NO POSTAGE
NECESSARY
IF MAILED
IN THE
UNITED STATES

Sports Car Market

KEITH MARTIN PUBLICATIONS
PO BOX 16130
PORTLAND OR 97292-9915

BUSINESS REPLY MAIL

FIRST-CLASS MAIL   PERMIT NO 890   PORTLAND OR

POSTAGE WILL BE PAID BY ADDRESSEE

NO POSTAGE
NECESSARY
IF MAILED
IN THE
UNITED STATES

Sports Car Market

KEITH MARTIN PUBLICATIONS
PO BOX 16130
PORTLAND OR 97292-9915

BUSINESS REPLY MAIL

FIRST-CLASS MAIL   PERMIT NO 890   PORTLAND OR

POSTAGE WILL BE PAID BY ADDRESSEE

NO POSTAGE
NECESSARY
IF MAILED
IN THE
UNITED STATES

Sports Car Market

KEITH MARTIN PUBLICATIONS
PO BOX 16130
PORTLAND OR 97292-9915